The Formation of the New Testament

The Formation of the New Testament

Eduard Lohse

Translated from the third German edition
by M. Eugene Boring

Abingdon
Nashville

DIE ENTSTEHUNG DES NEUEN TESTAMENTS

THE FORMATION OF THE NEW TESTAMENT

Library of Congress Cataloging in Publication Data

LOHSE, EDUARD, 1924-
The formation of the New Testament.
Translation of Die Entstehung des Neuen Testaments. Includes bibliographical references and indexes.
1. Bible. N.T.—Introductions. I. Title.
BS2330.2.L6413 225.6 80-27032

ISBN 0-687-13294-0

MANUFACTURED BY THE PARTHENON PRESS AT
NASHVILLE, TENNESSEE, UNITED STATES OF AMERICA

Contents

Foreword

It is hoped that this handbook will provide a convenient survey of the formation of the NT canon and of the individual NT writings, as well as an introduction to NT text criticism, thereby providing a basic knowledge of the discipline usually called Introduction to the NT. The material has been repeatedly revised for presentation in lectures, seminars, and colloquia with students, who have made many helpful contributions to its present form.

It is to be noted that in this presentation careful attention is given throughout to the significance of form-critical study of NT texts for the understanding of early Christian literature. A description of the formation of the NT in such a limited space calls for discrimination between the important and the less important. Accordingly, the selection of materials is made with a view to emphasizing the major issues, in order to illustrate the way in which historical-critical methods function in interpretation. In the dialogue with secondary literature (cited according to the abbreviations in RGG³) preference is given to foundational works, to works with an opposing point of view, and especially to the most recent literature which has not yet been discussed in other handbooks.

The counsel and critique of Dr. P. von der Osten-Sacken of Göttingen was helpful in the completion of the manuscript; Professor Dr. O. Kaiser of Marburg and Pastor A. Baumann of Hannover helped correct the page proofs. To them I hereby express my sincere gratitude.

Foreword to the Second Edition

In the second edition the book remains the same in outline and development. Minor corrections were made, suggestions from critical reviews were taken into consideration, supplementary material was added, and the bibliographies were brought up to date.

Foreword to the Third Edition

For the third edition a few minor corrections and additions have been made and the bibliographies have been expanded, in order to bring the account of the formation of the NT into line with the current state of research.

#1 The Task

Kümmel, W. G. "Einleitung in das NT als theologische Aufgabe" (1959), in *Heilsgeschehen und Geschichte,* 1965, 340-50.
Marxsen, W. "The Theological Approach to NT Introduction," in *Introduction to the NT*, 1968, 1-16.

a. The formation of the NT is usually dealt with in the discipline called Introduction to the NT. This term does not connote an introduction that sets forth the general and particular presuppositions necessary to the understanding of the NT writings. The concept introduction is rather so understood that General Introduction discusses the origin of the NT canon and Special Introduction deals with the composition of the individual writings. Who were the authors of the Gospels and the Letters? To whom were they written? What circumstances occasioned their writing? To answer these questions, first the relevant data within the writings themselves are assembled and critically examined. Then the claims in the early church tradition are investigated. To be sure, the early church only accepted writings into the canon that were supposedly written by an apostle. But those opinions which circulated in the early church must themselves be examined with the tools of historical-critical study. Finally, to NT introduction belongs the study of the history of the text and the discipline of text criticism. Have the writings of the NT been preserved intact, or have they suffered additions and omissions? From the multiplicity of manuscripts that have come down to us, how can that form of the text be restored which corresponds as exactly as possible to that which was written by the authors of the NT document themselves?

The task of an introduction to the NT is therefore to be distinguished both from the task of exegesis, which is concerned with the interpretation of the NT writings in detail, and from the task of NT theology, which is concerned with working out the theology contained in the NT documents. The boundaries between the disciplines, of course, sometimes cannot be sharply drawn. For example, a form-critical approach to the Gospels has immediate consequences for understanding the theology of the early church and the evangelists. One will interpret the Fourth Gospel differently if one regards the apostle John as its author.

And the picture of Pauline theology will change considerably if one advocates the view that the Pastoral Letters are among those written by the apostle himself.

These examples show that the question of the formation of the NT can only be answered by means of historical investigation. This task receives theological significance from the fact that the object that is investigated is comprised of the twenty-seven writings of the NT, which form the canon of the Christian church. While the scope of a history of early Christian literature would also include early Christian writings which were not accepted into the canon, an Introduction to the NT concentrates on the NT literature. God's word is spoken to us through the word of human beings. Therefore, the theologian is obliged to make a conscientious use of historical investigation, in a way appropriate to the subject matter, in order to understand the message of those first witnesses whose preaching was constitutive for the early churches.

b. In the early church and Middle Ages, there was as yet no historical investigation of NT writings. Of course, various opinions were handed on in the tradition as to authorship, addressees, and purpose of the biblical books—as in the so-called Muratorian Canon, (see p. 21), the Gospel prologues (see pp. 138, 153) and in the church fathers, but not until the advent of humanism did interest arise in philological and historical studies. If the rigid doctrine of inspiration, as advocated by post-Reformation Protestant Orthodoxy, left no room for questions from a historical perspective, the Enlightenment aroused a hitherto unknown interest in history.

The history of the discipline Introduction to the NT begins with the studies of the Catholic scholar Richard Simon. His three-volume work *Histoire critique du NT* (1689–93) evoked vigorous opposition, but also compelled his critics to venture into historical study themselves. On the Protestant side, the first significant work was written by Johann David Michaelis, whose book *Einleitung in die göttlichen Schriften des Neuen Bundes* (1750) in its later editions attained more and more independence from the beginning made by Simon. In the following decades Semler, De Wette, Eichhorn, Schleiermacher, and others opened the way for a broader acknowledgment of historical investigation of the writings of the NT. In the nineteenth century, the works of Ferdinand Christian Baur stood in the center of the debate. Baur sought to conceive the history of early Christianity in terms of the Hegelian philosophy of history. The thesis, formed by the Jewish Christianity of the early apostles, was followed by the antithesis, the law-free Gentile Christianity of Pauline coinage. The synthesis was attained by a mediating movement reflected by the Gospels and Acts, to which the finishing touch was given by the Gospel of John. In that each NT writing was studied with a view to determining just where it was to be located in this pattern of early Christian history, inquiry was made of each individual writing concerning its own tendency within the development from thesis through antithesis to synthesis. That is, so-called tendency-criticism *(Tendenzkritik)* was practiced. While this gave a strong impulse to historical work on the NT, the schema according to which the formation of the NT books was supposed to be explained was too rigid, for it is impossible to explain every early Christian writing in terms of the conflict between Jewish and Gentile Christianity. So Baur's views have been corrected on many points; the insight remains, however, that every NT writing is to be investigated in terms of its setting in the history of early Christianity.

Around the turn of the century many significant descriptions of the origin of the NT were published. H. J. Holtzmann's *Lehrbuch der historisch-kritischen Einleitung in das NT* (1885, [3]1892) is distinguished by a prudent critical approach. Th. Zahn's comprehensive work (1897–1899) offers an abundance of material, much of which is for apologetic purposes. The introductions to the NT by F. Barth (1908, [4,5]1921) and P. Feine (1913, [11]1950 Feine-J. Behm) have a rather conservative character. The critical counterpart to them was provided by A. Jülicher's textbook (1894, Jülicher-Fascher [7]1931). Catholic scholarship participated in the discussion through the works of J. Sickenberger (1916, [5,6]1939), H. J. Vogels (1925), M. Meinertz (1933, [2[5]]1950) and K. Th. Schäfer (1938, [2]1952).

While W. Michaelis (1946, [3]1961) published a book from the Protestant side in which he sought to defend the traditional opinions, A. Wikenhauser (1953, [4]1961) demonstrated how Catholic biblical scholarship acknowledged critical points of view, and worked with them within the boundaries set for it prior to the Second Vatican Council. J. Schmid undertook a complete revision of the book and expanded it to a comprehensive reference work (1972).

Critical discussion in the period after the Second World War resulted in two books: W. Marxsen's *Introduction to the New Testament* (1963, [4]1978) contains an introduction in which the theological significance of the discipline of introduction to the NT is indicated by selected examples. W. G. Kümmel's complete rewriting of the work by Feine-Behm thoroughly elaborates the scholarly discussion and offers a splendid resource for orientation concerning the problems presently discussed, in which an abundance of information is consistently combined with carefully weighed judgments (1963 12th edition of Feine-Behm; [17]1973).

Ph. Vielhauer's *Geschichte der urchristlichen Literatur* (1975) has not only dealt with the preliterary early Christian tradition and the origin of the written documents that were accepted into the NT canon, but his work, which is characterized by great methodical care, also discusses the early Christian apocryphal documents and the writings of the apostolic fathers. H. M. Schenke and K. M. Fischer have collaborated on an *Einleitung in die Schriften des Neuen Testaments,* the first volume of which is devoted to the Letters of Paul and the writings of the Paulinists, and closes with a survey of the continuing influence of Paul and the nurturing of his legacy by the Pauline school (1978).

H. Conzelmann and A. Lindemann have produced an *Arbeitsbuch zum NT* [Workbook to the NT] ([4]1979), which not only offers a survey of the formation of the NT writings, but also a section on methodology, an introduction to text criticism, a survey of the environment of early Christianity, a sketch of the ministry and proclamation of Jesus of Nazareth, and an outline of the history of early Christianity. At the same time, concrete assignments give the reader guidance in familiarizing himself with the methods of historical-critical study, and in checking the insights that result from their use.

Workbooks for the NT are also provided by J. Roloff, *Neues Testament* (1977) and K. Berger, *Exegese des Neuen Testaments* (1977).

A.

The Formation of the New Testament Canon

A.

Kümmel, W. G. "Notwendigkeit und Grenze des neutestamentlichen Kanons" (1950), in *Heilsgeschehen und Geschichte*, 1965, 230-59.
Käsemann, E., ed. *Das Neue Testament als Kanon*, 1970.
Campenhausen, H. v. *The Formation of the Christian Bible*, 1972.

#2 The Beginnings of the Formation of the Canon

a. The word *canon* means reed, yardstick, guideline (cf. Gal. 6:16), rule, norm. From the fourth century on, it was used in the early church as referring to the list of Holy Scriptures that have authoritative standing in the church. The Latin church took over the concept from the Greek, and understood it in the sense of *regula*. In the Scriptures that were acknowledged as canonical, the testimony to divine truth was given with binding authority. Which documents attained this authority in the ancient church?

b. The OT was acknowledged as Holy Scripture by the early Christian churches. To be sure, the synagogue did not resolve the question of the extent of the OT canon until the end of the first century A.D.; the Song of Solomon, Ecclesiastes, and Ezekiel were still disputed until their agreement with the Torah had been confirmed, thereby assuring that they belonged in the canon. In practice, however, the circle of OT Scriptures had already been closed in the time of Jesus and the first Christians. This is proved on the one hand by the way the OT is used in the texts of the community of Qumran, and on the other by earliest Christianity's usage of the OT, which is cited mostly as η γραφη or αι γραφαι ("the Scripture" or "the Scriptures," I Cor. 15:3-5) or *a parte potiori* as ο νομος ("the Law"). All three parts of the OT are named in Luke 24:44: παντα τα γεγραμμενα εν τω νομω Μωυσεως και τοις προφηταις και ψαλμοις ("everything written . . . in the law of Moses and the prophets and the psalms").

The Christian community reads the OT differently from Judaism: not as law, but as testimony to Christ, who is the end of the law (Rom. 10:4); for it is through the fulfilling of its promises that the real meaning of the Torah is revealed and thereby that the law is truly established (Rom. 3:31). The Scripture was therefore read as both coming from Christ and as having Christ as its subject matter, and was regarded by both Jewish and Gentile churches as incontestably the Word of God. Sentences from the OT were used in the so-called scriptural proofs, or taken up into the parenesis of the community. It was necessary that this understanding of the OT be defended against the objections of the synagogue, in order to ground the Christ-event in the fulfillment of the Scriptures.

c. The gospel of the crucified and resurrected Christ has as its content "what God promised beforehand through his prophets in the Holy Scriptures" (Rom. 1:2). Every part of the Scripture is seen in the light of the good news. Christ speaks in the Psalms, the words of the Prophets describe his work, and the Pentateuch shows by the example of Abraham what it means to believe in the God who raises the dead. For the Christian community, the gospel is the key which opens the door to the riches of the Scripture, the true contents of which the church discloses in its preaching of its Lord.

d. This understanding of Scripture is guided by the confession of Jesus as Lord. Words of the κυριος ("Lord") were transmitted in the tradition and instructed the community how disputed questions were to be settled. So the problem of whether Christians who have died will suffer some disadvantage over against those who are still alive at the time of the imminently expected parousia was settled with a λογος κυριου ("word of the Lord," I Thess. 4:13-18). Authoritative instructions on the question of marriage and divorce were provided by a dominical saying (I Cor. 7:10), as also with regard to the obligation of the community to provide support for the preachers of the gospel (I Cor. 9:14). The celebration of the Lord's Supper in the church specified what the Lord had commanded in the night in which he was betrayed (I Cor. 11:23-25). When the tradition contained no relevant saying of Jesus, Paul called specific attention to this fact: λεγω εγω, ουχ ο κυριος ("I say, not the Lord," I Cor. 7:12).

e. The apostle is a fully authorized messenger of the Lord, who claims for himself: δοκω δε καγω πνευμα θεου εχειν ("And I think that I have the Spirit of God," I Cor. 7:40). He speaks with the authority of the Spirit as αποστολος Ιησου χριστου ("apostle of Jesus Christ"). To be sure, the word of the apostle had to establish itself over against various objections, but nonetheless it found general acceptance in the churches. So his Letters were preserved, read in worship, and found a wider hearing. For the Christian community the Lord and the apostle both had binding authority and their words stood side by side, just as did the Law and the Prophets in the OT.

f. The early Christian writings, originally written for particular situations, were gathered into collections very early. Letters of an apostle were shared between congregations (Col. 4:16), copies made and collected. There must certainly have been such collections in the centers of the Pauline mission, Corinth and Ephesus. When in the second century the author of II Peter speaks of "all the letters of our beloved brother Paul" (3:15-16), he presupposes a collection of Pauline Letters. Ignatius of Antioch quotes from most of Paul's Letters, just as does Bishop Polycarp of Smyrna a little later.

The Gospels, which originated in different parts of the Roman Empire, immediately received a wide circulation. The papyrus fragment P^{52} (see p. 183) testifies that the Gospel of John was already known in Egypt ca. 125. Around the middle of the second century the author of the secondary ending of Mark (see pp. 133-34) knew all Four Gospels and composed a single harmonious Easter story from their data (Mark 16:9-20). Sayings of Jesus, which are ordinarily cited by the apostolic fathers from the oral tradition (see H. Koester, *Synoptische Überlieferung bei den apostolischen*

Vätern, 1957), are occasionally introduced as γραφη ("Scripture") (Barn. 4:14; II Clem. 2:4). What the Lord said was considered as authoritative as Holy Scripture. In the middle of the second century, Justin reported that "the Memoirs of the Apostles" were read in worship just as were the writings of the prophets (Apol. I, 66:3; 67:3). There was of course not yet a comprehensive descriptive term for the early Christian writings which were used in worship on a par with the OT Scriptures, but in regard to their authority, Gospels and apostolic Letters stood already on the same plane as the Law and Prophets. While the rabbis set about the collection of the oral tradition of the exposition of the law in the tractates of the Mishnah, in order thereby to establish the normative understanding of the Torah, the Christian community was collecting the writings from which they received that interpretation of the Scripture which was for them the valid testimony to Christ. Thus, there developed very early the beginnings of a collection of a NT canon, which contained both Gospels and apostolic Letters.

g. Around the middle of the second century Marcion rejected the OT, because the God of the OT was only the Demiurge who created the world, not the father of Jesus Christ. For his church the canon of the OT was replaced with a new canon of sacred writings, which consisted of the Gospel of Luke (from which Marcion excised the Jewish sections) and ten Letters of Paul (without the Pastorals). By setting forth this new canon, Marcion compelled the main body of Christians from its side to make binding decisions as to which early Christian writings it recognized as having canonical authority. Of course one can hardly say that the idea and reality of a Christian Bible were first created by Marcion, so that the church which differentiated itself from him conformed to his model (so von Campenhausen); for in fact clear beginnings toward the formation of a NT canon were already present before Marcion. But certainly Marcion's canon gave vigorous momentum to those developments already present within the main body of Christians, so that by the end of the second century the fundamental elements of the NT canon were basically already determined.

#3 The New Testament Canon Around A.D. 200

As the third century began, the development of a NT canon had already attained definite results, which can be documented in different areas of the ancient church and which exhibit an essentially uniform picture.

a. Irenaeus, a native of Asia Minor who later worked in southern France, knew and used all Four Gospels, and considered this so obvious that he philosophized concerning the givenness of the number four, relating the four living creatures of Ezekiel 1:10 and Revelation 4:7 to the Four Gospels. Moreover, he uses the Acts as well as all the Letters of Paul (except Philemon), and of the Catholic Letters I Peter and I and II John. Missing are II Peter, III John, Jude, James, and Hebrews. On the other hand, he does use the Apocalypse. So the determination of which Catholic Letters are canonical remains open.

b. Tertullian documents twenty-two NT writings for the West: four Gospels, Acts, thirteen Letters of Paul, besides I Peter, I John, Jude, and Revelation. He ascribes Hebrews to Barnabas, and does not include it in the canon.

c. Clement of Alexandria quotes in his extensive writings from all Four Gospels, fourteen Letters of Paul (including Hebrews), as well as I Peter, I and II John, and Jude. But the boundary of the canon is not sharply drawn. For on the one hand he includes pagan authors, by virtue of their having written under the influence of inspiration; and on the other hand he appeals to a wide range of early Christian writings such as the Apocalypse of Peter, the Letter of Barnabas and I Clement, the Didache and the Shepherd of Hermas, as well as the apocryphal Gospel of the Hebrews and the Gospel of the Egyptians, although he does not ascribe the same rank to these as to the four canonical Gospels.

d. The Muratorian Canon is the most important witness for the NT canon around A.D. 200. This document, named for the Milan librarian who discovered it in 1740, comes from the end of the second century and presents a list of the canonical books of the church in Rome. The extant text begins with the last words concerning Mark; the beginning, which doubtless dealt with Matthew, has been lost. The writings are not only listed in order, but also a few words concerning the origin and significance of each are given. The Gospel of John is expressly ascribed to the apostle John, Mark and Luke on the other hand to disciples of the apostle (Mark = interpreter of Peter; Luke = traveling companion of Paul). After Acts come thirteen Letters of Paul: I and II Corinthians, Ephesians, Philippians, Colossians, Galatians, I and II Thessalonians, and Romans were sent to seven churches, corresponding to the seven letters of Revelation 2–3. After the letters addressed to churches the letters to Philemon, Titus, and Timothy are listed. A letter to the Laodiceans is also mentioned as being in circulation, but is considered to be "forged in Paul's name for the sect of Marcion, as are other things which cannot be accepted in the catholic Church, for it is not tolerable to mix gall with honey." Finally the letters of Jude and II John are mentioned, and the Apocalypse of John along with the Apocalypse of Peter, because they have apostles as authors. But the Shepherd of Hermas "which was not composed until recently, in our time in the city of Rome" is to be read, "but cannot be read publicly to the people in church as among the Prophets, whose member is closed, nor as among the Apostles at the end of the times." Thus the catalog intends to include all NT writings in as complete a list as possible and to define clearly the boundaries of the canon.

Four Gospels, Acts, thirteen Letters of Paul, and a few Catholic Letters were generally acknowledged as NT Scripture. Apostolic authorship was considered an important criterion—as the Muratorian Canon clearly shows—but this was not understood too narrowly, since gospels written by disciples of apostles were acknowledged. Alongside the criterion of apostolic authorship, the ancient church also used criteria that were concerned with the contents of the writings, as the judgment of Bishop Serapion of Antioch (ca. 200) shows. One of his churches used the Gospel of Peter in its worship, a document with which the bishop was not personally familiar. When he examined this writing carefully and confirmed that it was Gnostic-docetic in content, he wrote "that, to be sure, most of it agrees with the true doctrine of our Savior, but some of it departs therefrom." He therefore concluded that this writing circulated falsely under the name of Peter. "For we know that such writings have not been handed down to us in the tradition" (Eusebius, H. E. VI, 12). The assertion that a writing goes back to an apostle was therefore not sufficient to assure it a place in the canon. Its validity could be acknowledged only after its contents had been examined. In this way the church sought to distinguish the early Christian testimony from later writings. Around 200 the canon of the NT was already fixed in its most important parts: Gospels, Acts, Letters of apostles. Disputes continued in the West over Hebrews, in the East over Revelation, as well as generally over the exact list of Catholic Letters. The problem of whether II Peter, II and III John, Jude, and James were to be numbered among the canonical books was thoroughly dealt with in the third and fourth centuries, and finally resolved affirmatively.

#4 The Closing of the New Testament Canon

a. In the Greek church, Origen, like Clement of Alexandria, did not yet know a conclusively fixed boundary between canonical and noncanonical books. He did hit upon a way of categorizing the writings so that they fell into the following groupings: (1) αναντρρητα ("unobjectionable") or ομολογουμενα ("acknowledged"), which were in general use in the church: Four Gospels, thirteen Letters of Paul, I Peter, I John, Acts, and Revelation; (2) αμφιβαλλομενα ("included/contested"), which are contested: II Peter, II and III John, Hebrews, James, and Jude; (3) ψεθδη ("false"), that is, books which were rejected as falsifications and therefore as bungled products of the heretics: the Gospels of the Egyptians, Thomas, Basilides, and Matthias.

This classification was then reformulated by Eusebius in the fourth century: (1) ομολογουμενα ("acknowledged") are the writings concerning which a united judgment prevails: Four Gospels, Acts, fourteen Pauline Letters (including Hebrews), I John, I Peter, to which many would add the Apocalypse; (2) αντιλεγομενα ("disputed") are the books to which there was objection. This latter group is composed of two subcategories: (a) Antilegomena which, however, are acknowledged by most Christians, γνωριμα ("acquainted with"): James, Jude, II Peter, II and III John; (b) Antilegomena which are regarded as inauthentic, νοθα ("illegitimate"): the Acts of Paul, the Shepherd of Hermas, the Apocalypse of Peter, the Letter of Barnabas, and the Didache; there were also many who consigned Revelation to this group, as Eusebius himself tended to do. (3) The apocryphal gospels are described as heretical writings, which are to be rejected.

If the last word about the delimitation of the canon had not quite yet been spoken in the time of Eusebius, it was not long before the final decision was made by the bishops of the early church. In his Easter letter of A.D. 367 Bishop Athanasius of Alexandria enumerated these twenty-seven books of the NT canon: Matthew, Mark, Luke, John—the opinion of that time was that this was their order of composition—Acts, followed by the Catholic Letters: James, I and II Peter, I, II, and III John (listed in this order from Galatians 2:9: James, Cephas, John), Jude; then the Letters of Paul, in which Hebrews was included, listed in final position among the letters addressed to churches; and finally, Revelation. During the times in which Athanasius was banished from Alexandria he had repeatedly been in the West and had there become acquainted with the high esteem in which the Apocalypse was held. Nevertheless, in the East the Apocalypse continued to have less significance than the other books, and did not attain uncontested authority until the Middle Ages. At the end of the list stand these words: "These are the springs of salvation, by which the thirsty can be abundantly refreshed. In them alone is the true religious teaching proclaimed. Let no one either add anything or take away anything."

b. The process of the fixation of the canon in the Latin church of the third and fourth centuries brought the Latin canon nearer and nearer to that of the East, from which especially Hebrews and the delimitation of the Catholic Letters were derived. By the end of the fourth century full agreement with the Greek church was reached in recognizing the same twenty-seven books, which was expressly confirmed by the synods of Hippo Regius (393) and Carthage (397).

c. In the Syrian church, at first the gospel harmony (Diatessaron) of Tatian (see pp. 239-40) prevailed in the worship usage. Not until the fifth century did Bishop Rabbula of Edessa succeed in suppressing the Diatessaron and having the separate gospels read in worship (see p. 240). Besides the Acts and fourteen Letters of Paul, the Syrian church used only three Catholic Letters (James, I Peter, I John), and thus only twenty-two canonical writings. Later, however, also II Peter, II and III John, Jude, and Revelation were able gradually to attain a position of authority in the church (as in the translations of Philoxenus of Mabug, 508, and Thomas of Harkel, 616 [see p. 240]), but they were still not valued as highly as the other Scriptures.

d. Like the medieval church, the leaders of the Reformation retained the NT canon of twenty-seven books. After the apostolic authorship of some writings, especially among the Catholic Letters, had become questionable already in the writings of the humanists, Luther undertook to make distinctions based on criteria of content. In the preface to James in the September–Bible of 1522 he wrote that the real touchstone for the evaluation of all the books was to determine whether or not they set forth Christ. "What does not teach Christ is not apostolic, though preached by Peter or Paul; and that which proclaims Christ is apostolic even if done by Judas, Annas, Pilate, or Herod." Critical distinctions are made on this basis: concerning James as "a right strawy epistle," because it emphasizes works so strongly; concerning Hebrews, because it denies the possibility of a second repentance; concerning Jude, because it is superfluous beside II Peter; and concerning the Apocalypse, because it does not manifest a genuine apostolic manner but is occupied with visions instead of prophesying in words that are clear and plain. Luther placed these books at the end of his NT in order to indicate that he classified them as belonging to a lower level than that of the other writings.

Against the critiques of the humanists and the reformers, the Tridentine Council of 1546 affirmed that all twenty-seven books were equally canonical. No distinction in their evaluation was permitted; Hebrews was listed among the Pauline Letters.

e. The question of a canon-within-the-canon is still with us. The delimitation of the NT canon was only accomplished by a long process in the ancient church and then brought to a conclusion by a decision by the bishops. In this process the ancient church exercised good judgment in excluding the apocryphal Christian literature. In the process of fixing the canon, the oldest writings thought to be traceable to the apostles were collected, and then were examined to see whether their contents could be regarded as authentic witness to the gospel. It was this which became the decisive criterion for the delimitation of the NT canon, for the NT documents witness to the proclamation of earliest Christianity that founded the church. The validity of this proclamation is, of course, not dependent on whether or not the individual writings were authored by apostles. But the twenty-seven writings are to be carefully examined as to how they witness to the kerygma and elaborate on it. In the question of "the canon-in-the-canon" Luther's pointing to "that which sets forth Christ" remains therefore entirely valid.

B.

The Formation of the New Testament Writings

I.

Forms and Types of Early Christian Preaching and Teaching

Prior to the time in early Christianity when written documents were composed, the gospel of Jesus Christ was promulgated, the faith was publicly confessed, worship was conducted, and the community instructed in how they should lead their life in obedience to the Lord—all of this done orally. Definite forms were thereby developed in which the preaching and teaching of the community were expressed. Of course these have not come down to us directly, but must be inferred from those written sources that are in part dependent on the oral tradition. The oral preaching and teaching of earliest Christianity can be reconstructed above all from the Pauline Letters, which are the oldest extant Christian writings. Though Paul occasionally refers expressly to tradition (I Cor. 11:23; 15:3), in other places he introduces previously existing phrases or sentences without any specific indication.

In order to be able to distinguish traditional material from its context, methodologically proven criteria are required: (1) often indications are found in the broader context that call attention to the appropriation of traditional material, as in introductory remarks (I Cor. 11:23; 15:3) or declarations about the content of the faith (Rom. 4:24-25) or of the confession (Rom. 10:9-10). (2) The quoted material frequently begins with a clearly-recognizable introductory word: οτι ("quote," "that," I Cor. 15:3; I Peter, 2:21; 3:18) or ος ("who," Phil. 2:6; I Tim. 3:16). (3) Often the traditional passage has a firm formal structure: *Parallelismus membrorum* (I Cor. 15:3-5; Rom. 4:25) or strophic arrangement (Phil. 2:6-11; Col. 1:15-20). A noticeable heaping-up of relative clauses (Phil. 2:6-11) or a participial style (Rom. 1:3-4) are clues to the presence of preformed units of material. (4) The vocabulary of the quotation may differ clearly from the author's usual choice of words (see below to I Cor. 15:3-5; Phil. 2:6-11). Traditional sections are often deficient in the use of the article. (5) Frequently the author of the letter has given his own interpretation to the material he has taken over, by conspicuously inserting here and there an idea especially important to him (thus in Rom. 3:25: δια πιστεως ("to be received by faith"); in Phil. 2:8: θανατου δε σταυρου ("even death on a cross"). (6) Certain expressions in the quotation—of predominately christological content—recur in other places within the NT likewise as formalized expressions, as for example the reference to Christ's office as Son of David (Rom. 1:3-4; II Tim. 2:8), the expression ωφθη ("he appeared/was seen," I Cor. 15:5; I Tim. 3:16) or the schema of the humiliation and exaltation of Christ (Phil. 2:6-11; I Tim. 3:16). (7) Finally, a quotation may also be recognized by the circumstance that it is often not completely integrated into the context. Thus I Corinthians 15 only makes use of the statement about the resurrection, and not that of the death of Christ (I Cor. 15:3-5). Often an expository application is joined to the traditional passage; I Corinthians 15:6ff elaborates the reference to the resurrection of Christ, while Colossians 1:21-23 appends an *applicatio* to the hymn of 1:15-20, which elaborates both the consolation and the demand inherent in the reconciliation brought about through Christ.

#5 Early Christian Confessions

Cullmann, O. *The Earliest Christian Confessions*, 1949.
Conzelmann, H. "Was glaubte die älteste Christenheit?" (1955), in *Theologie als Schriftauslegung*, 1974, 106-19.
Kramer, W. *Christ, Lord, Son of God*, 1966.
Wengst, K. *Christologische Formeln und Lieder des Urchristentums*, [2]1974.

a. In the preaching of earliest Christianity, the crucified and risen Christ was proclaimed as Lord. No complete example of a sermon from the earliest Christian preaching has been preserved. Still, inferences can be drawn regarding the different forms of early Christian proclamation from the NT letters, for the living speech of preaching has determined the style of the early Christian letters in many places. First Corinthians specifically sets itself forth as written instruction for the congregation that is to be read aloud in worship (16:19-24). And Hebrews is described as λογος της παρακλησεως ("word of exhortation," 13:22), through which the congregation is encouraged and admonished. Preaching included exposition of the Scripture, elaboration of the kerygma, responding to current issues, ethical instruction, and instruction by means of somewhat catechetical collections of teaching material. Jewish forms of scriptural interpretation were included, as were the forms of preaching found in the Hellenistic synagogues and the style of the Cynic-Stoic diatribe used by wandering preachers to give ethical instruction. The speeches reproduced in Acts (2:14-39; 3:12-26; 4:9-12; 5:30-32; 10:34-43; 13:16-41; 14:15-17; 17:22-31) are constructed according to a firm pattern in which the cross and resurrection of Christ are described as the fulfillment of OT promises and which confront the hearers with a summons to repentance. To be sure, early Christian traditional material has been used in these speeches, but it has been so reformulated by the author of Acts that direct inference from the speeches of Acts to earliest Christian preaching is not possible.

A brief summary of early Christian missionary preaching is found in I Thessalonians 1:9-10.

> The conceptuality of these two verses proves the pre-Pauline origin of the formulation (see G. Friedrich, "Ein Tauflied hellenistischer Judenchristen," *Th.Z.* 21 [1965] 502-516): επιστρεφω ("turn") is found only here in Paul and is used in the early Christian missionary preaching as a technical term for conversion (Acts 9:35; 11:21; 14:15, and elsewhere); δουλευω ("serve") is combined with τω θεω ("God"), but elsewhere by Paul with τω κυριω ("the Lord") or χριστω ("Christ") (Rom. 12:11; 14:18; 16:18); God is described as ζωη ("living") and αληθινος ("true") in the OT-Jewish manner; αναμενω ("wait") is *hapax legomenon* for the NT; εκ των ουρανων (lit. "from the heavens") is found only here in Paul, who elsewhere always uses the singular ουρανος ("heaven") (I Thess. 4:16; I Cor. 15:47, and elsewhere); the participle ρυομενος ("delivers") recurs in Paul only in the quotation from Psalms 14:7 in Romans 11:26; the expression εκ της οργης της ερχομενης ("from the wrath to come") has no parallel in the Pauline corpus.

The early Christian preaching joined the Hellenistic-Jewish missionary preaching in demanding a renunciation of the vain idols and a turning to the one true God. To this was added the eschatological declaration that the Christians awaited the parousia of the Son of God, whom God had raised from the dead and who will appear as our Savior from the coming wrath of judgment. Whoever accepted this preaching confessed that Jesus had been raised from the dead and will save us on the Last Day.

b. To this kerygma that proclaims the gospel of God's deed in the cross and resurrection of Christ there corresponds the confession of those who accepted this message in faith. The confession is a public declaration of one's faith (Rom. 10:9: parallelism of ομολογεω/πιστευω ("confess/believe," Mark 8:38 par.; Matt. 10:33-34 par.; Luke 12:8-9; John 1:20; confession is the opposite of denial or being ashamed, Rom. 1:16). In the confession one proclaims: this Jesus who is testified to by the preaching is my Lord, is our Lord. In the worship service the cry rings forth: κυριος Ιησους ("Jesus is Lord," I Cor. 12:3) or κυριος Ιησους χριστος ("Jesus Christ is Lord," Phil. 2:11). The present κυριοτης ("lordship") of the crucified and risen Lord is lifted up in contrast to whatever other so-called gods and lords there may be (I Cor. 8:5). This concise confession is sounded forth as an acclamation similar to that affirmation with which every Jew confessed his faith in the God of Israel as the one God, creator and Lord of the world: "Hear O Israel, your God is one" (Deut. 6:4). This cry was also taken up in the earliest Christian confessions: Εις Θεος ("God is one," Rom. 3:30; Gal. 3:20; James 2:19), and this one God is precisely the God and Father who has revealed himself in Christ.

c. Since faith confesses Jesus Christ as Lord, it is based on the Christ-event, in which God has acted for us once and for all. The content of this faith is expressed in creedal formulas which are mostly composed in participial phrases, relative clauses, or οτι ("that")-clauses. The oldest creedal formulae are preserved in concise expressions: that God has raised Jesus from the dead (Rom. 10:9); οτι Ιησους απεθαςες και ανεστη ("that Jesus died and rose again," I Thess. 4:14); χριστος Ιησους ο αποθανων, μαλλον δε εγερθεις ("Christ Jesus who died, yes, who was raised," Rom. 8:34); χριστος απεθανεν και ανεζησεν ("Christ died and lived again," Rom. 14:9; cf. further Rom. 4:24-25; II Cor. 13:4, and elsewhere). Frequently the creedal formula is introduced by a specific reference to πιστις/πιστευω ("faith/believe").

The early Christian kerygma, recorded in confessional form, is summarized in I Corinthians 15:3-5 in carefully formulated phrases, which Paul cites as the gospel that had been delivered to him.

Concerning the pre-Pauline unit see J. Jeremias, *The Eucharistic Words of Jesus* (1966); H. Conzelmann, "On the Analysis of the Confessional Formula I Cor. 15:3-5," *Interpretation* 20 (1966) 15-25. The introduction (vv. 1-2) expressly refers to the reception and handing-on of tradition; παραδιδωμι/παραλαμβανω ("to hand over as tradition/to receive as tradition," v. 3) serve as technical terms for the citation of tradition. Verses 3-5 are preserved in *Parallelismus membrorum:* each of the two major οτι (that)-clauses, which speak respectively of the death and resurrection of Christ, is followed by a shorter οτι -clause, which underscores the preceding statement: και οτι εταφη—και οτι ωφθη ("and that he was buried"—"and that he appeared"). The vocabulary of vv. 3-5 is pre-Pauline. It is characteristic of Paul himself to speak of sin in the singular, by which he means a cosmic power (Rom. 5:12); εγηγερται ("he was raised") is used elsewhere to refer to the resurrection only in II Timothy 2:8 and I Corinthians 15:12ff as an echo of the tradition cited in vv. 3-5; ωφθη ("he appeared") is found elsewhere only in I Timothy 3:16, δωδεκα ("twelve") only here; otherwise Paul speaks of Cephas and the apostles, without giving their exact number. Whether vv. 3-5 go back to an originally Hebrew or Aramaic text (Jeremias) or rather were composed in a Greek that from the beginning had been strongly influenced by the LXX (Conzelmann) can no longer be clearly determined. But there can be no doubt that we have here a creedal formula, which goes back to the earliest Jerusalem church. In the context Paul himself calls attention to this origin: the earliest apostles εκεινοι, v. 11 ("they") and he deliver one and the same message, which is the foundation for faith: ουτως κηρυσσομεν και ουτως επιστευσατε ("so we preach and so you believed," v. 11). From v. 6 on the apostle elaborates and applies the quotation in such a way as to emphasize what it says about the resurrection of Christ, for this was the disputed point between him and those in Corinth who denied the resurrection.

The two affirmations concerning the death and resurrection of Christ, which are connected by formal parallelism, are related to each other in the closest possible way. Because Christ is risen, therefore it can be preached that his death happened "for our sins." But apart from the cross the testimony to the resurrection would not be properly understood. The Scriptures are appealed to as confirming this content of the Gospel, the Scriptures that testify to the truth of that preaching which is the basis of faith.

d. The content of faith was expressed in a variety of formulations. The discussion that follows I Corinthians 15:3-5 shows that Paul in no way felt himself slavishly bound to the exact text of a "sacred formula," but rather supplemented the tradition and thereby interpreted it. The apostle knew himself to be bound only to the mandate to preach the gospel (I Cor. 9:16-17). But this gospel comes to expression in different formulations, which disclose the content of faith, as in the brief statement of Romans 4:25: ος παρεδοθη δια τα παραπτωματα ημων και ηγερθη δια την δικαιωσιν ημων ("who was put to death for our trespasses and raised for our justification"). In the context, v. 24 refers only to the resurrection of Jesus as the content of the πιστευειν ("believing"). In v. 25, the death and resurrection of Jesus are referred to in a statement constructed in parallelism; again, the reference to "sins" in the plural corresponds to early Christian [but not Pauline] linguistic usage.

Another, somewhat different, early Christian creedal formula is cited by Paul in the introduction to the Letter to the Romans (1:3-4). By way of introducing himself to the Roman church, which does not know him personally, Paul refers to the good news as it is believed and confessed everywhere in the Christian world.

The pre-Pauline quotation is clearly distinguishable from the context (see E. Schweizer, *Neotestamentica*, 1963, 180-89; Kramer, *op. cit.* 108-111; H. Zimmermann, *Neutestamentliche Methodenlehre*, [4]1974, 192-202 [Lit.]; E. Linnemann, "Tradition und Interpretation in Rom. 1:3-4," *Ev. Th.* 31 [1971] 264-275). The tradition, introduced by περι ("concerning"), is preserved in the participial style, omits the article before all substantives, and is arranged in two lines: του γενομενου/του ορισθεντος ("who was descended"/"who was designated"). γενεσθαι εκ ("descend from, be born from") is found elsewhere in Paul only in Galatians 4:4; Jesus' office as "Son of David" is otherwise never mentioned in the Pauline corpus, except for II Timothy 2:8. The contrast between κατα σαρκα/κατα πνευμα ("according to the flesh/ according to the Spirit") is used only here by Paul to distinguish the earthly and the heavenly spheres, but cf. I Peter 3:18; 4:6; I Timothy 3:16. πνευμα αγιωσυνης ("Spirit of holiness") is unique in Paul, and is an obvious Hebraism (lit. "Spirit of holiness = Holy Spirit"). εξ αναστασεως νεκρων ("by his resurrection from the dead") is used only here in the Pauline Letters of the resurrection of Jesus. The phrase εν δυναμει ("in power") could however be Pauline, since the apostle frequently uses the concept δυναμις ("power"). In that case Paul would emphasize that Jesus had always been Son of God, but since the resurrection is Son of God in δυναμις, that is, that he reigns as the exalted Lord.

The form and content of the expression reveals that we have here a Jewish-Christian formulation. The earthly Jesus was Son of David; however, his office as Son of David was surpassed by his rank as Son of God to which he was appointed as the resurrected one (Ps. 2:7). But Paul joins the Hellenistic church in saying that Jesus did not first become Son of God at the resurrection, but that he was already Son of God as the earthly Jesus (Rom. 8:32) and as the preexistent Christ (Gal. 4:4). He interprets the traditional confessional formula from that point of view, by prefacing it with περι του υιου αυτου ("concerning his Son") and adding at the end, Ιησου Χριστου του κυριου ημων ("Jesus Christ our Lord"). At the beginning and at the conclusion of the Jewish-Christian formulation there now stand the two most important christological titles for Hellenistic Christianity, Son and Lord, which are specially emphasized by their positions.

#6 Early Christian Songs

Schille, G. *Frühchristliche Hymnen*, 1962-[2]1965.
Deichgräber, R. *Gotteshymnus und Christushymnus in der frühen Christenheit*, 1967.
Sanders, J. T. *The New Testament Christological Hymns*, 1971.

a. The early Christians praised Christ as the Lord in songs (Col. 3:16; Eph. 5:19) and sang Christian psalms (I Cor. 14:26). Such songs, or parts of them, are quoted in the letters of the NT. The author of the Apocalypse composed hymns modeled on early Christian singing of his time, in order to portray the praise of the redeemed for σωτηρια ("salvation"). Like the creedal formulas, the songs refer to the Christ-event; however they do not speak of it in the terse formulation of the creedal statement, but speak in elaborate expressions of the event, which can also be pictured in dramatic form. The songs are for the most part arranged strophically, and expressed in the elevated style of hymnic prose—not however in rigidly metrical verses.

b. An outstanding example of an early Christian Christ-hymn is presented by Philippians 2:6-11.

The pre-Pauline character of the song, the beginning of which is clearly marked by the ος ("who") of v. 6, is clearly demonstrated by its terminology (see E. Lohmeyer, *Kyrios Jesus*, 1927; E. Käsemann, "A Critical Analysis of Phil. 2:5-11" in *God and Christ, J. Th. Ch* [5](1968) 45-88; G. Bornkamm, "Zum Verständnis des Christushymnus Phil. 2:6-11, *Ges. Aufsätze* II, [2]1963, 177-87; Deichgräber, *op. cit.*, 118-133; R. P. Martin, *Carmen Christi*, 1967): μορφη ("form," vv. 6-7) and the phrases αρπαγμον ηγεισθαι, ισα Θεω ειναι ("count equality with God a thing to be grasped") are not otherwise found by Paul. κενοω ("empty") is used occasionally by Paul, however always in a negative sense, and in the active voice only in I Corinthians 9:15; but in v. 7 κενοω is used in a positive sense. σχημα ("form," v. 8) is found elsewhere only in I Corinthians 7:31; the use of δουλος ("servant/slave") as a description of human existence as such is without parallel; ταπεινοω ("to humble") is also used in II Corinthians 11:7; 12:21, but there it refers to the relation of the apostle to the church (see also Phil. 4:12). υπερυψοω ("to highly exalt") is not found elsewhere in Paul; χαριζομαι ("bestow, give") always means "to forgive" elsewhere in Paul (Rom. 8:32, and elsewhere): το ονομα υπερ παν ονομα ("the name which is above every name") is also unique, appearing otherwise as ονομα του κυριου, ονομα Ιησου χριστου ("the name of the Lord, the name of Jesus Christ") or the like (I Cor. 1:2, 10; 5:4; 6:11, and elsewhere).

The song is divided into two strophes. Verses 6-8 deal with the descent and humiliation of the preexistent Christ, who took on the form of a slave and was obedient unto death. Verses 9-11 speak of the exaltation of Christ, to whom God gave the name which is above every name, so that the whole cosmos cries out, "Jesus Christ is Lord." Into the humiliation-exaltation schema Paul has inserted his own theology of the cross, by the emphatic addition θανατου δε σταυρου ("even death on a cross," end of v. 8). This early Christian hymn is quoted in order to show the church at Philippi what φρονειν εν χριστω (lit. "to think 'in Christ,'" v. 5) means, what it means to live under the lordship of the *Kurios* (v. 5).

c. As is the case with the creedal statements, so also in the songs of early Christianity we can observe a rich variety of expressions. In Colossians 1:15-20 a hymn is quoted that celebrates the universal lordship of Christ.

In these verses we find a veritable parade of concepts, which elsewhere in Colossians, as in the whole Pauline corpus, are not found at all or are used only in another sense. See Käsemann, *op.*

cit., I, 34-51; E. Lohse, *Colossians and Philemon, Hermeneia*, 1971, *ad loc* [bib.]: εικων του Θεου ("image of God") serves as a christological predicate elsewhere only in the formalized statement of II Corinthians 4:4, ος εστιν εικων του Θεου ("who is the image of God"); in I Corinthians 11:7 it is said of man that he is εικων και δοξα Θεου ("the image and glory of God"). ορατος ("visible") is found only here in the NT, and though αορατος ("invisible") is found a few times (Rom. 1:20; I Tim. 1:17; Heb. 11:27), it is never used in contrast to ορατος ("visible"). The Pauline Letters never speak elsewhere of Θρονοι ("thrones"), and of κυριοτης ("dominion") only in Ephesians 1:21. The intransitive συνιστημι, perf. ("hold together") is not otherwise used by Paul. In reference to Christ Paul says απαρχη ("first fruits," I Cor. 15:20), never αρχη ("beginning"). πρωτευω ("be preeminent") and ειρηνοποιεω ("make peace") are *hapax legomena* in the NT, κατοικεω ("dwell") occurs elsewhere in the Pauline corpus only in Colossians 2:9 and Ephesians 3:17, in both cases in dependence on the hymn, and αποκαταλλασσω ("reconcile") only in Ephesians 2:16. The blood of Christ is mentioned by Paul only in connection with traditional early Christian expressions that deal with the substitutionary death of Christ (Rom. 3:25; 5:9; I Cor. 10:16; 11:25, 27; cf. also Eph. 1:7; 2:13); the combination αιμα του σταυρου αυτου ("blood of his cross") is however without parallel.

Thus language and style indicate that the section is a hymnic text, which has been taken over from the tradition. A solemn introduction calls the reader to worship (vv. 12-14); verses 15-20 are divided into two strophes, each of which begins with ος εστιν ("who [he] is," vv. 15, 18*b*). In each case there then follows a relative clause composed of christological affirmations, which is then followed by a substantiating οτι ("for")-clause. Verses 17 and 18*a* are each introduced by και αυτος ("and he [is]"), v. 20 by και δι αυτου ("and through him").

The hymn praises Christ as the Lord of both creation and reconciliation. The author of Colossians did not, however, take over the hymn unchanged, but interpreted it in the sense of Pauline theology. At the end of the first strophe the expression κεφαλη του σωματος ("head of the body") was originally understood cosmologically; σωμα ("body") means the whole cosmos, whose head is Christ. By the addition of της εκκλησιας ("the church") however, an ecclesiological understanding is conferred on the phrase: Christ is Lord of the whole cosmos, but for the time being he exercises his worldwide Lordship in the church. Verse 20 is overloaded in its present form: he has established peace δια του αιματος του σταυρου αυτου δι αυτου (lit. "through the blood of his cross, through him/it"). Thus the words δια του αιματος του σταυρου αυτου ("through the blood of his cross") can be recognized as an addition by means of which the author of the letter indicates that the cross of Christ is that place on which the cosmic reconciliation is founded, in the sense of the Pauline theology of the cross. In the continuing context the style shifts from affirmation (vv. 15-20) to address (vv. 21-23), in order to encourage the community with the message of reconciliation.

As a further example of an early Christian hymn we may mention I Timothy 3:16.

The hymnic character of this verse is clearly recognizable from its form, content, and language. See E. Schweizer, *Erniedrigung und Erhöhung bei Jesus und seinen Nachfolgern*, [2]1962, 104-8; Zimmermann, *op. cit.* 203-213 [bib.]; Deichgräber, *op. cit.* 133-37; W. Stenger, "Der Christushymnus in I Tim. 3:16," *Trier Theol. Zeitschr.* 78 (1969) 324-67. The statements are composed in parallel form, with the verb at the beginning in accord with Semitic style; three times the earthly and heavenly spheres are placed over against each other. Thereby σαρξ ("flesh") and πνευμα ("spirit") are used as in Romans 1:3-4; I Peter 3:18; 4:6 to mean the earthly and heavenly realms respectively. For ωφθη ("he appeared/was seen") cf. I Corinthians 15:5; δικαιοω (lit. "to justify") means being received up into the heavenly world (cf. John 16:8-10).

The prefaced introductory comment, και ομολογουμενως μεγα εστιν το της ευσεβειας μυστηριον, ("great indeed, we confess, is the mystery of our religion") refers to the following quotation. The quotation itself begins with ος ("who"), the variant reading Θεος ("God") being secondary (ΟΣ became ΘΣ). The lines are not arranged chronologically, but in terms of subject matter. The hymn expounds what it means that the preexistent one has been manifest in the realm of flesh, in order to praise Christ as revealer and redeemer.

In addition to those named above, the NT writings offer further examples of early Christian songs, among which are Ephesians 1:3-14; 5:14; I Peter 2:22-24 (25); Hebrews 5:7-10. The Christ-hymns, which could be sung in many different settings, had their primary *Sitz im Leben* in the regular worship of the community, in which songs were sung *"Christo quasi deo"* ("to Christ as to a god"), Pliny the Younger, *Ep*. X 96:7.

#7 Liturgical Traditions

Käsemann, E. "Liturgie im NT" in *RGG*[3], 4:402-4.
Bornkamm, G. "Das Anathema in der unchristlichen Abendmahlsliturgie," in *Das Ende des Gesetzes*, [5]1966, 123-32.
Jeremias, J. *The Eucharistic Words of Jesus*, [3]1966.
Hahn, F. *The Worship of the Early Church*, 1973.

a. The worship services, in which preaching, creedal confession, and songs were firmly situated, were at first held in a variety of forms without rigid structures. Synagogal tradition was influential in Jewish-Christian circles, as can be recognized from the adoption of certain liturgical expressions: "amen" (I Cor. 14:16), "halleluia" (Rev. 19:1, 3, 6), as well as fixed forms of prayer (the Lord's Prayer). In Gentile-Christian churches the worship was usually less structured, as is seen in the example of the Corinthian church, whose worship was characterized by the free sway of the Spirit *(Enthusiasmus)* (I Cor. 14). It is clear from I Corinthians that the preaching of the word was often combined with the Lord's Supper. The apostle's writing ends with liturgical expressions that prepare for the celebration of the Eucharist. The holy kiss was exchanged as a sign of mutual forgiveness, unbelievers were expelled (anathema), and with *Maranatha* the cry for the coming of the Lord sounded forth (I Cor. 16:22; cf. Rev. 22:20).

b. The celebration of the Last Supper is carried out in accordance with the instructions given the community in the tradition of Jesus' last meal (I Cor. 11:23-25; Mark 14:22-24 par.). The congregation, gathered in the name of Christ, eats the broken bread and drinks from the cup according to his words. It thereby solemnly proclaims the death of the Lord (I Cor. 11:26) and experiences the present activity of the Christ who has given himself up to death for all and who gathers his own together as the eschatological covenant community. Paul does not understand the Lord's Supper tradition as a sacred, untouchable formula, but interprets the traditional statements by emphasizing his own understanding of the σωμα ("body")-concept (I Cor. 11:24; 10:16-17). The participants, who receive the body of Christ given for them, are responsible for each other as members of the body of Christ. While Paul and Luke document the liturgical form of the eucharistic words as they were used in the churches of the Pauline mission, Mark and Matthew present a text that pairs σωμα/αιμα ("body–blood") rather than σωμα/διαθηκη ("body–covenant"). The substitutionary death of Christ is the foundation for the eschatological program of salvation in which the forgiveness of sins is made available.

Eucharistic tradition is also present in I Corinthians 10:16-17, where Paul interprets a traditional statement by emphasizing the ecclesiological significance of the concept σωμα ("body"). Liturgically influenced expressions are also taken up in Romans 3:24-26.

The pre-Pauline quotation begins with the relative clause introduced by ος ("who") in v. 25, and is distinguishable from its context by its vocabulary. See E. Käsemann, "Zum Verständnis von Röm. 3, 24-26 [1950/51], in *Exegetische Versuche und Besinnungen* I, [6]1970, 96-100; E. Lohse, *Märtyrer und Gottesknecht*, [2]1963, 149-54; J. Reumann, "The Gospel of the Righteousness of God," *Interpretation* 20 [1966] 432-52. ιλαστηριον (["Place of] expiation") is unique in Paul; προτιθημι ("put forward") is also used in Romans 1:13, but there in the sense of "intend." The αιμα χριστου ("blood of Christ") is only found where Paul is using traditional material (see p. 37); παρεσις ("passing over") = αφεσις ("forgiveness") is *hapax legomenon* in Paul; αμαρτημα ("sins") recurs only in I Corinthians 6:18, the plural in accord with early Christian [but not Pauline] usage; Paul speaks of God's ανοχη ("forbearance") elsewhere only in Romans 2:4.

The tradition taken up by Paul speaks of God's righteousness as his covenant faithfulness, which he has proven by publicly setting forth Christ as an expiation for sins and by forgiving the sins that he had earlier passed over in the time of his forbearance. Paul gives his own interpretation to this sentence by emphatically inserting δια πιστεως ("to be received by faith," lit. "through faith") between ιλαστηριον ("expiation") and εν τω αυτου αιματι ("by his blood"; word order is different in Greek) and elaborates the earlier tradition found in v. 26*b*: salvation is received through faith alone; for in the present eschatological *Kairos* God proves his righteousness in that he justifies the one who lives εκ πιστεως Ιησου ("from faith in Jesus"). Since the theme of forgiveness of sins is of special significance in the early Christian phrase cited by Paul, it probably had its *Sitz im Leben* in the celebration of the Lord's Supper. But one could also think of baptism in this connection.

c. A series of liturgical expressions contained in the NT letters refer to baptism and the baptismal worship service, for example I Corinthians 6:11 απελουσασθε—ηγιασθητε—εδικαιωθητε εν τω ονοματι του κυριου Ιησου χριστου και εν τω πνευματι του Θεου ημων ("you were washed, you were sanctified, you were justified in the name of the Lord Jesus Christ and in the Spirit of our God"). Baptism was performed in the name of the *Kurios*; the baptized person becomes thereby the property of the Lord. He is baptized εις χριστον ("into Christ," Rom. 6:3) and so becomes a member of the σωμα χριστου ("body of Christ," I Cor. 12:13). According to the extensive formula in Matthew 28:19 baptism was performed εις το ονομα του πατρος και του υιου και του αγιου πνευματος ("in the name of the Father and of the Son and of the Holy Spirit"). During the baptismal ceremony the confession κυριος Ιησους ("Jesus is Lord") was spoken (Rom. 10:9), and hymns to Christ such as Philippians 2:6-11 and Colossians 1:15-20 were sung. Through baptism the new creation was established, in which from then on the believer lives εν χριστω ("in Christ," II Cor. 5:17).

d. As among religious Jews, so also from the first Christians utterances of praise to God rang forth. Letters sometimes begin with doxologies: ευλογητος ο Θεος και πατηρ του κυριου ημων Ιησου Χριστου ("blessed be the God and Father of our Lord Jesus Christ," II Cor. 1:3; Eph. 1:3); but they are also found in the midst of the text (Rom. 1:25; II Cor. 11:31 and Rom. 9:5); in the latter instance, a colon must be placed after Χριστος κατα σαρκα ("according to the flesh [is the] Christ"); for the doxology refers to God. Besides the ευλογητος ("blessed")-expressions, those with δοξα ("glory") are also frequently used: αυτω η δοξα εις τους αιωνας ("to him be glory for ever," Rom. 11:36; cf. also Rom. 16:27; Gal. 1:5; Phil. 4:20, and elsewhere). In the oldest texts these declarations are always in reference to God, but in the later ones they also refer to Christ, as for example II Timothy 4:18: "The Lord will rescue me . . . ω η δοξα εις τους αιωνας των αιωνων. αμην ("to him be the glory for ever and ever. Amen").

Luke 2:14 contains a hymnic doxology.

The oldest form of the text had two lines, not three: δοξα εν υψιστοις Θεω / και επι γης ειρηνη εν ανθρωπος ευδοκιας ("Glory to God in the highest / and on earth peace among men with whom he is pleased"). (See C.-H Hunzinger, "Neues Licht auf Lucas 2:14," *ZNW* 44 [1952/53] 85-90; and "Ein weiterer Beleg zu Lucas 2:14 ανθρωποι ευδοκιας, *ZNW* 49 [1958] 129f; E. Vogt, "Peace Among Men of God's Good Pleasure" [1953] in K. Stendahl, ed., *The Scrolls and the NT*, 1957, 114-17; R. Deichgräber, "Lc. 2:14 ανθρωποι ευδοκιας, " *ZNW* 51 [1960] 132).

This short affirmation places this series of concepts over against each other: δοξα/ειρηνη - εν υψιστοις/επι γης - Θεω/εν ανθρωποις ευδοκιας ("glory/peace—in the highest/on earth—to God/among men with whom he is pleased"). Where God is given praise and glory "in the highest," there dwells the eschatological peace of God among "men with whom he is pleased," that is, the members of the eschatological community of salvation that he has chosen for himself (cf. the expression from the Qumran texts, "sons of the [divine] good pleasure," which is used in a different sense, 1QH IV 33f.; XI, 9; 1QS VIII, 6).

#8 Parenetic Traditions

Weidinger, K. *Die Haustafeln*, 1928.

Voegtle, A. *Die Tugend- und Lasterkataloge im NT*, 1936.

Wibbing, S. *Die Tugend- und Lasterkataloge im NT*, 1959.

Kamlah, E. *Die Form der katalogischen Paränese im NT*, 1964.

Käsemann, E. "Principles of the Interpretation of Romans 13," in *NT Questions of Today*, 1969, 196-216.

Lohse, E. *A Commentary on the Epistles to the Colossians and to Philemon*. [14]1971, 154-57.

Lohse, E. "Katechismus im Urchristentum," in *RGG*[3], 3:1179.

Crouch, J. *The Origin and Intention of the Colossian Haustafel*, 1972.

Dibelius, M., and Conzelmann, H. *A Commentary on the Pastoral Epistles*. [4]1972, 50ff.

Zimmermann, H. *Neutestamentliche Methodenlehre*, [4]1974, 165-69.

Dibelius, M. and Greeven, H. *A Commentary on the Epistle of James*. [11]1976.

Parenesis, i.e. exhortation to right living, is always and everywhere largely determined by tradition. So also early Christianity adopted traditional material, especially OT-Jewish proverbial wisdom and the ethical instruction of Hellenistic popular philosophy. Whatever appeared to be useful for the edification of the community was taken over from the rich treasury of experience, according to the principle: οσα εστιν αληθη, οσα σεμνα, οσα δικαια, οσα αγνα, οσα προσφιλη, οσα ευφημη, ει τις αρετη και ει τις επαινος ταυτα λογιζεσθε ("whatever is true, whatever is honorable, whatever is just, whatever is pure, whatever is lovely, whatever is gracious, if there is any excellence, if there is anything worthy of praise, think about these things," Phil. 4:8).

a. So-called catalogs of virtues and vices are frequently found in the hortatory sections of NT letters. Behavior to be avoided and duties to be fulfilled are placed over against each other, as are lists of people who have done evil and examples of virtue. Such lists are not formed *ad hoc,* but taken over from parenetic tradition. Similar catalogs were widespread in the Cynic-Stoic popular philosophy, whence they found entrance into the Hellenistic synagogue. On the other hand, Palestinian Judaism also knew catalog-like lists, which set forth right and wrong conduct, as for example in the "Manual of Discipline" of Qumran I QS IV, 2-14. The NT catalogs rest on this broad traditional base: the vice-catalogs Romans 1:29-31; 13:13; I Corinthians 5:10-11; 6:9-10; II Corinthians 12:20-21; Galatians 5:19-21; Ephesians 4:31; 5:3-5; Colossians 3:5, 8; I Timothy 1:9-10; II Timothy 3:2-4, and the virtue-catalogs Galatians 5:22-23; Philippians 4:8; Ephesians 4:2; Colossians 3:12; I Timothy 4:12; 6:11; II Timothy 2:22; 3:10; I Peter 3:8; II Peter 1:5-7. The enumerated virtues or vices therefore offer no information about the situation of the churches to which they are addressed; the traditions that have been taken over are rather for the purpose of instructing the community, somewhat catechetically, what is to be done and what is to be avoided. To make the tradition more relevant, one or another item from the catalog may be especially emphasized. For example, in Romans 1:29 αδικια ("wickedness") is placed at the beginning to emphasize the connection to 1:18: God's judgment fall on every ασεβεια and αδικια ("ungodliness and wickedness"). In I Corinthians 6:9 πορνοι ("immoral") stands at the beginning, because Paul is developing an argument against πορνεια ("immorality") in the church. And when the fruits of the Spirit (Gal. 5:22) are contrasted with the works of the flesh (Gal. 5:19) the emphasis falls on αγαπη ("love"), which is the fulfillment of the law (Gal. 5:13-15).

b. In the so-called tables of household duties *(Haustafeln)* the NT letters offer catalogs in which the various classes within the community are addressed one after the other: wives/husbands, children/fathers, slaves/masters. To each is declared what he or she is to do in his or her particular station in life: Colossians 3:18–4:1; Ephesians 5:22–6:9; I Timothy 2:8-15; Titus 2:1-10; I Peter 2:13–3:12. The Hellenistic popular philosophy offered instructions for people in various positions in life, which held up before them their respective duties. Such instruction was imparted in the Hellenistic synagogue to describe proper conduct in accordance with the Torah. The Christian community adopted such traditions, but developed the exhortations as directions that receive their authority εν κυριω ("in the Lord"). At the same time a critical norm was thereby developed so it could be decided which traditions could properly be adopted and how they might be adapted. Parenetic material was set forth with the intention of illustrating what obedience to the Lord means in the circumstances of everyday living.

c. The Christian manner of life in the world is set forth in parenesis. Wisdom traditions, collected as a series of proverbs, expand the rich treasury of material derived from experience. Such proverbial material, amplified by themes from popular philosophy and the Christian sayings-tradition (which has various parallels in the Sermon on the Mount) has been collected in the Letter of James into a somewhat catechetical arrangement (see pp. 204-5). The Christian manner of life in the world had above all to authenticate itself in its relation to the state. This is dealt with in I Peter 2:13-17 at the beginning of a table of household duties *(Haustafel)*, and in Romans 13:1-7 in an independent passage (cf. also Titus 3:1). Romans 13 contains no specifically Christian directions, neither Christ nor love being mentioned, but presents what everyone must find binding who follows his conscience as a responsible citizen and conducts himself so as to gain public approval. It is thus a matter of a pre-Christian tradition that was taken up into the instruction of the community. Only by means of its wider context does this tradition take on a Christian connotation. For the whole parenetical section of Romans stands under the superscription that Christian worship is to take place precisely in the midst of the everyday world (Rom. 12:1-2).

d. The catalogs of duties in the Pastoral Letters set forth what one who holds an ecclesiastical office was supposed to do and the qualifications for the office (bishops, I Tim. 3:1-7; Titus 1:7-9; presbyters-elders, I Tim. 5:17-19; Titus 1:5-6; deacons, I Tim. 3:8-13; widows: I Tim. 5:3-16). These catalogs are for the most part based on tradition. In the Hellenistic world there were similar catalogs that enumerated the characteristics and tasks that must be present in a στρατηγος ("praetor, chief magistrate") or holder of a high political or military office. This pattern was then adopted in regulations for church order and so adapted that it delineated the standards for officers in the church.

e. Firm collections of parenetic material were formed quite early. Materials were collected that could be used for the instruction and indoctrination of the community. In I Corinthians 4:17 Paul wrote that he was sending Timothy to Corinth, ος υμας αναμνησει τας οδους μου τας εν Χριστω ("who will remind you of my ways in Christ"). These "ways" show how one should live his or her life (cf. the Jewish concept of Halakah, i.e. instruction concerning the right way according to the Torah). In Hebrews 6:1-2 the major elements of an early Christian catechism are listed just as they were used in the prebaptismal instruction. It contains the following sections: repentance from dead works, faith in God, instruction about baptism, laying on of hands, resurrection of the dead, and eternal judgment. In this enumeration it becomes clear how Christian instruction was patterned after the model of the Hellenistic-Jewish mission to the Gentiles. More extensive didactic complexes are then developed in the so-called "Two-Ways Catechism" (Barnabas 18-20, Didache 1-6). Such comprehensive passages are not yet present in the NT; still, in the NT parenesis reference is often made to complexes of ethical instruction which were widely circulated in the churches, as I Thessalonians 4:1-12; 5:13-22; or Romans 12-13. These sections do not provide instructions that have been called forth by particular situations or questions in the churches, but traditional materials are elaborated upon in order to direct the church to what is permanently valid and accordingly how it is to conduct itself.

II.

The Composition of Early Christian Letters

#9 Letter and Epistle

Deissmann, A. *Light from the Ancient East*, [4]1928.
Roller, O. *Das Formular der paulinischen Briefe*, 1933.
Doty, W. *Letters in Primitive Christianity*, 1973.
Berger, K. "Apostelbrief und apostolische Rede, Zum Formular frühchristlicher Briefe." *ZNW* 65 (1974):190-231.

a. A *letter* serves to cultivate relations and facilitate exchange of ideas between sender and receiver when they are geographically separated. It originates at a particular time, and speaks from a definite situation to a particular set of circumstances of the addressees. This is different from a writing in which the letter form is only the framework for a literary essay. This letter form is not directed to definite addressees, but is set forth as a tract addressing a wide circle of readers, as, for example, the philosophical letters of Cicero and Seneca. In distinction from real letters this artificial form has been called an *epistle* (Deissmann). To be sure, this designation is not entirely satisfactory, since the word "epistle" itself means the same as "letter"; but this terminology is still in general use.

Are the NT letters real letters, or epistles representing theological treatises? The apostle Paul refers in his writings to concrete congregational relationships, so there can be no doubt that his writings are real letters. The typical letter form is of course sometimes distended by their contents: creedal formulas, songs, sermonic passages, interpretations of scripture, parenesis, and theological discussions have their place. Nonetheless, the whole content of each letter serves for the immediate instruction and admonition of a particular congregation. Whether epistles are to be found among the Deutero-Pauline and other NT letters is something to be examined from case to case. James is rather like a tract; also one might consider whether Ephesians, I John, and Hebrews are more like letters or epistles. But since the authentic Letters of Paul are written from a particular situation of the apostle to a particular situation in a certain church, there can be no doubt that they are not epistles, but real letters.

b. The composing of a letter is not to be thought of in terms of modern letters. Ancient letters were consistently very short, 250 words or less, so that the whole content could be written on a single page. The letter that was written by the Roman officer Claudius Lysias to the governor Felix comprises only five verses (Acts 23:26-30). This extent corresponds to the normal length of a Greek personal letter, which was a brief communication beginning with the names of the sender and receiver and the greeting Χαιρειν ("greeting," lit. "rejoice") and concluding with the wish ερρωσο ("be strong," i.e. "healthy"). So also in the Orient letters were consistently short and introduced with a bipartite formula. First the names of the sender and receiver were given. Then followed the greeting in the form, "Peace be with you" (Dan. 3:31). Letters were mostly written in one's own hand, especially since scribes had to be paid dearly. A sheet of papyrus served as writing material, with something like a thick watercolor being used as ink. The letters were written in *scriptio continua* with a reed pen. The completed letter was rolled up, tied with a cord, and sealed. The address of the receiver was written on the outside of the papyrus roll, and the letter was then entrusted to a carrier.

If a letter was dictated verbatim, the composition took a correspondingly long time. Comprehensive writings such as

Romans or I Corinthians could not possibly have been written in one day. But in addition to verbatim dictation, the ancient world used another technique. A scribe noted key words on a wax tablet, which he then used as a guide in composing the letter. The conclusion of the letter was always written in the sender's own hand, so that the receiver would have no doubt as to who was the author of the letter.

How did Paul compose his letters? In Romans 16:22 the scribe who actually wrote the letter, Tertius, greets the church in his name. So the long letters to churches were dictated by Paul to a scribe, while he supposedly wrote a short letter such as Philemon in his own hand. But how did Paul dictate—verbatim or in key phrases, which the scribe then elaborated in the completed letter? Roller has vigorously advocated the thesis that Paul dictated to a secretary who then undertook the composition of the letter on the basis of key phrases he had noted down. To support this, Roller points out that at the beginning of the Pauline Letters so-called co-senders are named, which occurs only rarely in ancient letters. Roller infers therefrom that the named co-workers of the apostle participated in the composition of the letter. He adds a further argument: five of the Pauline Letters originated in prison (Phil., Philem., Col., Eph., II Tim.). In the terrible circumstances that prevailed in ancient prisons, it would have been impossible for Paul to have written a letter with his own hand; he could only have given key phrases to a helper, who used them as the bases for the composition of the letter. It was Timothy who served in this role for the most part, but in the case of the Pastoral Letters it must have been someone else, which explains their linguistic and stylistic differences from the other Pauline Letters. How should we evaluate this secretary-hypothesis?

Since the Pauline authorship of Colossians, Ephesians, and II Timothy is disputed, their references to the prison situation cannot with certainty be evaluated as historical data. A short writing such as Philemon could in fact have been written by Paul himself in prison. So it remains to examine Philippians, which did originate in prison and which begins with the names of both Paul and Timothy (1:1). The content of the letter clearly reveals, however, that Timothy did not share in its composition. For 2:19-24 commends Timothy to the church as a trustworthy assistant of the apostle in such exalted language, that such self-congratulation should not be attributed to Timothy himself. But if in this case it is clear that Timothy did not participate in composing the content of the letter itself, it follows that Paul himself is responsible for the content of the other letters as well. Thus he dictated the letters verbatim, and a scribe wrote them down sentence by sentence (Rom. 16:22). The apostle wrote the last lines himself (Gal. 6:11; I Cor. 16:21). A messenger then delivered the letter to the church (Rom. 16:1), which was then read aloud in the worship service of the gathered congregation.

#10 Authenticity and Pseudonymity

Sint, J. A. *Pseudonymität im Altertum,* 1960.

Balz, H. R. "Anonymität und Pseudepigraphie im Urchristentum," *ZThK* 66 (1969):403-46

Speyer, W. *Die literarische Fälschung im heidnischen und christlichen Altertum,* 1971.

Metzger, B. M. "Literary Forgeries and Canonical Pseudepigrapha," *JBL* 91 (1972):3-24.

Rist, M. "Pseudepigraphy and the Early Christians," in *Studies in NT and Early Christian Literature*. Edited by D. E. Aune, 1972, pp. 75-91.

Brox, N. *Pseudepigraphie in der heidnischen und jüdisch-christlichen Antike,* 1977.

a. The name of the authors of only a few NT writings are confidently known. Paul places his name emphatically at the beginning of his letters, which he combines with the claim to be an authorized apostle of the exalted Lord. His claim for the truth of the gospel which he preaches is over his own signature. Whoever doubts his apostleship thereby attacks the message proclaimed by him (Gal.). The author of the Apocalypse also names his own name, John—in distinction to Jewish apocalyptic, in which the name of the actual author is concealed behind that of some famous saint of the past (see p. 221). The author of the Apocalypse also names his own name, John (Rev. 1:1, 4, 9; 22:8) in distinction to (or from) Jewish apocalyptic in which the name of the actual author is concealed behind that of some famous saint of the past.

b. Apart from the Pauline Letters and Revelation, which give the names of the authors unambiguously, the NT contains a series of writings that give neither the author's name nor any information from which the identity of the author can be inferred, e.g. Hebrews and I John, which are somewhat like theological treatises, and the Synoptic Gospels and the Gospel of John. Later tradition undertook to attribute these writings to definite authors. Since apostolic authorship was a requirement for recognition by the church at large (see p. 22), it was desirable to attach the names of apostles or at least of disciples of the apostles. As a result of this the originally anonymous writings became pseudonymous—an event that has many parallels in antiquity. In the Greco-Roman world medical texts were regularly attributed to Hippocrates, anonymous speeches to Demosthenes, and philosophical speculations with mysterious content to Pythagoras. The OT-Jewish tradition ascribed wisdom traditions to King Solomon, who was regarded as the Wise Man par excellence, and regarded King David as the poet who composed the Psalms. Through such connections with famous men it was sought to confirm the authority of anonymous writings.

c. Like ancient literature in general, so also early Christian literature contained various writings that were known under the name of a pseudonymous author from the very beginning. A famous example is presented by the pseudo-Platonic letters, which were circulated in the name of the revered philosopher. In Judaism various saints of the OT were alleged to be the authors of all the apocalyptic literature, in order thereby to promote acceptance for these writings. It is therefore not surprising that also pseudonymous writings emerged in early Christianity. Thus, for example, the author of II Peter is doubtless literally dependent on Jude (see pp. 216-17). The author of II Peter conceals his name behind that of another, who enjoyed uncontested authority in the readership to which he wanted to direct his message. This authority was accorded by the ancient church to the apostles and their teaching. Whoever composed a writing for which he, or the circle in which he stood, wanted to obtain general acceptance in the churches, not only had to be guided by this norm for the content of his writings, but also placed the name of an apostle at the beginning of his writing. In this regard the authentic letters of Paul served as a standard-setting model. The Pauline Letter formulas were taken over not only in the Deutero-Pauline writings, but also in other documents such as I Peter and Revelation (1:4-8). Paul's name was prefaced to the Deutero-Pauline Letters.

The authority of an apostle was invoked in order to settle disputes with heretics and to solidify church order. In this way it was intended that the binding word of an apostle was allowed to speak again into the new situations in which the churches of the second and third generation found themselves. Where it was desired to hold fast to the apostolic traditions, it was necessary to be concerned that the new tasks which emerged be carried out under the authority of an apostle. The origin of pseudonymous writings is therefore not properly understood when they are described as falsifications and thereby given an a priori negative judgment. Rather, the conditions that led to the production of pseudonymous literature must be kept in mind. This means that the Deutero-Pauline and other pseudonymous writings in the NT are to be evaluated in terms of this material issue: did they succeed in holding fast to the early Christian kerygma while at the same time expressing it in new ways?

#11 The Chronology of Early Christian History

Deissmann. *Paul*, [2]1927, 261-86.
Finegan, J. *Handbook of Biblical Chronology*, 1964.
Suhl, A. *Paulus und seine Briefe—Ein Beitrag zur paulinischen Chronologie*, 1975.
Jewett, Robert. *A Chronology of Paul's Life*, 1979.

a. The dating of NT writings, especially the Pauline Letters, requires that we distinguish between absolute and relative chronology. No NT document is provided with a statement giving its exact date. But the Gospel of Luke and Acts do in fact refer to events of secular history, and Paul's Letters mention particular periods in the life of the apostle. Paul did not make his first contact with the earliest Jerusalem church until three years after his conversion (Gal. 1:18). Fourteen years later he journeyed to the "apostolic conference" in Jerusalem (Gal. 2:1). This means that about sixteen years elapsed between Paul's conversion and the "apostolic conference." (Parts of years were counted as full years in antiquity.) Acts reports that Paul spent one and a half years in Corinth (18:11) and two and a fourth years in Ephesus (19:8, 10). With the help of this data concerning relative chronology, the information from the letters and from

Acts can in fact to some extent be correlated. But an exact chronology can only be established if an absolutely fixed point can be found to which the relative chronology can be related.

b. This date is provided by the so-called Gallio inscription. In Acts 18:12 it is said: "But when Gallio was (or became) proconsul of Achaia, the Jews made a united attack upon Paul and brought him before the tribunal (of the proconsul)." As a senatorial province, Achaia was administered by a proconsul whose term of office was one year. Acts 18:12 accordingly declares: when Gallio arrived in Corinth as the new proconsul, the Jews dragged Paul into his court. So the question is, When did this Gallio (the brother of the philosopher Seneca) enter upon his office? An inscription from Delphi, published for the first time in 1905, contains a letter from the Emperor Claudius to the city, in which certain privileges are confirmed. This inscription refers to Gallio as proconsul in Achaia, and gives its date as the twenty-sixth acclamation of Claudius. The twenty-second to twenty-fourth acclamations, each of which followed a military victory, took place in the eleventh year of Claudius' reign, and the twenty-seventh occurred before August 1, A.D. 52. So the twenty-sixth acclamation is to be dated in the spring of 52. This was within the period of Gallio's term of office as proconsul of Achaia. Since the term of office began in late spring or early summer, Gallio probably began his term in the early summer of A.D. 51. (Possible, but less probable, the early summer of 52.) At that time Paul had to withdraw from Corinth. If one counts back one and a half years (according to Acts 18:11), Paul came to Corinth at the end of 49 or the beginning of 50. According to Acts 18:2 he found there the married couple Aquila and Priscilla who had been forced to leave Rome because Emperor Claudius had banned the Jews from the capital (see p. 75). According to the historian Orosius (who did not write until the fifth century) the edict of Claudius against the Jews was promulgated in A.D. 49. This data coincides exactly with the calculations derived from the Gallio inscription.

From this fixed point, which has been attained with the help of the Gallio inscription, further calculations forward and backward can be made with the help of the relative chronology.

c. For the time before Gallio's term of office the following may be ascertained: before Paul reached Corinth at the end of 49 or the beginning of 50, he visited the churches listed in the report of the so-called second missionary journey of Acts 15:36–18:22. That would take up the year 49. The apostolic conference is then to be dated in A.D. 48. From here we may proceed further with the help of the data in Galatians 1-2, (see above p. 51). By subtracting the sixteen years derived from Galatians 1-2, we arrive at a date of about A.D. 32 for the conversion of Paul. The death of Jesus, who was condemned by Pontius Pilate (governor of Judea 26-36), probably falls in the year 30 (see J. Jeremias, *The Eucharistic Words of Jesus*, 1966, 36-41).

d. A few dates may also be ascertained for the time after the beginning of Gallio's term of office. Paul left Corinth in mid-year of 51 and concluded the so-called second missionary journey, returning to Caesarea via Ephesus (Acts 18:22). Paul began the so-called third missionary journey (Acts 18:23ff) in A.D. 52 at the earliest. First he visited churches in Galatia and Phrygia, then he settled down in Ephesus for two and a fourth years (Acts 19:8, 10). From Ephesus he traveled via Macedonia to Corinth, where according to Acts 20:3 he remained for three months. Here he wrote the Letter to the Romans, before he boarded the ship for the trip to Jerusalem (see p. 77). The three months' stay in Corinth must have been during the winter, since travel by boat could not be continued until the following spring. So the time in Ephesus is to be dated about 53–55, and that in Corinth about 56. From Corinth the apostle first went through Macedonia, where he boarded a ship in Philippi in order to deliver the collection to Jerusalem. The trip went via Troas and Miletus to Caesarea, and from there to Jerusalem. Here Paul was arrested and brought back to Caesarea as a prisoner. According to Acts 24:27 Paul was imprisoned two years in Caesarea. If Paul returned to Jerusalem in 57, then the years 57-59 would be the dates for his Caesarean imprisonment. But some uncertainty remains. Acts 24:27 mentions the changing of procurators from Felix to Festus. But this cannot be exactly dated. Felix became procurator in 52/53, and Festus succeeded him in office, continuing until his death in 62. But we do not know for sure when his term of office in Judea began. Paul's imprisonment in Caesarea ended because he appealed to Caesar and was transported to Rome for his case to be decided. In Rome Paul was imprisoned two years, according to Acts 28:30-31. Neither Acts nor Paul's Letters provide any further information. Did death end Paul's Roman imprisonment, or was he once again set free? If he was set free, it is perhaps possible to relate the data in the Pastorals to this time (see pp. 99-100). Was Paul able to realize his plans to travel to Spain (Rom. 15:24)? According to I Clem. 5:7 he reached "the limits of the West." But this assertion could be simply an inference from Romans 15:24; for what an apostle planned, he will certainly have done. In any case there is no firm data beyond Acts 28:30-31, so that reliable documentation of a trip to Spain and a second Roman imprisonment is not available. We should therefore accept as most probable that Paul was executed in Rome shortly after A.D. 60. His death is not to be related to the Neronian persecution of A.D. 64. Since the early church had not yet developed a cult of apostles and martyrs, no detailed account of the death of Paul was preserved, as was also the case with Peter.

III.

The Authentic Letters of Paul

#12 The First Letter to the Thessalonians

Eckart, K. G. "Der zweite echte Brief des Apostels Paulus an die Thessalonicher," *ZThK* 58 (1961):30-44.

Kümmel, W. G. "Das literarische und geschichtliche Problem des ersten Thessalonicherbriefes" (1962), in *Heilsgeschehen und Geschichte,* 1965, 406-16.

Best, E. *The First and Second Epistles to the Thessalonians,* 1972.

Schmithals, W. "The Historical Situation of the Thessalonian Epistles," in *Paul and the Gnostics,* 1972, 123-218.

Friedrich, G. "1. Thessalonicher 5, 1-11" (1973), in *Auf das Wort kommt es an, Gesammelte Aufsätze,* 1978, 251-78.

a. Contents: In chapters 1-3 the usual thanksgiving section is greatly extended, first surveying the previous activity of the apostle (1:2–2:16) and then reporting events after he left the Thessalonian congregation (2:17–3:13). Chapters 4-5 respond to two questions from the church (4:13–5:11), surrounded by parenetic material (4:1-12; 5:12-24). Then follow the final greetings and conclusion (5:25-28).

b. The church at Thessalonica was founded by Paul. Thessalonica was a significant center of commerce, and the capital city of the Roman province of Macedonia. According to the portrayal in Acts 17:1-15 Paul at first preached in the synagogue for three sabbaths with minimum results, then—corresponding to the schematized Lukan account—went from the Jews to the Gentiles, many of whom became believers. But then the Jews compelled the apostle to leave the city (Acts 17:13). Since he himself was prevented from returning (2:18), he sent Timothy (3:1, 5), and received fresh reports from Thessalonica upon his return.

c. Timothy's report was the occasion of writing the letter (3:6). There is some conflict between the data of Acts and that of the letter. According to the letter Timothy was sent from Athens to Thessalonica and returned to Paul—at Corinth (3:1, 5-6). The account in Acts is different in that Paul set out alone from Berea to Athens, while Timothy and Silas at first remained behind in Berea, but then were informed through the Bereans who had conducted Paul to meet him as quickly as possible. They then met him in Corinth (18:5). Acts therefore mentions nothing of Timothy's trip back to Thessalonica, supposedly because in Acts the activity of Paul's co-workers recedes completely behind the work of the figure who plays the leading role—Paul as missionary to the Gentiles.

Timothy brought good news. But uneasiness had arisen because some members of the congregation had suddenly died. Will they participate in the salvation soon to appear at the parousia? Paul answers this question by citing a word of the Lord from the oral tradition, and elaborates by explaining that at the parousia those who have fallen asleep will be awakened and along with the living will be taken in a festive procession to meet the returning Lord (4:13-18). A second question directed to the apostle likewise concerns the eschatological expectation. It is answered with instruction περι δε των χρονων και των καιρων ("concerning the times and the seasons," 5:1).

The composition of this letter could not have been too long after the departure of the apostle from the church. The concern that the church might doubt the reliability of the apostle (2:1-12), and the necessity to give further instructions about the eschatological expectation (4:13–5:11), make clear that the letter was intended to solidify his relationship with the young church. Thus the church must have been founded in A.D. 49 (see pp. 52-53), and the letter written in A.D. 50 in Corinth. A later origin, e.g. during the so-called third missionary journey, can therefore not be considered.

The letter's course of thought is well-rounded and closely linked together. It is therefore a mistake to attempt to dissect such a unified letter into different writings (so most recently Schenke-Fischer; cf. Kümmel's proper critique of Eckart and Schmithals). Since the section 5:1-11 is also determined by an immediate expectation that the eschaton could come any moment, it cannot be seen as a later insertion (contra Friedrich).

#13 The Letter to the Galatians

Lütgert, W. *Gesetz und Geist,* 1919.

Oepke, A. *Der Brief des Paulus an die Galater,* ³1965.

Schlier, H. *Der Brief an die Galater,* ⁵1971.

Schmithals, W. "The Heretics in Galatia," in *Paul and the Gnostics,* 1972, 13-64.

Mussner, F. *Der Galaterbrief,* 1974.

Betz, H. D. "Geist, Freiheit und Gesetz," *ZThK* 71 (1974):78-93.

———. "The Literary Composition of Paul's Letter to the Galatians," *NTS* 21 (1974/75):353-79.

———. *A Commentary on Paul's Letters to the Churches in Galatia,* Hermeneia, 1979.

a. Contents: The section 1:6-9 which directly follows the introductory greeting (1:1-5) lets us see immediately the sharpness of the debate in which this letter is engaged. In distinction from all of Paul's other letters, not one word of the customary thanksgiving is found. Paul must combat two charges (1:10-21): (1) what he preached was a "man's gospel," κατα ανθρωπον, because he wanted to please men, and (2) his official standing was παρα ανθρωπου ("from man"), so he was not a legitimate apostle.

Paul first countered the latter charge (1:10–2:21) by explaining that his apostleship was not conferred through men. Independent of the authorities in Jerusalem (1:10-24), later expressly recognized by them (2:1-10), he had successfully defended his gospel even against Peter in Antioch (2:11-21).

A reminder of the early days of the Galatian church (3:1-5) serves as a transition to a defense of the Pauline gospel, which is carried through by scriptural proofs using two texts from the Pentateuch (3:6–5:12). In this section Paul shows that everyone who reads the Law rightly must hear in it the testimony for justification by faith. The doctrine of justification by faith is grounded in the example of Abraham's faith (3:6-9) and in the story of the two sons of Abraham (4:21-31). After the first scriptural proof, the relationship of faith and law is dealt with (3:10–4:7) and applied to the Galatians (4:8-20). The second scriptural proof is followed by the either/or question: slavery under the law or the freedom of the gospel (5:1-12)?

Then follows the parenetic section (5:13–6:10) and the closing greeting written in his own hand (6:11-18).

b. The letter is addressed to the churches of Galatia. Two different answers have been given to the question of where this Galatia is to be located: (1) According to the so-called South-Galatian theory, the province is intended. After the death of the last Galatian King Amyntas (25 B.C.), his country, located in the midst of Asia Minor, became Roman territory. The Romans combined Galatia with Pisidia, Isauria, Lycaonia, Phrygia, Paphlagonia, and Pontus into one province, which extended all across Asia Minor from the southwest to the northeast, comprising about a third of Asia Minor, and which could be called simply "Galatia." If Galatia refers to this province, then Paul could be addressing the churches of South Asia Minor founded on the first missionary journey and mentioned in Acts 13–14, churches composed primarily of Jewish Christians. Since the apostle had been to their churches twice according to 4:13, the letter would then have been written on the so-called second missionary journey. To support this view the following types of evidence are presented: (a) we know of the establishing of these churches and their continued existence from Acts; (b) the line of argument followed in Galatians presupposes a familiarity with the OT by the readers that would have been present only in erstwhile Jews; (c) Paul elsewhere prefers to use the names of provinces when he is giving geographical information, so that Galatia is also to be understood as referring to the province.

(2) The North Galatian theory, advocated by most exegetes, understands Galatia to be the region of Galatia in central Asia Minor, in which the Galatians who originally came from Gall settled in the third century B.C. (Schlier, Oepke). There is no report of the founding of churches in this region. According to Acts 16:6 and 18:23 Paul twice passed through Galatia (cf. Gal. 4:13). According to the North Galatian theory the letter must have been written during the further course of the so-called third missionary journey. That this view is correct is supported by the

following evidence: (a) The direct address of the recipients as "Galatians" (3:1) would be meaningless if the readers are thought of as being in the southern part of the province, for they would not at all have belonged to the Galatian people. So the inhabitants of the old region of Galatia must be meant. (b) The readers are unmistakably addressed as erstwhile pagans who earlier did not know God, worshiped idols, which were not really gods (4:8), and who were enslaved by the elemental spirits of the universe (4:9). (c) It is not always the case that Paul thinks in terms of provinces when giving geographical information. In Galatians 1:21 Syria and Cilicia are mentioned in the sense of regions (for Jerusalem belonged at that time to the province of Syria!), and in I Thessalonians 2:14 Judea is mentioned in the sense of a region, not a province.

So Paul writes to the churches founded by him in the heart of Asia Minor. A severe sickness, concerning which no details have been preserved, caused the apostle to interrupt his journey for a while in Galatia, and then the opportunity was available to bring the gospel to the Gentile Galatians (4:13). A second visit followed—that is presupposed by το προτερον ("the first time, at first")—and after that people suddenly appeared who aroused the church against Paul. This was the occasion for the Letter to the Galatians, which was written in the further course of the so-called third missionary journey—probably during Paul's stay in Ephesus (ca. A.D. 53–55).

c. From outside the church false teachers penetrated the congregations; they threw suspicion on Paul, charging that he was not a legitimate apostle and attacking his gospel (1:10-12), and claimed that they brought the true and complete gospel (1:6-9). Because Paul wanted to please men (1:10) he had withheld the law from the Galatians. But the complete gospel included the law, so circumcision must be practiced (5:2; 6:12), the Jewish feasts must be observed (4:10), and the laws concerning food and ritual purity must be followed (2:11-21). Only the one who could produce for inspection those works demanded by the law could be righteous before God.

Paul proceeds against the false teachers with cutting acidity, in that he describes them as ravagers of the churches who have perverted the good news into its opposite (1:6-9). Whoever accepts this teaching is obligated to keep the whole law, thereby loses Christ (5:2), and falls back again into that slavery in which he once lived as a pagan (4:9-10).

If it is immediately apparent from the Pauline polemic that Paul is combating Judaizers, the question is also to be asked whether Paul had to contend with other tendencies at the same time, or whether the doctrine he approved had itself already been influenced by other ideas. Lütgert advocated the thesis that Paul struggled not only with the Judaizers, but also with a second group characterized by spirit-enthusiasm. There was conflict in the church between the Judaizers and the spirit-enthusiasts (5:15). Paul dealt with the pneumatics (6:1) somewhat sparingly, in order to direct his main attack against the Judaizers. But 5:15 is certainly concerned with personal differences between members of the congregation (rather than party-differences), and Paul addresses the whole community with πνευματικοι ("spiritual" [ones]), not just a part of it. Thus Lütgert's thesis has rightly been rejected by most exegetes.

A modified form of Lütgert's position has been adopted by Schmithals, who considers the false teachers to have been the advocates of a Judaizing Gnostic movement. The traits which Lütgert divides between two groups are seen by Schmithals as characteristics of a single movement. As pneumatics (6:1), the heretics not only teach the law, but also speak of the enslaving elemental cosmic spirits (4:9) and they emphasize "freedom" (5:1, 13), which belongs alone to those who have attained to true knowledge. The thesis developed by Schmithals has been accepted by a few exegetes and has led to the supposition that since Paul lacked exact information he did not recognize how Gnostic the teaching he opposed really was (Marxsen). But the false teaching at Galatia cannot be simply identified with that of Colossae (see p. 88), and one must be careful in affirming that Paul had only insufficient understanding of the situation. That the Judaizers may have made use of syncretistic concepts such as στοιχεια (του κοσμου) ("elemental spirits," 4:9) still does not prove the specifically Gnostic character of their ideas. πνευματικοι ("spiritual" [ones], 6:1) is certainly not a label applied to his opponents, but is rather to be understood as an address to the whole community (see above). And the concept of freedom in 5:1, 13 is used in the specifically Pauline sense—without any recognizable Gnostic ideas in the background. Therefore we can hardly conclude from the Galatian letter that the beginnings of the churches in Galatia and even Paul's own early days were characterized by an intensive spirit-enthusiasm (so Betz). The false teaching against which Paul directed his attack is in any case clearly to be described as Judaizing legalism. Against the proclamation of the necessity of keeping the law for salvation, Paul set forth the truth of the gospel, which can tolerate no additions or supplementation.

Paul's letter obviously accomplished its purpose. That is clear not only from the fact that Galatians was preserved, but also from I Corinthians 16:1 where Paul mentions the Galatians as among the Gentile churches which had taken an offering for the Jerusalem church. This collection was taken a little later under the direction of the apostle. The debate carried through in Galatians conclusively settled the issue that the church was not to remain a Jewish sect, but as the people of God composed of both Jews and Gentiles was to testify to the gospel to the whole world.

#14 The First Letter to the Corinthians

Lütgert, W. *Freiheitspredigt und Schwarmgeister in Korinth*, 1908.

Weiss, J. *Der 1. Korintherbrief*, 1910.

Schlatter, A. *Die korinthische Theologie*, 1914.

Wilckens, U. *Weisheit und Torheit*, 1959.

Dinkler, E. "Korintherbriefe," in *RGG*[3], 4:17-23.

Hurd, J. *The Origin of I Corinthians*, 1965.

Schenk, W. "Der 1. Korintherbrief als Briefsammlung," *ZNW* 60 (1969):219-43.

Conzelmann, H. *I Corinthians: A Commentary on the First Epistle to the Corinthians*, Hermeneia, 1975.

Schmithals, W. *Gnosticism in Corinth*, 1971.

———. "Die Korintherbriefe als Briefsammlung," *ZNW* 64 (1973):262-88.

a. Contents: The loosely connected sequence of individual sections of the letters are united by the common theme of the edification of the church. It is from the perspective of this leitmotif that the apostle responds to individual reports and questions which he has received from the community. After the letter's introduction (1:1-9) Paul turns first to the problem of disputes in the congregation of which he had been informed by Chloe's people (1:11) (1:10–4:21). Christ may not be divided

(1:12). The church lives from the gospel alone, and the gospel's content is the word of the cross (1:18)—not human wisdom (1:18–3:23). Therefore the community should not be scandalized by the lowliness of the apostle (chapter 4). Chapters 5 and 6 deal with moral abuses in the congregation: the case of incest (5), going to court before pagan judges (6:1-11), and immorality with harlots (6:12-20).

In 7:1–11:1 the apostle responds to questions from the Corinthian church: the question of whether or not Christians should marry (chapter 7) and whether or not to eat meat sacrificed to idols (8:1–11:1). Verse two of chapter 11 through chapter 14 contains an extensive section in which instructions for the meetings of the congregation are given. They are concerned with the veiling of women in the worship (11:2-16), the proper celebration of the Lord's Supper (11:17-34), and the spiritual gifts, which are to be evaluated by their contribution to the edification of the community (12:1–14:40). Chapter 15 carries through the debate with those in Corinth who deny the resurrection. Chapter 16 deals with business and personal matters and concludes with the personal greeting in the apostle's own hand (vv. 19-24).

b. The church at Corinth was founded by the apostle during his year and a half of residence in the city which began at the end of 49 or the beginning of 50 and lasted until the middle of 51 (see pp. 51-52). Corinth had been destroyed by the Romans in 146 B.C., then rebuilt at the order of Caesar, and had been capital of the senatorial province of Achaia and residence of the proconsul since 29 B.C.. Since the city is favorably located for commerce, it quickly recovered its significance. Sea traffic and business brought many foreigners to Corinth, and thereby an increase in the port city's pleasure-seeking and a relaxing of moral standards.

Acts gives only a brief report of the beginnings of the church. Paul arrived in Corinth from Athens, and at first stayed with Aquila and Priscilla, who had been forced to leave Rome on account of the edict of the Emperor Claudius against the Jews (see p. 75), and through them he found work as a tentmaker (18:2-3). He taught every sabbath in the synagogue (v. 4), then Silas and Timothy came to him from Macedonia (v. 5, see p. 56). His preaching of Christ brought him into conflict with the Jews (v. 5), so that Paul had to leave the synagogue and turn to the

Gentiles (v. 6). He was received into the house of the proselyte Titius Justus (v. 7)—from the Jews to the Gentiles! As a special success of the ministry of the apostle, it is emphasized that the ruler of the synagogue became a Christian (v. 8; I Cor. 1:14). Many other Corinthians believed and were baptized (v. 8). But when they proceeded against Paul and brought him before the tribunal of the proconsul Gallio, he was forced to leave Corinth (vv. 12-18). He embarked in Cenchreae, the outer harbor of Corinth, and traveled via Ephesus to Caesarea.

This terse account is confirmed and supplemented by data from the letter itself. Paul founded the church (3:6; 4:15) by bringing the gospel to Corinth (15:3-5). The expression ουκ οιδατε ("do you not know?") recurs often in the letter, referring back to instructions given to the community when Paul was with them (3:16; 5:6; 6:2-3, 9, 15-16, 19, and elsewhere). The members of the church came for the most part from the lower classes of society (1:26-28), including slaves (7:21; 12:13), but also a few rich people belonged to the congregation (11:21-22). The church was composed of various kinds of people, which corresponds to our picture of the city itself. Soon after Paul was compelled to leave the city, Apollos came to Corinth. The information which Acts gives about him is unclear, in that it indicates that he at first knew only the baptism of John the Baptist, then taught in Corinth, and later received Christian baptism (18:24–19:7). Paul does not mention Apollos' having originally come from the group of John's disciples, but he acknowledges his ministry: "I planted, Apollos watered" (3:6); that is, he continued the work of the apostle. Paul therefore supported the request expressed by the Corinthians that Apollos might visit them again (16:12). In Corinth there were people who proudly appealed to him: "I belong to Apollos" (1:12). As it was believed in the mystery religions that the initiatory rite established an abiding relationship between the initiate and the mystagogue, so also in the Christian community it was thought that the baptized person was brought into a firm relationship which was highly significant for his life. It was obviously not Apollos' fault that such groups were formed—for Paul affirms his ministry (3:6; 16:12)—but the fault of his partisans.

The slogans listed in 1:12 indicate that in addition to those who considered themselves to be disciples of Paul and Apollos respectively there were also those who claimed to belong to Peter.

Although the missionary activity of Peter is referred to in 9:5, there is no particular reason to believe that Peter had been in Corinth. So it must have been the case that Christians from outside Corinth joined the Corinthian church, Christians who came from a region where a Semitic language was spoken—for they use the Aramaic name Cephas—and who emphasize as a special distinction that they had become Christians through Peter.

The different influences which in this way had become effective in the community resulted in the situation that the proudly proclaimed slogans—I belong to this one, I to that—were used in polemical sense, since each knew himself to be borne along by the exalted feeling that comes from possessing the Spirit. A fanatical spirit-enthusiasm had seized the whole church (Lütgert, Schlatter, Schmithals, Wilckens). In the awareness of being filled by the powers of the Spirit and of wisdom, the pneumatics thought that the eschaton was already present (4:8), so that they scorned the miserable appearance of the apostle (4:1ff), and condescendingly had the notion that nothing earthly really concerned them any longer. All that matters is the possession of the πνευμα ("spirit"); what one does with the body, and what will happen to the σωμα ("body") matters not at all. They boast of the freedom they have received, so that everything is permitted: παντα μοι εξεστιν ("all things are lawful for me," 6:12; 10:23). Whether one commits incest (5:1-13), others visit prostitutes (6:12-20), or some renounce marriage on the ground of a disdain for the body (chapter 7), is finally immaterial to the Spirit-people. They eat food sacrificed to idols without giving it a thought, because of course they have the right knowledge that the gods don't really exist (8:1). Women stride without their veils into the worship service, where the powers of the coming world can already be experienced in the present, where a meal of those drunk with the Spirit is celebrated (chapter 11). Ecstatic speech as a phenomenon of the Spirit is vastly overrated (chapters 12-14). And they will hear nothing of a future resurrection of the dead, because by the resurrection of Christ the spiritual reality has already broken in (chapter 15). To be sure, this "Corinthian" theology does not yet contain a developed Gnostic mythology. But the proud self-awareness of the pneumatic who feels himself exalted over everything earthly has those features which a short time later were clearly expressed in Gnostic doctrine.

It may be that the brief expression εγω δε Χριστου ("I belong to Christ," 1:12) is also to be explained in terms of this spiritualist movement. The interpretation of these words is presently contested. The problem may not be solved by simply regarding this phrase as a later gloss (so J. Weiss, Wilckens, and others), for the question μεμερισται ο Χριστος ("is Christ divided?") in 1:13 is part of a chiastic structure which must include the εγω δε Χριστου ("I belong to Christ") of the preceding verse (cf. also II Cor. 10:7). It has often been supposed that we have here the motto of the so-called "Christ party," which considered itself superior to all the other parties. But the letter nowhere speaks of such a party. We might rather suppose that in this slogan the pneumatic, proud self-awareness of being the true Christians is expressed. Since this Spirit-enthusiasm permeated the whole church—not just particular groups—Paul addresses all members of the community and reminds them of the gospel which they have received and accepted, in order to use that as the basis for his discussion of what the church is and should be.

c. The composition of this letter had already been preceded by an exchange of correspondence. In 5:9 Paul mentions an earlier letter in which he had said to the church that they should not associate with immoral people. The Corinthians reacted to this with the sulky counter-question of how this was possible in their city (5:9-10). The apostle then clarified that he had not spoken of the immoral people in the world in general, but that some relationships belong strictly to church life, and that those guilty of immorality, greed, and idolatry were not to be included. This previous letter has not been preserved.

Various attempts have been made to reconstruct this lost letter. The loose structure of I Corinthians has made it possible to lift out various passages and to attribute them to the "previous letter," which must have included instructions concerning proper sexual conduct according to 5:9. J. Weiss attributed 10:1-22; 6:12-20; 9:24-27; 11:2-34 to that letter; Dinkler 6:12-20; 9:24-27; 10:1-22; 11:2-34; 12–14; Schmithals, who at first dismantled the two Corinthian letters into six separate writings, now argues that there were originally nine independent letters, of which I Corinthians 11:2-34 is the oldest. Schenk dissects I Corinthians into four separate letters, the so-called "previous letter" containing I Corinthians 1:1-9; II Corinthians 6:14–7:1; I Corinthians 6:1-11; 11:2-34; 15; 16:13-24. Schenke-Fischer attributes 6:12-20; 9:24–

10:22; 11:2-34; 13; 15 to the "previous letter." None of these suggestions can be called persuasive. The fact that in I Corinthians different issues are discussed in a loosely connected series is easily explained from the occasion of the letter (see below).

Hurd has attempted to reconstruct the "previous letter" by another route, namely on the basis of allusions in I Corinthians which point back to the earlier exchange of correspondence. He supposes that the previous letter must have dealt not only with the issue of marriage, but also with the question of eating meat sacrificed to idols. But these are precisely the themes also dealt with in the so-called "Apostolic Decree" (Acts 15:20, 29). From this he infers that Paul himself stood near the position of the Corinthian enthusiasts, but that after the apostolic conference he was obligated to enforce its decisions also in Corinth. This was the purpose of the letter mentioned in 5:9, against which the Corinthians protested. The counter-response of the apostle is represented by our I Corinthians. The dialogue between Paul and the church therefore is supposed to have developed in such a way that the position of the apostle changed under the influence of circumstances. This reconstruction however requires a complete distortion of the facts of the matter, for Paul knows absolutely nothing of such decisions as are described in Acts 15:20, 29 (Gal. 2:1-10), and underwent no alteration in his views as a result of the apostolic conference. First Corinthians does show that the themes πορνεια ("sexual immorality") and meat sacrificed to idols were important issues in the dialogue with the Corinthian church. But a reconstruction of the letter mentioned in 5:9 is not possible.

First Corinthians was occasioned by two factors: (1) through "Chloe's people"—slaves or domestic servants?—Paul had received reports of the situation in the church (1:11). In chapters 1–6 Paul responds to this situation of which he had heard indirectly, cf. 5:1 ακουεται ("it is reported"): cf. also 11:18 ακουω ("I hear"), utilizing information reported to him. (2) A letter from the church was written to the apostle in which was posed a series of questions to him. Stephanas, Fortunatus, and Achaicus, who were presently with Paul (16:17), presumably brought this letter. In 7:1 Paul begins to respond to the Corinthian's questions: περι δε ων εγραψατε ("now concerning the matters about which you wrote"). Six points are indicated as referring specifically to the Corinthians' questions, each introduced by περι δε ("concerning"): (1) concerning marriage and celibacy (7:1); (2) concerning virgins (7:25), whether or not they should get married in view of the eschaton's already having begun; (3) concerning meat sacrificed to idols (8:1); (4)

concerning spiritual gifts (12:1); (5) concerning the collection (16:1) which the Gentile Christian churches were gathering for the original Jerusalem church; (6) concerning Apollos (16:12). The oral and written reports and questions which came to the apostle account for the rather disconnected train of thought in the answer which he gives to the church in I Corinthians. Nevertheless, the variety and multiplicity of problems dealt with which tends to fragmentize the letter does not represent a haphazard structure, but on the contrary everything discussed by the apostle is oriented to the resurrection of the dead (chapter 15) and is dealt with from the point of view of serving the edification of the community.

Ephesus is named in 16:8 as the place where the letter was written. Paul intends to remain there until Pentecost and has already sent Timothy on ahead to Corinth—obviously by the land route (4:17). To facilitate his being welcomed when he arrives, Paul includes a recommendation for him to the church in the letter which was sent directly (16:10-11). Since I Corinthians was written in the spring near the end of his stay in Ephesus (16:8), and since Paul was there from 53 to 55 (see p. 53), the composition of I Corinthians is to be dated in the spring of 55.

#15 The Second Letter to the Corinthians

Hausrath, A. *Der Vier Capitel-Brief des Paulus an die Korinther,* 1870.

Lietzmann, H. *An die Korinther I/II,* ³1931 (Lietzmann-Kümmel, ⁵1969).

Käsemann, E. "Die Legitimität des Apostels," *ZNW* 41 (1942):33-71.

Bultmann, R. "Exegetische Probleme des zweiten Korintherbriefes" (1947), in *Exegetica,* 1967, 298-322.

Fitzmyer, J. A. "Qumran and the Interpolated Paragraph in 2 Cor. 6:14–7:1" (1961), in *Essays on the Semitic Background of the NT,* 1971, 205-17.

Bornkamm, G. "The History of the Origin of the So-Called Second Letter to the Corinthians," *NTS* 8 (1962):258ff.

Gnilka, J. "2. Kor. 6, 14-7, 1 im Lichte der Qumranschriften und der Zwölf-Patriarchen-Testamente," in *Neutestamentliche Aufsätze für J. Schmid,* 1963, 86-99.

Friedrich, G. "Die Gegner des Paulus im 2. Korintherbrief" (1963, in *Auf das Wort kommt es an, Gesammelte Aufsätze,* 1978, 189-223.

Georgi, D. *Die Gegner des Paulus im 2. Korintherbrief,* 1964.

Barrett, C. K. "Paul's Opponents in II Corinthians," *NTS* 17 (1970/71):233-54.

a. Contents: The letter falls naturally into three extensive sections: 1–7, 8–9, 10–13. In 1–7 the relationship of the apostle to the church is discussed in terms of the apostolic office. Paul first speaks of his previous relations with the church (1:12–2:13), then presents a comprehensive apologia for the apostolic office (2:14–7:4) in which its glory (2:14–4:6) is contrasted with its lowliness and humiliation (4:7–6:10). By means of a direct appeal to the church and by relating his personal experiences Paul hopes to establish a new relationship of trust between apostle and church (6:11–7:16).

Chapters 8–9 deal with the offering which the Gentile churches were collecting for the mother church in Jerusalem.

Chapters 10–13 debate with opponents who have recently appeared, repulsing their slanderous attacks against Paul (10:1–11:15), and containing the apostle's own "boasting" (11:16–12:10), both on the ground of his suffering (11:16-33) and on the basis of his pneumatic experiences (12:1-10). Then the defense against his opponents is concluded (12:11-18), the impending visit of Paul to Corinth is announced (13:1-10), and the letter brought to a close (13:11-13).

b. After I Corinthians (= I.) had been sent, the situation was changed by a series of events involving the apostle and the church. The visit of Timothy to Corinth mentioned in I 4:17 obviously had no results, for the relation of Paul to the Corinthians became so bad that he suddenly decided to change his plans (cf. I 16:8) and to return immediately to Corinth—a visit not mentioned in Acts. First Corinthians presupposes that Paul had previously been in Corinth only once: the time when the church was founded; II 12:14 and 13:1 however announces the impending visit as the third. So Paul must have made another visit to Corinth between I and II Corinthians. But the attempt to clarify the situation misfired. Some sort of episode must have occurred in which a member of the congregation outrageously insulted the apostle (II 2:5; 7:12). The exact circumstances and the identity of the one who did it—Paul refers to him merely as αδικησας ("the one who did wrong")—are unknown and cannot be determined. In any case this event brought Paul's relationship to the community to an extreme crisis. Paul had to leave Corinth and return to Ephesus. From there he wrote a letter—the so-called intermediate letter or painful letter—to Corinth, which according to II 2:4, 7:8-9 and 12 he wrote in the midst of great internal turmoil. Titus made a trip to Corinth and delivered this letter (2:13; 7:6, 13-14). Thereafter Paul remained in Ephesus only for a short time, for he had gotten into a situation there in which his life was in danger (1:8-11), so he went via the land route to meet Titus (2:12-13) and found him in Macedonia (7:5ff). Titus brought him surprisingly good news. The church had punished the offender and was proceeding with the plans to take the offering for Jerusalem. Encouraged by these reports, Paul writes to Corinth. In the light of these events one would expect a letter in which previous differences are smoothed over, but strangely enough chapters 10–13 present us once again with the sharpest polemics against Paul's opponents.

c. Opponents of Paul emerged in Corinth who had not been present in the church at the time when he wrote I Corinthians. They were Jewish Christians (11:22) who penetrated the community from outside (11:4) and who established themselves in the eyes of the church by letters of recommendation (10:12, 18). They claimed to speak to the church with the authority of apostles (11:5, 13; 12:11). Their message was different from that of Paul (ευαγγελιον ετερον, "a different gospel," 11:4), whom they declared to be no apostle at all, since he could not possibly produce the proper credentials (13:3, 7), and had not even dared to avail himself of the genuine apostle's right of financial support from the congregation (11:8-9). Instead, they claimed that Paul, sly rascal that he is, robbed the congregation under the pretense of taking an offering for the Jerusalem church (11:8-9; 12:16). After all, Paul makes such a curious impression. In person, he is seen to be a small and rather ordinary man, who can hardly make a decent speech (11:6); but from a distance, he writes imposing letters (10:1-2, 9-10). The community which knew Paul as a missionary, and also as the author of letters, was obviously very impressed by the appearance of these people. They had to distinguish true from false apostles, and thereby settle the issue of the legitimatization of an apostle.

The problem of how these opponents of Paul can be more exactly identified is still disputed among scholars. F. C. Baur considered them Judaizers; but there is not a word about law, sabbath, or circumcision, so that the opponents are to be described as Jewish-Christians (11:22) but not as Judaizers. Lütgert, Bultmann, and Schmithals (see p. 61) are of the opinion that the opponents are the same Spirit-enthusiasts as in I Corinthians, who claim to be the true Christ-people (10:7) who alone have the true knowledge (11:6), and who brag about their spiritual experiences (12:1ff). But I Corinthians nowhere presupposes Jewish-Christian opponents, so we may not use information from I Corinthians to delineate the opponents in II Corinthians. It is rather a matter of so-called apostles who came into the church from outside, and then of course made common cause with the spirit-enthusiastic efforts already present in the church. Käsemann would like to explain the incontestable Jewish-Christian character of the opposition as well as their apostolic claim by regarding them as emissaries of the mother church in Jerusalem who appeal to the original apostles (so also Barrett). This would explain the respectful reception they were accorded by the church, on the one hand, and the severity of the struggle, in which apostle stood against apostle, on the other. The Jewish-Christian character and apostolic claims find an impressive explanation in this interpretation; but the fact is that nowhere is the Jerusalem church referred to—neither in connection with the letters of recommendation nor in connection with apostleship. Thus Friedrich has attempted to describe the opponents as members of the Stephen group of Acts 6 and 7, who appealed to ecstatic-visionary experiences and set themselves forth in the churches as charismatic preachers. But that disciples of Stephen might have made their way to Corinth must remain an unprovable supposition; and the scanty reports concerning the Stephen group offered by Acts do not suffice to make points of contact with Corinth probable. Georgi has connected the emergence of the opponents in Corinth with the widespread presence of wandering preachers who claimed to be inspired with divine powers. The preachers who so impressed the Corinthian church were Hellenistic Jewish-Christians who appealed to letters of recommendation from other churches, and who exhibited effective demonstrations of the Spirit which accompanied their ministry as its legitimatization. This explanation would account both for the Jewish-Christian character and the missionary zeal of these so-called apostles. However, a degree of uncertainty remains in any attempt to exactly describe the position of these newly arrived opponents, for Paul sometimes polemicizes against the claims of these opponents, but other times against the criteria used by the Corinthians to judge between these new apostles and Paul himself as an apostle. The decisive thing in the eyes of the Corinthians was whether or not demonstrations of the Spirit and signs of divine power could be presented. From this point of view they obviously found the "super-apostles" preferable to the paltry results of Paul's ministry.

The apostle defends himself fiercely. The attack on his apostleship is carried out by those who preach another Jesus and who have another spirit (11:4). If he didn't seem to have the imposing appearance of a pneumatic (10:1-10), he too could boast of belonging to Israel (11:22) and of ecstatic experiences (12:1-10). But if it is a matter of boasting, then he will boast of suffering and weakness. Since Christ was crucified in weakness (13:4), his servants can only be recognized when the power of Christ finds its full expression in their weakness (12:9). So one may only boast εν κυριω ("in the Lord"). In the debate with his opponents Paul warns the church that he will come soon and straighten things out. There can be no doubt that the passionate argument of 10–13 is genuinely Pauline. But we must ask whether it was originally composed as part of one and the same letter as chapters 1–9.

d. Whether II Corinthians is an editorial composition which has been composed by joining together parts of several letters is a question that has been discussed for a long time. The break between chapters 9 and 10 can hardly be explained by supposing that Paul had a sleepless night between composing the two parts (Lietzmann), or by supposing he was interrupted during the course of dictating the letter (Kümmel). Hausrath thinks that the harsh tone and language of chapters 10–13 are to be explained by the hypothesis that we have here the so-called intermediate letter or painful letter (2:4; 7:8-9, 12). This supposition has been both widely accepted and met with justifiable objections. For example, there is nothing in 10–13 about the αδικησας ("the one who did wrong"), although the "painful letter" was a reaction to the way he had mistreated Paul. (Hausrath went astray on this point by supposing that the αδικησας ("the one who did wrong") was to be identified with the incestuous person of I Corinthians 5. If 10–13 is to be attributed to the intermediate letter, then it must have contained considerably more, so that 10–13 could only be a large fragment of this writing.

The letter contains other gaps in its train of thought which have given rise to critical reflections. In 6:14–7:1 we have a self-contained unit which can easily be removed from the context—7:2 joins well to 6:13—and is distinguished by its un-Pauline vocabulary which is strongly reminiscent of the Qumran texts (Fitzmyer, Gnilka). Thus it is a matter of either a secondary insertion or a pre-Pauline fragment which has been inserted here. It is also noticeable that the problem of the offering is discussed twice, chapters 8 and 9. Finally we may notice that the personal report of 2:12-13 finds its continuation in 7:5ff, so that 2:13–7:4 (apart from 6:14–7:1) forms a self-contained unit.

G. Bornkamm has combined these various observations into a carefully argued theory of the composition of II Corinthians. The gap between 9 and 10 is so striking that there must be a seam here. Chapters 10–13 represent a fragment of the "painful letter"—not the whole letter, since there is no mention of the αδικησας ("the one who did wrong"). A later editor placed this section at the end because it corresponded to a firm pattern to conclude a writing with warning against false teachers (cf. the conclusions of Gal. and Rom. as well as Did. 16). But neither is the remaining part of the letter a unity. Into the personal report 1:8-11; 2:12-13; 7:5-16, which may be read as a smooth sequence, a long apologia for the apostolic office has been inserted, a section which still presupposes a close relationship to the church (2:14–7:4). From this it may be inferred that this section must have been written the earliest of all the sections of II Corinthians. After this letter the situation in Corinth suddenly worsened, so that Paul's trip there became necessary, the episode in which Paul was insulted occurred, and then the "painful letter" to which 10–13 belongs was written. This writing, delivered by Titus, improved the situation, so that Paul could finally send a letter of reconciliation to Corinth which contained all sorts of reports and information (1:1–2:13; 7:5-16; 8; 13:11-13). Chapter 9, which begins with yet another new discussion of the arrangements for the offering is probably to be assigned to a different, independent writing.

Thus the analysis results in the following original order: apologia for the apostolic office (2:14–7:4), then the painful visit and the "painful letter" (10–13) which moved the community to a reconciliation with Paul, then the letter of reconciliation from Paul (1:1–2:13; 7:5-16; 8; 13:11-13). Chapter 6, verse 14 through 7:1 is to be considered a non-Pauline section not related to the rest of II Corinthians, and chapter 9 is part of an independent letter. All the parts deal with the essence and legitimacy of the apostolic office. The apologia 2:14–7:4 and the "painful letter" originated in Ephesus, the letter of reconciliation in Macedonia after the reunion with Titus. The letters followed one another rapidly in a series which was apparently completed during a brief period within the years 55–56.

We may accept Bornkamm's reconstruction of the process by

which the different fragments were combined to produce the present form of the letter: chapters 10–13 were placed at the end for the reason given above. The letter of reconciliation provided the framework for the other sections. Chapter 9 was inserted after chapter 8 because of similar content. The apologia found an appropriate place following 2:13. By means of the connection with 2:14, the trip from Ephesus via Troas to Macedonia is seen as a segment of the triumphal procession in which God leads the apostle through the world. A good connection was also made at the end of this inserted section, in that 7:5 takes up the theme of θλιψις ("affliction") named in 7:4.

Unlike the case of I Corinthians, in which the loose chain of thought is a result of responding to various reports and questions from the church, in II Corinthians the gaps in the present form of the letter—especially between chapters 9 and 10, but also between 2:13 and 2:14—can only be satisfactorily explained by positing a secondary editorial process. Supporting evidence is provided by the fact that our II Corinthians is not documented prior to the time of Marcion. So it may be supposed that the different fragments were brought together at the beginning of the second century under the leitmotif of the legitimacy of the apostolic office, not only in order to preserve the impressive letter which was thereby attained as the legacy of the apostle, but also above all to facilitate its use in the worship service.

#16 The Letter to the Romans

Lietzmann, H. *An die Römer,* [4]1933 ([5]1971).

Friedrich, G. "Römerbrief," in RGG[3], 5:1137-43.

Michel, O. *Der Brief an die Römer,* 1955, [13]1966.

Munck, J. *Paul and the Salvation of Mankind,* 1959.

Luz, U. "Zum Aufbau von Rm 1–8," *ThZ* 25 (1969):161-81.

Klein, G. "Paul's Purpose in Writing the Epistle to the Romans" (1969), in *The Romans Debate,* ed. Karl P. Donfried, 1977.

McDonald, J. "Was Romans XVI a Separate Letter?" *NTS* 16 (1969/70):369-72.

Bornkamm, G. "Romans as Paul's Testament," in *Paul,* 1971, 88-96.

Minear, P. S. *The Obedience of Faith: The Purposes of Paul in the Epistle to the Romans,* 1971.

Borse, U. "Die geschichtliche und theologische Einordnung des Römerbriefes," *BZ NF* 16 (1972):70-83.

Schmithals, W. "The False Teachers of Romans 16:17-20," in *Paul and the Gnostics,* 1972, 219-38.

Käsemann, E. *Commentary on Romans*, 1980.
———. *Der Römerbrief als historisches Problem*, 1975.
Wilckens, U. *Der Brief an die Römer I*, 1978.

a. Contents: The theme of the righteousness of God (1:16-17) determines the course of thought of the whole letter. After the address and greeting (1:1-7) the introductory paragraph of the letter leads up to a statement of its thesis (1:8-17). The first major section deals with the gospel as the power of God for everyone who believes (1:18–8:39). The revelation of the wrath of God against Gentiles and Jews (1:18–3:20) serves as the background for the revelation of God's righteousness (3:21–8:39). For the revelation of the righteousness which comes by faith (3:21-31), a scriptural proof is provided by the example of the righteousness of Abraham who had faith (chapter 4). Chapters 5–8 respond to the question, What does it then mean that the one who is righteous on the basis of faith shall *live* (1:17)? Paul first shows that, although life is always a future reality grasped by hope, it is nonetheless already present (5:1-11). Just as sin, and through sin, death, were able to enter the world through Adam, so righteousness and life have come through Christ (5:12-21). Then the apostle discusses how sin has lost its ruling power over those who have faith (6:1–7:6). Those who have been baptized into Christ have died to sin and are alive to God in Christ Jesus (6:1-11). Therefore sin can no longer reign over them, and they are called to the obedient life of those who have been justified (6:12-14, 15-23). They now live in the new life of the Spirit, not in the old life ruled by the letter of the law (7:1-6). The question, What then is the significance of the law, leads to an excursuslike section which describes the slavery of humanity under the law (7:7-25). This major section is concluded by a discussion of life in the Spirit and the assurance of the coming consummation (chapter 8).

Also the question of the destiny of Israel is handled from the perspective of the major theme, the righteousness of God. After an introductory lament over Israel, Paul speaks of God's election and reprobation (9:6-29), contrasted with Israel's guilt (9:30–10:21), and in conclusion speaks of God's promise for Israel (chapter 11).

Finally, the parenesis is also subjected to the main theme of the letter. Those who have received the righteousness of God are called to obey. Chapters 12–13 contain exhortations concerning the conduct of Christians in their external relations, 14:1–15:13

guidance for life within the church, especially concerning how "strong" and "weak" can live together in the same church.

The letter's conclusion follows in 15:14–16:27. The apostle's plans are explained (15:14-33), with a long list of greetings (16:1-23) and a final doxology (16:25-27).

b. No information is available about the beginning of the Roman church. The letter presupposes that in Rome there already existed a church whose faith was known in the whole world (1:8). Paul had been intending to visit them for some time (1:10ff), but had so far been hindered from doing so (15:22ff). The letter nowhere mentions the names of missionaries who first brought the gospel to Rome. Nor is the apostle Peter mentioned, who was later supposed to have been the first bishop of the church at Rome. To be sure, it should be considered historical fact that Peter suffered martyrdom in Rome a short time after Paul's own death there, but neither of them founded the church. It rather originated through anonymous, unknown Christians. Certainly Christians from Jerusalem came to Rome very early (cf. Acts 2:10) and brought the Christian message with them. A large Jewish community lived in Rome. The first Christians probably came from these circles, which also included proselytes and so-called God-fearers.

That the beginnings of the Roman church must have been among Jewish-Christians is also evident from the so-called Jewish edict of the Emperor Claudius (see p. 52): *Judaeos impulsore Chresto assidue tumultuantes Roma expulit*. ("Since the Jews constantly made disturbances at the instigation of Chrestus, he expelled them from Rome.") (Suetonius, *Vita Claudii* 25.) This short account mistakenly supposes that a certain Chrestus—a common name among slaves—created disturbances among the Jews. In fact, there were probably disputes within the Jewish community regarding the Christian message. Claudius took this as an occasion to expel the Jews from Rome. The Jewish Christians were also affected by the edict (cf. Acts 18:2, see p. 52). The Christian community continued to exist by virtue of its non-Jewish membership, so that henceforth it was composed of Gentile Christians. The emperor Nero (A.D. 54–68) repealed the edict of Claudius and permitted the Jews to return to Rome. Thereupon many came back, so that the Christian community again had a Jewish-Christian contingent. But the Gentile Christians remained obviously in the majority. They are addressed especially in Romans 9–11, so that they do not forget that they have been grafted into the olive tree of Israel (11:13ff). Other places in the letter also indicate that the originally Jewish-Christian church (cf. the Jewish-Christian confession of Rom. 1:3) was at the time of the writing of the letter composed predominately of Gentile Christians (1:5-6; 15:14-16). The section 14:1–15:13 is concerned with the question of how the Gentile-Christian majority should live together with the Jewish-Christian minority.

c. Different presuppositions were present at the writing of the Letter to the Romans than was the case with the other Pauline Letters. Elsewhere he writes to churches which he had founded and whose situations he knows very well. But he has never seen the Roman church, and now addresses it for the first time. The occasion is named in 15:22-25. Paul regards his missionary task in the eastern part of the empire as completed—churches have been founded which will themselves provide for the continuing expansion of the gospel—and now would like to move westward, as soon as he has delivered the offering to Jerusalem. He considers himself a debtor to Greeks and barbarians, schooled and unschooled (1:14), and must be a witness of the good news to all. Before the apostle begins a new missionary work in Spain, he would like to relate himself to the church in the capital in order to assure himself of their support. Through this letter he prepares the way for this new period of his ministry by laying before the Roman church his gospel of the righteousness of God. Paul must reckon with the fact that the community has already heard various things about him, possibly not all of them good. Thus they are to arrive at their own judgment concerning the apostle's message on the basis of the letter itself. That is the explanation for the didactic, carefully weighed character of the argument of the document, which is still a letter [*Lehrbrief*: a letter of the sort which describes an apprentice's task and binds him to service (Michel)]—and not a treatise. Nor is the letter a complete Pauline systematic theology—among other things the Lord's Supper is missing—but contains the exposition of the Pauline understanding of the gospel as a revelation of the righteousness of God.

G. Bornkamm would like to describe the Roman letter as the testament of Paul, which he wrote down in advance of his trip to Jerusalem. Above all, chapters 9–11 are to be understood in view of the imminent debate with the leaders of the Jerusalem church with which Paul was faced. But it is precisely chapters 9–11 which can hardly be understood as preparatory work for the Jerusalem trip. The letter is addressed to Rome—and without side glances at the Jerusalem church. The fact that Romans is more carefully worked out on the basis of fundamental principles is to be explained by the reasons which Paul himself gives (see above).

G. Klein raises the question of why Paul wanted to preach the gospel in Rome although this was contrary to his principle not to work in someone else's territory (15:20), and answers: Paul did not consider the Roman church as a proper apostolic church, grounded on the apostolic foundation (I Cor. 3:10). Thus as a commissioned apostle he wanted to bring them the gospel and thus constitute them as a valid congregation. But such polemically influenced considerations are far from Paul's mind. Rather, his task of witnessing to the gospel to both Jews and Greeks must be fulfilled precisely in Rome. Paul speaks with respect of the Roman congregation (1:8), is cautiously hesitant about his own ministry which he wants to perform in Rome συμπαρακληθηναι εν υμιν ("that we may be mutually encouraged," 1:12), and indicates his agreement with the content of the confession which had obviously been considered authoritative in the Roman church from the very beginning (1:1-4) as being the common possession of all Christians. He presupposes that he confesses his faith in one and the same Lord with the Roman Christians, stands with them in the same fellowship of faith and love, and therefore can ask for their support for his missionary plans in the west.

P. S. Minear would like to explain the origin of the Roman Letter in terms of the relationships within the Roman church, which had come to the point that the opposition between quarreling parties prevented the whole congregation's coming together for regular worship. To be sure, Paul refers in chapters 14–15 to the differences of opinion which existed within the congregation; but in 15:22ff he names his real reason for writing.

Paul wrote Romans in Corinth, from where he is about to set out for Jerusalem to deliver the offering (15:22-25). The deaconess Phoebe from the congregation in Cenchreae, the suburban harbor of Corinth, is to take the letter with her to Rome (16:1). During his three-months stay in Corinth (Acts 20:3) Paul had found lodging with a certain Gaius (16:23). The letter was written after the Corinthian correspondence, and thus is to be dated A.D. 56.

d. A special problem is presented by the question of the relation of chapter 16 to the rest of the letter. The concluding doxology (16:25-27), which is to be recognized as post-Pauline on the basis of its vocabulary (the eternal God, the only wise God), stands at different points in the letter in different manuscripts. Marcion ended Romans at 14:23, so that chapters 15 and 16 are lacking in his text. He obviously omitted chapter 15 from anti-Jewish considerations, because Christ is there described as διακονος περιτομης ("a servant to the circumcised," 15:8). Marcion created a continuing uncertainty in the later textual tradition concerning the position of the concluding doxology. Many manuscripts place it after 14:23, P^{46} after 15:33, and other witnesses after 16:23. It is certain that chapter 15 belongs to the preceding chapters. But chapter 16 presents difficulties. There is no doubt about the Pauline character of the chapter. But whether the long list of greetings was really an original part of Romans has been disputed in the scholarly discussion. It seems strange that Aquila and Priscilla, who had been in Ephesus a short time before (I Cor. 16:19), should now be in Rome (16:3), and likewise that Epaenetus, one of the first in Asia Minor to become a Christian, should be in Rome at the same time (16:5). Thus many scholars have supposed that Romans 16 was originally sent to Ephesus, Phoebe took Romans 1–15, separate from chapter 16, with her to Rome, and en route delivered Romans 16 to Ephesus, then continued on to Rome with chapters 1–15. In Ephesus a copy of Romans 1–15 was made, to which chapter 16 was joined, so that the form of Romans which has come down to us, Romans 1–15 + 16, is to be traced back to the Ephesian church (Friedrich and others). Other exegetes suppose that chapters 1–15 and chapter 16 were first combined in Egypt (Munck and others). If chapter 16 was originally a short letter to the Ephesians, one could more readily understand why 16:17-20 abruptly lashes out against Gnosticizing false teachers (Schmithals), which is not to be expected in a letter to Rome (Käsemann).

Against this view it is objected that Romans 16 cannot really be understood as an independent letter, especially since there are no other examples in antiquity of a letter which consists almost exclusively of greetings (Kümmel). But this argument has recently been refuted, for in fact a few examples have been discovered of ancient letters composed mostly of greetings (McDonald). Thus it is in principle conceivable that Romans 16 was originally sent not to Rome, but to Ephesus, and only secondarily joined to Romans 1–15.

However, this thesis is not absolutely certain. One can readily understand that Paul, who had not yet been able to visit the Roman church, would have his reasons for wanting to use the long list of greetings to call attention to the considerable number of church members in Rome he already knew and through whom he already had a relationship to the church. Aquila and Priscilla were mobile people, sometimes in Corinth, sometimes in Ephesus, and possibly returned to Rome after the repeal of Claudius' edict against the Jews (see p. 75). In that time when the security of the Pax Romana made safe travel possible, a Christian from Asia Minor such as Epaenetus could easily have moved to Rome. Finally, the remaining names on the list could have been found as readily in the world capital Rome as in Ephesus. A brief concluding warning against false teachers could have been placed at the end of the document as a general warning even if there were no immediate reason for it in the congregation being addressed. So there is no compelling proof that Romans 16 could not have been a part of the original letter to Rome. On the contrary, it is very possible that the list of greetings belongs to Romans from the beginning (Lietzmann, Kümmel, Wilckens).

For the rest, the literary integrity of Romans is almost universally acknowledged. Schmithals however argues that two originally independent letters of Paul to Rome were first combined by the editor of the oldest collection of Paul's letters, who also joined chapter 16 and the concluding doxology to this letter. Schenke-Fischer attribute 14:1–15:13, along with chapter 16, to a letter originally addressed to Ephesus.

#17 The Letter to the Philippians

Deissmann, A. *Light from the Ancient East*, [4]1928.
Lohmeyer, E. *Der Brief an die Philipper*, 1930.
Köster, H. "The Purpose of the Polemic of a Pauline Fragment (Phil. III)" *NTS* 8 (1961/62) 317-32.
Bornkamm, G. "Der Philipperbrief als paulinische Briefsammlung" (1962), in *Gesammelte Aufsätze IV*, 1971, 195-205.
Gnilka, J. *Der Philipperbrief*, 1968.
Schmithals, W. "The False Teachers in the Epistle to the Philippians," in *Paul and the Gnostics*, 1972, 65-122.
Friedrich, G. *Der Brief an die Philipper*, 1976.

a. Contents: Following the address (1:1-2) and introductory paragraph (1:3-11) come reports and parenesis (1:12–3:1) which include first a report of the apostle's own situation (1:12-26), then admonitions to unity in the congregation (1:27–2:18) which receive their theological grounding through the citation of a hymn to Christ (2:6-11). Then come two notes about Timothy and Epaphroditus (2:19-30), and then the call to "rejoice in the Lord" of 3:1 seems to sound the note for the last stanza of the letter. But then 3:2 unexpectedly begins a sharp warning against false teachers which extends to 4:1. Only then is the letter brought to an end with exhortations, a renewed call to joy, and grateful acknowledgment of the gifts received from the Philippians (4:2-20). Greetings and benediction conclude the letter (4:21-23).

b. The church in Philippi was a result of the missionary work of Paul when he first came to Europe on the so-called second missionary journey in A.D. 49 (Acts 16:12-40). In this city which was named after its founder Philip of Macedon, the father of Alexander the Great, only a few Jews were to be found, though it was favorably located for travel and commerce. They had no synagogue, but only a small place for prayer (Acts 16:13). According to the report in Acts, Paul began his missionary work in Philippi here, and won Lydia, a businesswoman who dealt in purple goods, to the Christian faith. Paul's freeing a girl from a spirit of divination led to some tumultuous disputes, as a result of which he was thrown into jail. Acts pictures his imprisonment and miraculous release with full details. Paul himself only briefly mentions that he had to endure conflicts and mistreatment (Phil. 1:30; I Thess. 2:2). The names mentioned in the letter prove that the church was primarily composed of Gentile Christians (12:25ff; 4:2-3, 18). Despite the short time that Paul had been able to remain with the church, he felt his relationship to them was very close. Only from them had he received gifts (4:15-16); otherwise he earned what he needed to live by working with his own hands, in order not to hinder the preaching of the gospel (I Cor. 9:18). The apostle expresses his special thanks for the demonstration of their close relationship to him (4:10-20).

c. Chapter 3 contains a sharp polemic against false teachers, whose position is difficult to determine exactly. In 3:2 they are called dogs, evil-workers, those who mutilate the flesh. These words point to people of Jewish origin, who trust in the flesh. If they boast of their Jewish lineage, so Paul could also make such claims, but he had counted it all loss for the sake of Christ

(3:4-11). A fresh beginning is made in 3:17, and the community is told that there are unfortunately many who live as enemies of the cross, whose God is their belly, whose glory is their shame, who are only interested in earthly things (3:18-19). But we should hardly think that a second group is intended here, to be distinguished from those described in 3:2ff; rather it is a matter of describing the same false teachers more closely. Thus they cannot simply be described as Judaizers, nor can they be identified with the false teachers of Galatians (contra Schmithals). They are more like those opponents of Paul to whom he responds in II Corinthians 10-13, but there the demand for circumcision is missing, to which Philippians 3:2 alludes. So we should probably characterize the false teachers of Philippians as a Gnosticizing Jewish-Christian group which combined their pride in belonging to Israel with the self-consciously superior attitude of those who advocate a libertine ethic (Koester). In their view circumcision is a charm against the loss of salvation, of which they suppose themselves to be certain. Paul objects that the Christian who has been justified for the sake of Christ is not yet at the goal, but is still en route. Because he has been grasped by Christ, he strains forward to what lies ahead, looking toward the goal of the future consummation (3:12-14, 20-21).

d. The abrupt change in 3:2 raises the question of the literary unity of the letter (Schmithals, Bornkamm, Gnilka, Friedrich). Except for chapter 3, the whole letter is permeated by a tone of joy, which the apostle proclaims despite his imprisonment and possible imminent death. No joyful word is heard in chapter 3; it rather contains an extremely sharp call for separation from the false teachers. It is thus very likely that 3:2–4:3 originally belonged to another letter, the conclusion to which is apparently found in 4:8-9. Perhaps the section 4:10-20 should also be considered a part of an independent letter of thanks, which originally stood at the beginning of the correspondence between Paul and Philippi (Bornkamm). Philippians in its present form is therefore an editorial combination of more than one letter. Into the joyful letter (1:1–3:1; 4:4-7, 21-23) a polemic against false teachers has been inserted which contains a reference to the apostle as a model (3:17) and ends with a corresponding parenetical section (4:8-9).

From Paul's correspondence with the church in Philippi the

following parts have thus been preserved: A 4:10-20; B 1:1–3:1; 4:4-7, 21-23; C 3:2–4:3, 8-9. In the second century, Bishop Polycarp of Smyrna wrote a letter to the Philippians, in which he referred to the *letters* which Paul had written them (3:2). This could indicate that Polycarp in fact knew of more than one letter to Philippi. The editor did not place the polemic against false teachers at the end, as in II Corinthians, but arranged his materials so that the eschatological outlook was emphasized in 4:5, and so that the letter concludes with the spotlight on the close relationship which bound apostle and church together (4:10-20).

e. The time and place of writing may be ascertained with any degree of confidence only for 1:1–3:1; 4:4-7, 21-23. Paul is in prison (1:7, 13, and so forth) and expresses his gratitude to the community for the gift which they had sent him. The Philippians had heard that the apostle was confined in jail, and they sent Epaphroditus to him as their representative (2:25). While he was with Paul he became critically sick, and the Philippians learned of this (2:26-27). Paul in turn learned of their worry about Epaphroditus, and sought to reassure them in his behalf (2:27-28). So several communications had gone back and forth. There is no indication of where the apostle was imprisoned. It is only mentioned incidentally that the whole πραιτωριον had come to know that Paul was imprisoned because of his testimony to the gospel and not as a criminal (1:13). The trial of Paul could end with the death sentence (1:20; 2:17); but he still hoped to be freed and to be able to visit the church (1:26; 2:24). Among those greeted in the letter's concluding comments, οι εκ της Καισαρος οικιας ("those of Caesar's household") are mentioned (4:22). In the traditional view, still often advocated today, Rome is therefore to be considered the place of writing. Against that view is the fact that according to Romans 15:24, 28 Paul planned to travel from Rome to Spain, but in Philippians intends to visit the Philippian church. In addition, the distance between Rome and Philippi is so great that it is hardly conceivable how the repeated exchange of reports between apostle and church referred to in 2:25-30 could have occurred. The distance factor likewise speaks against the supposition that the letter was written during Paul's imprisonment in Caesarea (Lohmeyer), where there was a πραιτωριον ("praetorium"), which once had been Herod's palace (Acts 23:35).

The close contact which Paul had been able to maintain with the church makes it probable that the place of his imprisonment was not too far from Philippi. Thus Ephesus comes immediately to mind (Deissmann and others). Of course Acts says nothing about Paul's having been arrested in Ephesus, but Paul was often jailed in the course of his ministry (II Cor. 11:23), and the allusions to the severe suffering which he had endured during his Ephesian ministry (I Cor. 4:9; 15:32; II Cor. 1:8-11) make it easy to suppose that he had to spend some time in prison also in Ephesus. A group of the Praetorian Guard was stationed in Ephesus, and tomb inscriptions include names of members of the domus Caesaris, that is, emancipated slaves of the imperial household. According to 4:22 Paul's mission also had some results in these circles. In that case, the letter of 1:1–3:1; 4:4-7, 21-23 probably was written in Ephesus about A.D. 55. Since 3:2–4:3, 8-9 has no references to imprisonment, we may suppose that this section was written somewhat later, possibly while Paul was in Corinth in A.D. 56 (Gnilka). But this can be no more than a supposition. In any case, the fragment of the letter of thanksgiving 4:10-20 should be placed at the beginning of Paul's correspondence with the church in Philippi.

#18 The Letter to Philemon

Knox, J. *Philemon Among the Letters of Paul*, [2]1959.
Lohse, E. *A Commentary on the Epistles to the Colossians and to Philemon*, Hermeneia, 1971.
Stuhlmacher, P. *Der Brief an Philemon*, 1975.

a. Contents: After the greeting (1-3) and thanksgiving (4-7) Paul presents his petition to Philemon in behalf of the runaway slave Onesimus, namely that he would receive him back as a Christian brother (8-20). Brief reports and greetings conclude the letter (21-25).

b. The letter is addressed to Philemon whose slave Onesimus has run away and sought refuge with Paul. The apostle respects the property rights of the master and sends Onesimus back. He sends along with him the Letter to Philemon, which is to facilitate a benevolent reception for the slave by the master. Αγαπη ("love") is set forth as the norm for the conduct of both slave and master, who are to deal with each other as brothers. Since the letter to the Colossians specifically refers to Onesimus

(4:9) and Archippus (4:17) as belonging to the church at Colossae, we should suppose that Philemon also lived there.

According to Knox, Archippus, not Philemon, was the master of Onesimus, and thus was also the recipient of the letter. The Letter of Philemon is in fact the "Letter to the Laodiceans" mentioned in Colossians 4:16, and Philemon was thus a prominent member of the church in Laodicea. Paul wrote to him primarily so that he could send the letter on to Colossae and use his own influence with Archippus in behalf of the runaway slave. This is what is intended by the reference to the διακονια ("ministry") of Archippus in Colossians 4:17. But this reconstruction is only attained by an arbitrary combination of statements from Colossians with those of Philemon, and has no support from the text of Philemon itself. To be sure, Philemon 1:1-2 introduces Apphia, Archippus, and the house-church as addressees in addition to Philemon, because the Onesimus affair concerns the whole church. But when the apostle then turns to address the recipient of the letter in the singular (vv. 2, 4), there can be no doubt that Philemon, who is mentioned first, is the one intended.

c. Time and place of writing can be determined only with a modest degree of probability. Paul sits in jail (vv. 1, 9-10, 13, 22-23), obviously not too far from Philemon's place of residence, since the runaway slave was able to make his way to Paul unmolested. So it is probable that this letter too was written during the Ephesian imprisonment (see p. 82) around A.D. 55.

IV.

The Deutero–Pauline Letters

#19 The Second Letter to the Thessalonians

Harnack, A. v. "Das Problem des 2. Thess.," *SBA*, 1910, 560-78.
Weiss, J. *Earliest Christianity*, 1959.
Bultmann, R. *Theology of the NT*, 1951, 1955.
Braun, H. "Zur nachpaulinischen Herkunft des zweiten Thessalonicherbriefes" (1952-53), in *Gesammelte Studien zum NT und seiner Umwelt*, [3]1971, 205-9.
Trilling, W. *Untersuchungen zum zweiten Thessalonicherbrief*, 1972.
Lindemann, A. "Zum Abfassungsweck des zweiten Thessalonicherbriefes," *ZNW* 68 (1977) 35-77.

a. Contents: After the greeting (1:1-2) and introductory thanksgiving (1:3-12), the community is given instructions to the effect that the parousia will not come as quickly as many suppose (2:1-12). First must come the great apostasy, the disclosure of the ανθρωπος της ανομιας ("man of lawlessness," 2:3), and the κατεχον ("that which restrains," 2:6) or κατεχων ("he who restrains," 2:7), through whom the mystery of lawlessness is at present restrained, must be taken out of the way. Only then will the lawless one be revealed, whom the Lord Jesus will slay with the breath of his mouth (2:8). Accordingly, no one should be deceived by false reports or even "by a letter purporting to be from us, to the effect that the day of the Lord has come" (2:2). To the apocalyptic section there is then joined a renewed thanksgiving and exhortation of the community (2:13–3:5) and directions for church discipline in the face of the ατακτοι ("the undisciplined"), who are living in idleness in view of the nearness of the End (3:6-16). The letter ends with a final greeting purporting to be from Paul's own hand (3:17-18).

b. The relationship of II Thessalonians to I Thessalonians is characterized by a clash with regard to the contents. The author of I Thessalonians expects the parousia to occur soon (4:13ff; 5:1ff), but II Thessalonians teaches that there will be a delay before the Day of the Lord arrives. J. Weiss thus supposed that the order of the two letters is to be reversed: II Thessalonians was sent along with Timothy on his trip to visit the church; then the ατακτοι of II Thessalonians 3:11 are again referred to in I Thessalonians 5:14 which came later. Also, the strong emphasis on the Pauline authorship (II 2:2; 3:17) is only fully understandable if the letter is the first sent to the church. Finally, the comment that it is not necessary for the community to be instructed about the times and seasons (I Thess. 5:1) presupposes the teaching of II Thessalonians 2:1-12. But it is hardly conceivable that Paul first advocated that Christ should not return before an extended interval, only shortly thereafter to switch over to a near-expectation.

Harnack suggested that II Thessalonians was not directed to the whole church, but only to its Jewish-Christian party, as can be recognized by the many allusions to the OT, in contrast to the language of I Thessalonians. But the address of II Thessalonians 1:1 is exactly the same as I Thessalonians 1:1, and it is extremely unlikely that apocalyptic expectations were only alive among the Jewish-Christian members of the church.

c. The contrast between the respective contents of I and II Thessalonians finds a sufficient explanation only when the post-Pauline origin of II Thessalonians is accepted, which is supported by two items of evidence in particular. (1) Of course Paul himself often made use of apocalyptic ideas in order to emphasize his eschatological affirmations (I Thess. 4:13-18; I Cor. 15:20-28), but nowhere else does he portray the details of an apocalyptic drama. The purpose of II Thessalonians 2:1-12 is not to describe the coming of Christ, but rather to explain why the parousia must lie some extended distance in the future (Braun). (2) The rest of II Thessalonians contains an abundance of very similar linguistic echoes of I Thessalonians; a third of the vocabulary is common to the two letters (e.g. I Thess. 3:11 Αυτος δε ο Θεος και πατηρ ημων και ο κυριος ημων Ιησους κατευθυναι την οδον ημων προς υμας: ("now may our God and Father himself, and our Lord Jesus, direct our way to you"); II Thessalonians 3:5: ο δε κυριος κατυθυναι υμων τας καρδιας ("may our Lord direct your hearts"). Thus I Thessalonians was obviously used in the composition of II Thessalonians. This use was with the intention of correcting misunderstandings which could result from reading I Thessalonians. II Thessalonians seems like a commentary to I Thessalonians, which interprets the expectation of the soon-coming of the End found there by adding the limitations that first all sorts of things must happen which have not yet come on the scene (Bultmann). It is not necessary to infer from this, however, that the author of II Thessalonians intended to replace I Thessalonians by having his letter alone accepted as genuine (Lindemann). Second Thessalonians then apparently originated near the end of the first century, in circles which read and interpreted the Pauline Letters. This time for the composition of the letter is indicated by the "somewhat hackneyed and formalized instructional language" (Trilling) in which the author speaks. Second Thessalonians was soon acknowledged to be an authentic commentary to I Thessalonians, so that it was already quoted by Polycarp—his Letter to the Philippians 11:4 alludes to II Thessalonians 3:15—and was accepted by Marcion into his canon.

#20 The Letter to the Colossians

Lohmeyer, E. *Der Brief an die Kolosser*, 1930.
Dibelius, M., and Greeven, H. *An die Kolosser*, ³1953.
Lohse, E. *A Commentary on the Epistles to the Colossians and to Philemon*, 1971.
Lähnemann, J. *Der Kolosserbrief*, 1971.
Bujard, W. *Stilanalytische Untersuchungen zum Kolosserbrief*, 1973.
Schweizer, E. *Der Brief an die Kolosser*, 1976.

a. Contents: Following the greeting (1:1-2), the thanksgiving is extended so far that it not only deals with the good condition of the church (1:3-8), but also contains praise and a hymn (1:12-20), and its application to the community (1:21-23), including even a discussion of Paul's apostolic office (1:24–2:5). The didactic section carries on a sharp debate with false teachers (2:6-23). Their view that homage is to be paid to the elemental spirits of the universe is opposed by the affirmation that Christ is lord over all the universe (2:6-15). From this it is inferred that the rules imposed by the false teachers can have no binding force (2:16-23).

The parenetic part (3:1–4:6) is introduced by an appeal to seek the things that are above (3:1-4), with the challenge to put on the new person (3:5-17), to which a table of household duties *(Haustafel)* is added (3:18–4:1), rounded off with brief concluding exhortations (4:2-6). Reports and greetings conclude the letter (4:7-18).

b. The church in Colossae was not established by Paul, but by Epaphras, a disciple of the apostle (1:1; 4:12-13). Colossae, a city in Asia Minor situated in the upper valley of the Lycus River, had once been an important place, but then declined in significance and was overshadowed by its neighbor cities, Laodicea and Hierapolis (4:13, 15-16). The members of the church were predominately Gentile-Christians (1:21; 2:13). The picture portrayed by the letter describes, in generalized terms, a church that is obedient to the apostolic gospel, and thus manifests typical characteristics which show how a church lives from faith, love, and hope (1:4-5). In traditional expressions, a picture is given of how good Christians everywhere should live in αγαπη εν πνευματι ("love in the Spirit," 1:8).

c. False teachers have penetrated the community, who have not yet had any noticeable results (2:4, 8, 20), but who still represent a danger against which the church must be emphatically warned. Their teaching is primarily characterized by two fundamental traits: (1) It contains speculations concerning the στοιχεια του κοσμου ("elemental spirits of the universe," 2:8, 20), which are thought of as powerful angelic beings (2:18). As cosmic powers, they determine not only the course of the world, but also the destinies of individual human beings, who must therefore take care to pay them the proper respect (2:18).

Although the doctrine is named φιλοσοφια (lit. "philosophy," 2:8), that does not mean it is a matter of critical thinking and reflective judgment in the sense of classical Greek philosophy. The word φιλοσοφια here rather connotes religious ideas and expectations which are mediated and appropriated through the cult. (2) The service rendered to the elemental spirits includes the observance of specified δογματα ("legal demands," 2:14). Rules which require the exact observance of certain days (2:16) and the avoidance of prohibited foods and drinks (2:16, 21) must be carefully obeyed. The legal character of this doctrine is clearly reminiscent of the Judaizing requirements imposed by the false teachers of Galatia (see pp. 59-60), but is distinguished from the latter in that the Colossian false teaching is not based on the necessity of keeping the Mosaic law for salvation, but is related to the worship of the στοιχεια του κοσμου ("elemental spirits of the universe"). Thus the false teaching contains obvious syncretistic characteristics and has incorporated Jewish legalism along with other things in the colorful texture of its speculations. Against this doctrine it is affirmed that Christ is Lord of the whole universe and therefore all the divine fullness dwells in him (1:19; 2:9). Fullness of life therefore is found in Christ alone, and not through the worship of elemental spirits and angelic powers (2:10). Whoever has been baptized into Christ has died and risen with him, and has therefore died with him to the elemental spirits, so that these powers of destiny neither threaten him nor make legal demands on him. The freedom of Christians is grounded in the cosmic scope of the Christ-event, through which they are redeemed from the enslaving power of the elemental spirits and enabled to live a life in obedience to God.

d. The question of the time and place of writing presents a few problems. According to 4:3-4, 10, 18, Paul is in prison, but no indication of the place is given. The traditional view locates the place of writing in Rome, a view already expressed in the subscript later added to the letters: εγραφη απο Ρωμης δια Τυχικου και Ονησιμου ("written from Rome by Tychicus and Onesimus," KL *al*). Besides Rome, Ephesus has also appeared as a possibility in recent discussions. But if Colossians had been written by Paul in Ephesus, then it must have been written before Romans, perhaps also before II Corinthians. But such an early date must be absolutely excluded, since the theology of

Colossians indicates it must certainly have been written later than the major Pauline Letters. There is no reason to regard the letter as having been composed in Caesarea (Lohmeyer, Dibelius-Greeven). None of Paul's co-workers mentioned in 4:7-14 are mentioned in Acts' report of Paul's Caesarean imprisonment (23:23–26:32). Schweizer advocates the hypothesis that Timothy composed the letter in Ephesus with the apostle's authorization (cf. contra above pp. 48-49). If Rome is accepted as the place of origin the possibility would remain open that Paul's theology had undergone some development since the composition of the major letters, as the ideas of the aging apostle focused more and more on the mystery of the divine plan of salvation.

However, two important categories of evidence speak in favor of accepting the view that the letter is of post-Pauline origin: (1) The language and style of the letter are considerably different from that of the major Pauline Letters. There are thirty-four *hapax legomena* in Colossians. Among these are προακουω ("hear before," 1:5); αρεσκεια ("the desire to please," 1:10); πιθανολογια ("beguiling speech," 2:4); απεκδυσις ("the putting off," 2:11); χειρογραφον ([handwritten] "bond, certificate," 2:14). An additional twenty-eight words found in Colossians are also found elsewhere in the NT, but not in the other Pauline Letters, among which are αποκειμαι ("lay up," 1:5) συνδουλος ("fellow servant," 1:7; 4:7); δειγματιζω ("make a public example of," 2:15); εορτη ("festival," 2:16). Moreover, Colossians has a series of words found elsewhere in the NT only in Ephesians, e.g.: αποκαταλλασσω ("reconcile," 1:20, 22); απαλλοτριοομαι ("estrange," 1:21); ριζοομαι ("root," 2:7). The presence of several of these rarely used words can be explained by the debate with the φιλοσοφια ("philosophy"), but not all. On the other side, such important Pauline words are absent as δικαιοσυνη ("righteousness"); δικαιοω ("justify"); δικαιωμα ("righteous deed"); δικαιωσις ("justification"); ελευθερια ("freedom"); ελευθεροω ("set free"); νομος ("law"); πιστευω ("believe"); words which one would expect to be used in connection with the argument against the false teaching in Colossae.

Even more important than deviations from the Pauline vocabulary are differences in style (Bujard). Frequently expressions are composed of words which are derived from the same root, as εν παση δυναμει δυναμουμενοι (lit. "be empowered with all power," 1:11) or αυξει την αυξησιν του Θεου (lit. "grow with a growth from God," 2:19). Synonyms are juxtaposed, as προσευχομενοι και αιτουμενοι (lit. "praying and asking," 1:9) or τεθεμελιουμεοι και εδραιοι ("stable and steadfast," 1:23). Especially characteristic is the heaping up of dependent genitive expressions as εν τω λογω της αληθειας του ευαγγελιου (lit. "in the word of truth of the gospel," 1:5); εις την μεριδα του κληρου των αγιων (lit. "for the portion of the inheritance of the saints," 1:12) or το πλουτος της δοξης του μυστηριου τουτου ("the riches of the glory of this mystery," 1:27). Finally, in comparison with the major Pauline Letters the difference in sentence structure and the way in which clauses follow one another are to be noted. Colossians is characterized by a liturgical-hymnic style, in which long sentences are formed by one clause leading to another so that sometimes veritably endless chains of richly worded expressions are linked together into overloaded constructions. Thus the thanksgiving sentence begun with ευχαριστουμεν ("we thank") in 1:3 doesn't really end until 1:23. Relative clauses, inserted qualifications, participial expressions, and incidental comments blow up the sentence into a balloon which almost pops. A single, unwieldy sentence is also found in 2:8-15. This peculiarity of language and style cannot be satisfactorily explained by appealing to the special situation created by the debate with the false teaching or by claiming that the aging apostle was becoming a bit senile. Rather it indicates that in Colossians the traditions of the Pauline school are taken up and reinterpreted, by means of which the Pauline theology was elaborated to meet new situations (Lohse).

(2) These observations are confirmed by a comparison of the theology of Colossians with that of the major Pauline Letters. The Christology of Colossians goes beyond the statements found in the major letters in that it develops a cosmic breadth, affirming that the whole fullness dwells bodily in Christ (2:9) and that he is the head of all rule and authority (2:10). Ecclesiology is related most closely to this Christology: Christ is the head of the body—but that means, της εκκλησιας ("the church," 1:18). This does not refer, as in the major Pauline Letters, to the individual congregation, but to the church extended throughout

the world as the Body of Christ, which as σωμα ("body") is subject to its κεφαλη ("head"). This concept of the church is more closely explained in connection with the apostolic office. The apostle (1:24) is minister of the gospel (1:23) as he is also minister of the church (1:25), and the church is obligated to obey his word. However, the apostolic word is so coordinated to the teaching handed on in the tradition that confession and apostleship are related to each other in such a way that one cannot be thought of without the other.

It corresponds to this emphasis on apostolic teaching that eschatology recedes into the background in Colossians. "Hope" refers to the hoped-for reward which is already prepared for the faithful in heaven (1:5). In place of a temporal expectation directed toward a future fulfillment, we find a kind of thinking oriented spatially, which distinguishes below and above, earthly and heavenly (3:1-4). As a result of the subsiding of eschatology the understanding of baptism underwent important changes. While according to Romans 6:4 the Christian has died with Christ, but lives his life toward the future resurrection, Colossians says that we have already died and risen with Christ (2:12-13; 3:1). The resurrection to the new life has then already happened, so that the future event is no longer named resurrection of the dead, but the revelation of the life that had already been given and is now hid συν χριστω εν τω Θεω ("with Christ in God," 3:3). So what the Christian should do is: τα ανω φρονειτε ("seek the things that are above," 3:1).

These differences which represent a contrast to the major Pauline Letters compel one to conclude that Paul was not the author of the letter, but that a disciple of Paul, who was well-versed in Paul's theology, composed the letter with the intention of letting the word of the apostle be heard in the situation created by the appearance of the "philosophers" in the churches of Asia Minor. Following the example of the apostle he chose the letter form, which he filled with material from the traditions of the Pauline school. To form the list of greetings (4:7-18) he used the names and information found in Philemon 23-24 (cf. also Philemon 2, 10-11), and added reports and data from the circle of the apostle's co-workers. At the beginning of the list stand the greetings from his assistants (4:10-14), and only then the apostle's own greetings (4:15-18). His co-workers continued his work; thus they are spoken of more extensively and are commended to the church as ministers of the Lord legitimized by Paul himself. The intimate contacts with tradition from the Pauline school and the close connection to Christianity in Asia Minor suggest Ephesus as the letter's place of origin. Since Ephesians presupposes the existence of Colossians, the latter must not be dated too late—thus about A.D. 80.

#21 The Letter to the Ephesians

Harnack, A. v. "Die Adresse des Eph," *SBA* 1910, 696ff.
Käsemann, E. "Epheserbrief," in *RGG*[3], 2:517-20.
Mitton, C. L. *The Epistle to the Ephesians*, 1951.
Schlier, H. *Der Brief an die Epheser*, 1957 = [6]1968.
Gnilka, J. *Der Epheserbrief*, 1971.
Fischer, K. M. *Tendenz und Absicht des Epheserbriefes*, 1973.
Barth, M. *Ephesians*, 1974.
Lindemann, A. *Die Aufhebung der Zeit—Geschichtsverständnis und Eschatologie im Epheserbrief*, 1975.

a. Contents: The letter is clearly divided into a didactic (chapters 1–3) and a parenetic part (chapters 4–6). The didactic part deals with the one church of Jews and Gentiles. This theme is already present in the introductory hymn of praise (1:3-14) and intercession (1:15-23). Then the doctrine of the church is developed, the church which is God's eschatological new creation (2:1-10), in which the promise of the incorporation of the Gentiles is fulfilled (2:11-22) and which is founded on the apostolic teaching (3:1-13). A prayer of thanksgiving concludes the didactic section (3:14-21).

The parenesis is based on this doctrine of the church and describes the life of the new people of God. The first fundamental principle which is developed is that the unity of the Spirit is to be preserved amidst all the variety of spiritual gifts (4:1-16). Then the challenge is given to put off the old nature and to put on the new nature (4:17-24). To this is added a long list of individual exhortations (4:25–5:21) and an extensive table of household duties *(Haustafel)* (5:22–6:9). The parenesis is concluded with a description of the Christian's spiritual armor (6:10-20), a brief report concerning Tychicus, and a final blessing (6:21-24).

b. The character of Ephesians corresponds more to a

theological treatise than to a letter. The unity of the church of Jews and Gentiles is described in a systematically arranged structure of long theologically packed sentences. It is noticeable that the readers appear not to know the apostle personally at all (1:15; 3:2ff; 4:21), but are rather told: "You have heard of the stewardship of God's grace that was given to me for you, how the mystery was made known to me by revelation, as I have written briefly" (3:2-3). Paul could not have addressed the church in Ephesus, which he knew so well, in this way.

In addition to this observation based on the contents of the letter, there is important evidence from text criticism. In the salutation of the letter (1:1) the words εν Εφεσω ("in Ephesus") are lacking in our oldest extant manuscript P[46], also in the valuable minuscule, 1739, and in Marcion and Origen. In the uncials ℵ and B it was not originally present but has been added in a later hand. This evidence requires the conclusion that the address "in Ephesus" is a secondary addition and that the letter could not originally have been sent to the Ephesians. This of course raises the question, To whom was this document addressed? Two answers are advocated in the discussion:

(1) The letter could have been addressed to Laodicea instead of Ephesus. This was already the view of Marcion, who listed our "Ephesians" in his canon as "Laodiceans." Even today many exegetes believe that Ephesians is the letter mentioned in Colossians 4:16 written to the church in Laodicea (Schlier). But why the original address should have disappeared is hardly explainable. Harnack supposed that the name of the Laodicean church was later eliminated because according to Revelation 3:14-22 it was lukewarm and indolent. But where was there a court in early Christianity which could have decided that a church's name was to be erased, and how could such a judgment have been carried out? Thus the Laodicean hypothesis cannot be persuasive.

(2) Supposedly Ephesians was not written for an individual congregation, but was composed as a kind of circular letter directed to "the saints who are also faithful in Christ Jesus." Then the name of whatever church was being addressed could be inserted at the appropriate place as the contents of this circular letter were read aloud in the churches. Since the letter is doubtless concerned with the churches of Asia Minor (Eph. 6:21-22 = Col. 4:7-8), later the name of the most significant

church in Asia Minor remained firmly attached to the salutation, so that the letter secondarily became known as the letter to the Ephesians.

The theme of the *una sancta ecclesia* is dealt with in such a way that ecclesiology is developed on the basis of Christology. Christ, the head, is in heaven, and the church is his body embracing the whole world. The dividing wall which separated Jews and Gentiles from each other has been taken away, so that both belong to one people of God. For the elaboration of this doctrine Ephesians makes use of religious ideas from the environment which flow in from Gnostic contexts on the one side—e.g. the picture of the cosmic Anthropos (1:10; 2:14-18; 4:8-11) or the concept of the marital relation of Christ and the church (5:25-32)—and on the other side from genuine Jewish tradition—e.g. the portrayal of the spiritual armor (6:10-20) which has close parallels in the description of the struggle of the sons of light against the sons of darkness in the Qumran texts. The author of Ephesians felt no need to mark himself off polemically against Gnosticizing false teachers, but was able to make theological use of ideas taken from his environment in order to describe the relationship of the church to Christ, since he conceived ecclesiology as a function of Christology.

c. Ephesians' theology and chain of thought point clearly to the post-Pauline origin of the writing. There are two decisive lines of evidence for this conclusion.

(1) The language and style of Ephesians deviate considerably from the major Pauline Letters. While Paul calls the devil ο σατανας ("Satan, the adversary," I Cor. 5:5), Ephesians uses the term ο διαβολος ("the devil, the slanderer," 4:27; 6:11). Only in Ephesians (and there five times!) is heaven described as τα επουρανια (lit. "the heavenly" [places], 1:3, 20; 2:6; 3:10; 6:12). On the other hand, a number of specifically Pauline concepts are missing. Paul speaks almost without exception of sin in the singular as a cosmic power (Rom. 5:12), but Ephesians speaks of sins in the plural (2:1), adopting the expression for the forgiveness of sins common in the churches (1:7). In addition to observations relating to the distinctive vocabulary and word usage, the stylistic peculiarity of Ephesians is also important. Lengthy sentence constructions (1:3-14; 1:15-23; 2:1-10) contain a heaping up of genitive connections, participial expressions, and

relative clauses, which make the liturgical-hymnic character of the style clearly recognizable. As in Colossians (see p. 91) the adoption of tradition from the Pauline school is evident, which helped create the letter's overburdened manner of expression.

(2) Ephesians stands in a close hereditary relationship to Colossians. While Colossians is engaged in debate with false teachers, Ephesians is able to develop its ideas in the form of a meditative recital. Nonetheless, extensive common material is shared by the two letters, including not only the terminology they use in common—e.g. σωμα, κεφαλη, πληρωμα, μυστηριον ("body, head, fullness, mystery")—but especially the substance of the letters themselves. Christ is the head of his body, the church. He has triumphed over the spiritual powers; peace has been established through his blood; the parenesis contrasts the Christian's old nature with the new; in the table of household duties the different classes of people in the church are addressed one after the other. It is conceivable that these common elements are to be accounted for not by literary dependence of one letter on the other, but by an independent use of liturgical and parenetic traditions (so Käsemann). But his hypothesis does not sufficiently explain the mutual interrelationship between the two letters, for Ephesians 6:21-22 agrees verbatim with Colossians 4:7-8, so that a direct connection between the two letters must exist. In that case Ephesians must be literarily dependent on Colossians. If one compares the two tables of household duties, for example (Col. 3:18–4:1, Eph. 5:22–6:9), it is immediately clear that the tersely formulated sentences of Colossians have been extensively elaborated in Ephesians, and have been provided with a comprehensive basis in which specifically Christian arguments are much more developed than in the Colossians passage. The cosmic Christology of Colossians which was developed in opposition to false teaching has been elaborated into a nonpolemical doctrine of the church.

Once it is accepted that Ephesians stands in a literary relationship to Colossians, the decisive blow is given to the possibility of describing Ephesians as the work of the aging apostle (contra Schlier). Rather, just as in the case of Colossians, Ephesians was produced within the developing Pauline school tradition in Asia Minor (Gnilka). Thereby the continuity with Pauline theology was maintained, in that the doctrines of justification (2:1ff), of the spiritual gifts (4:7ff), and of the one people of God composed of both Jews and Greeks were developed as an elaboration of ideas already present in the major Pauline Letters. The worldwide church, which stands under its heavenly head, is understood as a structured church, which rests on the foundation of the apostles and prophets (2:20). The apostles are the "holy apostles" (3:5), in addition to whom prophets, evangelists, pastors, and teachers are enumerated (4:11). Charisma is therefore coordinated with official structures. One can recognize here a further development which not only surpasses the major Pauline Letters, and also goes beyond Colossians, but which still does not make clear the structures in which the various offices are ordered. As in Colossians, the eschatological expectation oriented to the future has been replaced with a conceptuality oriented in terms of space, which distinguishes above and below, heavenly and earthly. The resurrection of the believer has already occurred in baptism (2:5); salvation has already been received by grace, and those who have been awakened from death have already been raised up into the heavenly world (2:6).

Since Ephesians originated after Colossians, it is to be assigned a date near the end of the first century. The letter quickly found widespread acceptance, so that Ignatius already presupposed that his readers knew it (Ign. to Eph. 3:4). Shortly thereafter the Letter of Polycarp (1:3) also referred to Ephesians (2:5, 8, 9).

#22 The Pastoral Letters

Campenhausen, H. v. *Polykarp von Smyrna und die Pastoralbriefe*, 1951.

Strobel, A. "Schreiben des Lukas? Zum sprachlichen Problem der Pastoralbriefe," *NTS* 15 (1968/69):191-210.

Spicq, C. *Lés Epîtres Pastorales*, [4]1969.

Brox, N. *Die Pastoralbriefe, 1969.*

Dibelius, M., and Conzelmann, H. A Commentary on the Pastoral Epistles, Hermeneia, 1972.

Since the eighteenth century the two letters to Timothy and the Letter to Titus have been studied as one unit, the Pastoral Letters. Thereby the character of these letters has been appropriately described, for they contain instructions and exhortations for the conduct of the pastoral office in the leadership of the church. Although in the form of letters to individual persons, they obviously present instructions concerning the correct organization and administration of the church and the demarcation of true from false doctrine, instructions which claim general validity.

a. Contents: In I Timothy, polemic against false teaching alternates with prescriptions for church order. After the opening greeting (1:1-2), first comes a defense against false doctrine (1:3-20), then an extensive discussion of questions of church order (chapters 2–3). Then follows a renewed debate with the false teachers (4:1-10), and then again material concerning the life and order of the church (4:11–6:2). The last chapter returns once again to the struggle against false doctrine (6:3-19), and is concluded with a brief admonition (6:20-21).

These same themes are handled in the Letter to Titus. To the opening greetings (1:1-4) there is joined a description of Titus' assignment on Crete, which includes both the appointment of elders and the debate with false teachers (1:5-16). Questions of church order are then discussed again, including at the end the problem of defense against the false teachers (2:1–3:11). The letter concludes with greetings and reports (3:12-15).

In II Timothy, after the introductory greeting (1:1-2) Timothy is given a lengthy challenge to fearless confession (1:3–2:13). Then once again comes a polemic against the false teachers, whose appearance belongs to the phenomena to be expected in the last days (2:14–4:8). What is required is to remain steadfast to the orthodox church and not to be concerned with fruitless disputes about words. At the end, the personal situation of the imprisoned disciple is described, who addresses the urgent plea to Timothy to come to him soon, before it is too late (4:9-22).

b. The addressees of the letters are Paul's closest co-workers. According to Acts 16:1-3, Timothy was the son of a Jewish-Christian mother and a pagan father, whose home was in Lystra in Asia Minor. Paul took him on his missionary journeys as a companion and co-worker. He is mentioned several times as co-sender of Paul's letters (I Thess. 1:1; II Thess. 1:1; II Cor. 1:1; Phil. 1:1; Philem. 1; Col. 1:1). He made trips to Thessalonica (I Thess. 3:1-2, 6), Corinth (I Cor. 4:17;

16:10) and Philippi (Phil. 2:19, 23) as the apostle's representative. He accompanied the apostle in delivering the offering to Jerusalem (Acts 20:4). He spent some time in Ephesus according to I Timothy 1:3; II Timothy 1:15ff; 4:11ff; the leadership of that church was in his hands. The letters are for the purpose of giving him instructions for the execution of this assignment.

Titus is not mentioned in Acts. He was a Gentile Christian who accompanied Paul to the apostolic conference in Jerusalem (Gal. 2:1); there Paul withstood the demands of the false brethren and refused to have Titus circumcised. He is mentioned several times in II Corinthians as an assistant of the apostle (2:13; 7:6ff, 13ff). According to Titus 1:5 he is located on Crete, entrusted with the leadership of the churches. The letter is intended to give him help in the execution of this office.

The assignments which Timothy and Titus are called upon to fulfill are thoroughly similar to those of a governor of a province, for in the areas for which they are responsible they are to execute their official duties with independence, to preserve order, to appoint officials, and to carry out the tasks assigned to them by the apostle, whose rank is higher than theirs. The literary form in which these mandates are clothed by the Pastorals is thus comparable to the directives, decrees, edicts, and precise instructions issued in letter form by the administrators in the Hellenistic governments (Spicq). On the other hand, II Timothy is distinguished from I Timothy and Titus in that it is more personal and composed somewhat like a testament.

c. The post-Pauline origin of the Pastorals is evident from a series of compelling arguments:

(1) The data contained in the Pastorals concerning the external details of the situation of the apostle's co-workers and of the apostle himself do not agree with the other reports of the life and ministry of Paul handed on in the tradition. First Timothy presupposes that shortly before the writing of the letter Paul had worked together with Timothy in Ephesus. Paul had then traveled to Macedonia, but Timothy had remained in Ephesus (1:3). According to Titus, the apostle had been in Crete, Titus had remained there (1:5), and after he had fulfilled his assignment, was to rejoin the apostle in Nicopolis, where Paul had decided to spend the winter (3:12). This probably intends to refer to the Nicopolis in Epirus. Second Timothy is then

supposedly written some time later. Paul is in prison in Rome (1:8, 16-17; 2:9). He has already been through serious legal proceedings, but has been saved from the mouth of the lion (4:16). Almost all the brethren have forsaken him; only Luke still stands by him (4:11). Timothy should come quickly and bring Mark with him (4:11). From Troas he should bring the cloak and the books which Paul had recently left there (4:13). It is incidentally mentioned that Paul had also been in Corinth and Miletus (4:20). It is not said where Timothy himself is. The reference to Troas (4:13) and the greetings to Aquila and Priscilla (4:19) suggest Ephesus.

This data from the Pastorals cannot be harmonized with the information about Paul's life provided by Acts and the other letters of Paul. According to Acts 20:1, Paul left for Macedonia, after remaining in Ephesus two years and three months (Acts 19:8, 10). But Timothy was not left behind by Paul, but went with him, and later was sent on ahead to Troas (Acts 20:4). Thus I Timothy could not have been written during the so-called third missionary journey. According to Acts and the other Pauline Letters, Paul was never in the region mentioned in Titus. Of course Acts 27 tells of a stormy sea journey along the coast of Crete, but that could not possibly have offered any opportunity for establishing and organizing churches. On the so-called third missionary journey Paul visited the cities of Troas, Corinth, and Miletus (Acts 20), which are mentioned in II Timothy (4:13, 20), But since Timothy accompanied him on that trip, there would have been no need for the kind of further communications as are found in II Timothy 4. So it is clear that the data from the Pastorals cannot possibly find a satisfactory place within the ministry of the apostle as it is portrayed in the narrative which ends at Acts 28.

But perhaps they can find a place in the time after a "first" Roman imprisonment? The hypothesis according to which Paul was released from his Roman imprisonment and realized his plan for a missionary trip to Spain, though supported by various arguments, remains an unprovable supposition (see p. 54). Moreover, one must then believe that not only in the West, but also renewed missionary programs in the East were carried out, if a place is to be found for the regions of Crete and Asia Minor mentioned in the Pastorals. With the adoption of the hypothesis that Paul wrote the Pastorals in the time between 63 and 67, the obvious differences between the Pastorals and the other Pauline Letters is also supposed to be explained, because Paul writes as an old man and his style has correspondingly changed (Spicq). But such hypotheses are "a flight into an unknown land" (Dibelius).

(2) Language and style of the Pastorals deviate considerably from the other letters of Paul. The Pastorals use a total of 848 different words (in addition to 54 proper names). Of these, no less than 306 are missing from the other letters of Paul. A large number of new expressions emerge, e.g. σοφρων, σωφονιζω, σωφοσυνη, σωφρονισμος ("sensible, train, modesty, self-control"; the words are all related in Greek); ευσεβης, ευσεβεω, ευσεβεια ("godly, do religious duty, godliness," the words are all related in Greek); συνειδησις αγαθη or καθαρα ("good or clear conscience"); πιστος ο λογος ("the saying is sure"); παραθηκη ("deposit, that which has been entrusted"); φιλανθρωπια ("loving-kindness"); χρηστοτης ("goodness"); επιφανεια ("appearing"); μακαριος Θεος ("the blessed God"). On the other hand, specifically Pauline concepts are lacking, such as δικαιοσυνη Θεοθ ("the righteousness of God"); εργα νομου ("works of the law"); σαρξ ("flesh"); σωμα ("body"); ελευθεροω ("set free"); ενεργεω ("be at work in"); καυχαομαι ("boast"), among others. The vocabulary and style of the Pastorals stand much closer than the other letters of Paul to the cultivated Hellenistic Greek spoken by philosophers and literary authors and in sophisticated circles.

If one determines the average length of the words in the various writings of the Pauline corpus, the results (according to O. Roller, see pp. 46-48) are for the Pastorals: I Timothy = 5.58, Titus = 5.66, II Timothy = 5.26 letters per word. In the other letters of Paul the words are somewhat shorter, with Philemon the shortest at 4.66, and I Thessalonians the highest at 5.02. Roller would like to explain the differences by means of his secretary-hypothesis, in that he posits the use of a different secretary for the writing of the Pastorals. But this hypothesis cannot be maintained (see p. 48). Rather, the considerable differences in language and style over against the other Pauline Letters only serve to strengthen the case against Pauline authorship.

(3) The debate with false teachers is directed against the same group in all three letters. They come from among the περιτομη ("circumcision," Titus 1:10), and want to be teachers of the Law (I Tim. 1:7). They occupy themselves with myths and human commandments (Titus 1:14) or myths and genealogies (I Tim. 1:4; 4:7), and thus promote foolish inquiries and controversies about the Law (Titus 3:9). This obviously refers to Gnostic speculations, which make use of OT materials—as was often the case also in later Gnosticism—and were involved in speculative interpretations of OT genealogical tables. The observance of food laws concerned with ritual purity indicates a Jewish origin (Titus 1:14-15). But there is no Judaism present of the type found among the Galatians (see pp. 59-60), but a peculiar combination of Jewish legalism and Gnostic speculations. People boasted of a higher knowledge (Titus 1:14; I Tim. 6:20), advocated an ascetic life-style, forbade marriage, and prohibited the enjoyment of certain foods (I Tim. 4:3; Titus 1:14-15). Obviously the spiritual reality should not be contaminated with earthly matter. Since it was believed that the resurrection had already occurred (II Tim. 2:18), the pneumatic had obtained a salvation that could never be lost, which exalted him above everything earthly.

When I Timothy 6:20 warns against the αντιθεσεις της ψευδωνυμου γνωσεως ("contradictions of what is falsely called knowledge," or "the 'Antitheses' of the so-called Gnosticism"), this cannot possibly refer to the "Antitheses" of Marcion, for Marcion, who rejected the OT, could not have developed speculative reflections on OT genealogies. The doctrine that the Pastorals combat rather manifests features which resemble the φιλοσοφια opposed in Colossians (see p. 88).

The debate with this doctrine is executed differently in the Pastorals from the way it is done in Paul's Letters or in Colossians, in that the latter present carefully developed theological arguments. The Pastorals simply declare a sharp separation between false and true doctrine, in that they censure the dissolute life-style of the false teachers and represent their appearance as the fulfillment of a prophecy made by the apostle himself; in the last days some will fall away from the faith (I Tim. 4:1), and the time is coming when some will not hold fast to sound doctrine, and will seek teachers to suit their own likings, who will tickle their ears (II Tim. 4:3). Whoever follows the false teaching falls away from the θγιαινουσα διδασκαλια ("sound doctrine," I Tim. 1:10; II Tim. 4:3; Titus 1:9; 2:1) and turns his back on the orthodox church. Thus over against the false doctrine, now considered to be heresy, there emerges a developing orthodoxy, advocated by the constituted church.

(4) The Pastorals place a strong emphasis on correct doctrine. To be sure, the Pastorals also exhibit a series of genuine Pauline formulations, in that they speak of the mercy of God to sinners, of which Paul himself is chief (I Tim. 1:12ff), of justification not on the basis of works (Titus 3:5), and in that praise is given for the manifestation of the saving grace of God in Christ (II Tim. 1:10-11; Titus 2:11ff; 3:4ff). But the Pauline theology has been further developed by the continuing Pauline school. The content of right religion (I Tim. 3:15-16: ευσεβεια) is the creedal formulation of the developing early catholic church. The Pastorals contain no christological affirmations formulated by the author himself, but use exclusively formalized expressions taken over from the tradition which name Christ as the mediator between God and humanity, who has give his life as a ransom for all (I Tim. 2:5-6). Faith, emphasized so strongly in Pauline theology, in the Pastorals has become correct belief, which can be listed as one among other Christian virtues (I Tim. 4:12). Since πιστις ("faith") has thus lost its primary significance, it is not surprising that without embarrassment the demand for good works can again be emphasized. The καλα εργα ("good works") are the evidence that God's grace has prepared and equipped the members of the community for the new life (I Tim. 2:10; 5:10; 6:18: πλουτειν εν εργοις καλοις ("be rich in good deeds," II Tim. 2:21; 3:17). Christ gave himself for us—thus is described the goal of Christ's work in Titus 2:14—in order to redeem us from all ανομιας και καθαριση εαυτω λαον περιουσιον, ζηλωτην καλων εργων ("iniquity and to purify for himself a people of his own who are zealous for good deeds"). Since the church is the pillar and ground of the truth (I Tim. 3:15; II Tim. 2:19), it bears the responsibility for the correct preaching and teaching of God's revelation in Christ. The tradition therefore receives an appropriately high valuation, and the recipients of the letter are charged to preserve the deposit (παραθηκη) entrusted to them (I Tim. 6:20; II Tim. 1:12, 14; 2:2).

The eschatological expectation has receded, and the church of the correct doctrine has begun to adjust itself to the world, so that the ideal of a Christian "bourgeoisie" develops (Dibelius). Thus, for example, the picture of the ideal bishop makes extensive use of instructions in proper conduct which had already been collected and used in Hellenistic popular philosophy (I Tim. 3:1-7). The requirements which a philosophically educated person should fulfill are taken over as the standard for the Christian life (see p. 45).

(5) The church order of the Pastorals has outgrown that found in the authentic Letters of Paul. A series of different offices has been developed. The πρεσβυτεροι ("elders, presbyters," I Tim. 5:17; Titus 1:5) form the board of the πρεσβυτεριον ("council of elders, presbytery," I Tim. 4:14). The leadership of the church has been committed to the επισκοπος ("bishop," I Tim. 3:1; Titus 1:7), whose task it is της εκκλησιας του Θεου επιελεισθαι ("care for God's church," I Tim. 3:5). The διακονοι ("deacons") are assigned services to perform for the congregations (I Tim. 3:8-13), and also widows look after charitable work (I Tim. 5:1-16). Ordination to the office of the ministry of the word is accomplished by the laying on of hands (I Tim. 4:14; II Tim. 1:6; cf. I Tim. 5:22). Charisma and office are so coordinated to each other that the working of the spiritual gifts functions through the official ministries (II Tim. 1:6). Evangelists (II Tim. 4:5) and teachers (I Tim. 4:11ff; Titus 2:1, 15) serve as ministers of the Word. A hierarchy of officers begins to emerge, in which Timothy and Titus take care of the leadership of the church as representatives of the apostle, and exercise oversight over all the other office bearers.

Although the Pastorals originated in the post-Pauline period, they are thoroughly committed to the advocacy of Pauline theology. They accomplish this however by the adoption of material from the tradition of the Pauline school, which they adapt to enable the apostle to address a changed situation. The mention of personal details concerning the situation of Paul is intended to strengthen this claim. The picture of Paul in the Pastorals corresponds to the ideas prevalent in those circles which sought to preserve the legacy of Paul's theology at the transition from the first to second century. The composition of the Pastorals can best be thought of as having occurred in Asia Minor, probably in Ephesus, where the Pauline school continued to develop its traditions.

It is scarcely possible to guess the name of the unknown author of the Pastorals. Nonetheless, various attempts have recently been made to discover his identity. V. Campenhausen has called attention to the points of contact which exist between the Pastorals and the letter of Polycarp to Smyrna. They have in common the (for the NT) *hapax legomena* ματαιολογια ("vain discussion"), εγκρατης ("self-controlled"), διαβολος ("slanderer," adj.), and διλογος ("double-tongued"), and the expression ο νυν αιων ("this world, the present age") is found in both. But one cannot conclude from this that Polycarp was the author of the Pastorals. Since Polycarp wrote to the Philippians in his own name, it is difficult to understand why he should have issued the Pastorals under the pseudonym of Paul—quite apart from the fact that it is improbable that the Pastorals were not written until the middle of the second century.

On the basis of some agreements in terminology and language between the Pastorals and the two volumes of Luke-Acts, Strobel has attempted to show that Luke was the author of the Pastorals. Not only do both sets of writing have in common words which are rare elsewhere such as αγαθοεργω ("do good"), αχαριστος ("ungrateful"), and δυναστης ("ruler, sovereign, official"), but also grammatical constructions such as δει, εδει, δεον εστιν ("it is necessary, one must") and the Latinism δι ην αιτιαν ("for this reason, therefore"). Agreements are also found in certain phrases such as that Christ came into the world in order to save sinners (I Tim. 1:15; Luke 19:10), or that a worker deserves his wages (I Tim. 5:18; Luke 10:7). But such similarities prove no more than that in both writings a high level of Koine Greek is used; and the points of contact between the content of the two writings are to be explained on the basis of common Christian traditions which were adopted in both Luke and the Pastorals.

V.

Forms and Types of the Oral Jesus–Tradition

#23 Form Criticism of the Synoptic Tradition

Schmidt, K. L. *Der Rahmen der Geschichte Jesu*, 1919 = [2]1964.
Schniewind, J. "Zur Synoptiker-Exegese," *ThR NF* 2 (1930):129-89.
Dibelius, M. *From Tradition to Gospel*, [2]1934.
Bornkamm, G. "Evangelien, formgeschichtlich," in *RGG*[2], 2:747-53.
Bultmann, R. *The History of the Synoptic Tradition*, 1963.
Koch, K. *The Growth of the Biblical Tradition*, [2]1969.
McKnight, E. *What Is Form Criticism?* 1969.
Güttgemanns, E. *Candid Questions Concerning Gospel Form Criticism*, 1979.
Conzelmann, H. "Literaturbericht zu den Synoptischen Evangelien," *ThR* 37 (1972):220-72; 43 (1978):3-51.

a. There was a gap of several decades between the public ministry of Jesus and the writing down of his words and deeds by the authors of the Gospels. During this time, what was known about Jesus was handed on orally. The few instances in Paul's Letters which quote sayings of Jesus show that at the beginning the tradition about Jesus was in the form of individual stories and sayings. Thus Paul says in I Corinthians 7:10, "To the married I give charge, not I but the Lord, that the wife should not separate from her husband." Since a word of the Lord on the issue of divorce had been preserved, it constituted a binding rule for the church. In I Corinthians 9:14 a command of Jesus is quoted to the effect that the church is obligated to provide for the support of those who preach the gospel. Sayings of Jesus were used in the parenesis as instruction in the Christian way of life. Thus Paul bases his argument for the proper manner of observance of the Eucharist on the report of the Last Supper in the tradition (I Cor. 11:23-25). And to the Thessalonians, who are upset because some members of the church have died before the parousia, Paul responds with a word of the Lord from which they learn that at the parousia first those who have died will be raised, so that the church members who are still alive may together with the resurrected go in a festive procession to meet the returning Lord (I Thess. 4:15-18).

These examples from the Pauline Letters enable us to see that the sayings of Jesus received modifications as they were handed along in the oral tradition. They are without exception understood as the words of the Kyrios who speaks as the resurrected Lord to his church in the present (cf. II Cor. 12:8-9). The logia were formulated so as to be appropriate to the situation of the community, so that for example the early Christian concept of the ευαγγελιον ("gospel") is used for the content of what is preached (I Cor. 9:14), the title of the exalted Lord, Kyrios, is inserted into a saying of Jesus, and reference is made to the νεκροι εν Χριστω ("dead in Christ," I Thess. 4:15-16). The changed situation in which the community found itself necessarily meant that sayings which Jesus had spoken during his lifetime were reformulated in order to be appropriate to the new circumstances of the church which wanted to live according to the directions of its Lord.

Oral tradition, like folk narratives in general, is subject to strict forms and its own stylistic laws. Thus for example a fairy tale is introduced with the expression "once upon a time" and the conclusion presents the moral of the story. The form-critical study of the Gospels is guided by the question of which laws determined the oral tradition from and about Jesus before the material was fixed in writing. Making distinctions between different types of material is not for aesthetic purposes, but is an effort more precisely to determine the conditions under which the oral repetition of the individual units of tradition took place. The tradition of Jesus' sayings must be considered separately from the narrative tradition of his deeds—just as a similar distinction must be made between words and deeds in the prophetic tradition (e.g. Jeremiah) or between Halacha (i.e. legal religious instructions) and Haggada (i.e. narrative material) in the rabbinic tradition. The tradition of Jesus' preaching and that of his deeds did not follow the same course, but were affected by different conditions. Since the church allowed its issues and problems to influence the tradition, the form of the Jesus-traditions was thereby affected, even changed and expanded. In order to be able to classify an individual pericope within the history of the developing tradition as a whole, one must constantly be asking what was its setting in the life of the church *(Sitz im Leben)*.

b. In their foundational studies Dibelius and Bultmann made a similar distinction between the tradition of Jesus' words and that of his deeds. Dibelius began with the question of the conditions under which Jesus' sayings received their traditional forms. Since the preaching of the community stood at the source of its life, he explains the formation of different types of sayings on the basis of preaching and offers typical illustrations. Bultmann analyzed and cataloged all the materials in the Synoptic Gospels. He was concerned with the problem of the historical development of the synoptic tradition, and how this resulted in the formation of the small individual units of tradition. Both scholars attempted to discover the laws which governed the formation of the oral Jesus-tradition. Their pioneering works supplement each other and at the same time present criteria for mutual correction.

The sayings material is dealt with by Dibelius under the heading of parenesis. He correctly observed that—as the examples of the Pauline Letters already show—the proclamation of Jesus was handed on in the tradition primarily within a parenetic perspective. Dibelius does not discuss the total contents of the sayings tradition, but selects examples to illustrate maxims, metaphors, parables, prophetic calls, as well as brief and extended commandments. In contrast, Bultmann carried out a complete analysis of the sayings material, which he classified in the following types: apothegms, i.e. brief pericopes in which the accent is placed on the sayings of Jesus, especially in the conflict and didactic sayings; dominical sayings which, in distinction to the apothegms, are independent units of tradition without any sort of narrative context. This great complex of such dominical sayings is subdivided as follows: (1) logia in which Jesus speaks as wisdom teacher, e.g. Matthew 6:19-34; (2) prophetic and apocalyptic sayings—the Beatitudes for example—among which authentic sayings of Jesus are most likely to be found; (3) legal sayings and church rules—e.g. Matthew 18:15-22—the forms of which were affected by the needs of the church; (4) I-sayings in which the person of Jesus plays an essential role and which for the most part express the faith confessed by the community, e.g. Mark 2:17 par.; (5) similitudes and similar forms which form a firmly structured segment of the tradition, within which additions by the church can be distinguished from the oldest layer, as for example Mark 4:3-9 par. as distinguished from 4:13-20. This classification of the total contents of the speech material is more appropriate to the complex structure of the final form of the synoptic tradition than Dibelius' effort to arrange the whole sayings tradition into the one category of parenesis.

The narrative material was assigned by Dibelius to the following categories: the paradigm is characterized by its short, rounded-off form, in which the main point is a saying of Jesus, as for example in the story of plucking grain on the sabbath, in Mark 2:23-28 par., in which the emphasis falls on the saying of Jesus in vv. 27-28. It exhibits no biographical interest, but was used as a sermon illustration which placed a special stress on the saying of Jesus. The "tale" is distinguished from the paradigm in that it is characterized by an expansive style. Thus in the cycle of miracle stories in Mark 4:35–5:43 details of the maladies of the various persons are given in order to emphasize the difficulty of the healing. At the end the "choral conclusion" calls special attention to the fact that no one has seen anything like this before. The distinction between the terse report, as found for example in Mark 2:23-28 par., and the detailed description, as presented for example by Mark 5:1-43, has been rightly emphasized by Dibelius. But it still must be asked whether these may be divided into different categories as neatly as he supposes. "Paradigm" is a term from the rhetoric of antiquity, and a "tale" is an edifying narrative, a classification which pays no attention to the content.

The classification proposed by Bultmann is more appropriate, in that the conflict and didactic sayings generally correspond to Dibelius' paradigm, and the pericopes called "tales" by Dibelius are characterized as "miracle stories" in accordance with their content.

The other categories which Dibelius suggested for the narrative material are designated with reference to their content, but are not to be sharply distinguished from other categories. The "legend" is not a form, but a category based on the interests pursued in the content. It portrays the significance of the person it describes, as for example in the story of Jesus at the age of twelve, in which it is pictured that the end of his life already casts its shadow over his first public act. "Myth" intends to portray the cosmic significance of its subject's deeds, but is only used occasionally in the gospel tradition, as for example in the story of Jesus' transfiguration in Mark 9:2ff par.

In contrast to Dibelius, Bultmann divided the whole narrative material into miracle stories on the one hand, and stories and legends on the other, and then took into account the circumstance that the content of the traditions exercised more influence on the tradition process than their forms. The broad category of "miracle stories" is divided according to content into healing miracles and nature miracles. The category of narratives and legends includes the Passion story in particular, but also the pericopes such as Jesus' baptism or the triumphal entry, and in addition the Easter stories and the birth and childhood narratives.

The question, whether form-critical investigation of the Gospels can be made more precise or corrected by being combined with methods derived from a "linguistic-theological" approach to the NT (Güttgemanns) is still open and needs further clarification.

#24 The Tradition of Jesus' Preaching

Cf. bibliography to #23.

Bornkamm, G. "Formen und Gattungen im NT," in *RGG*³, 2:999-1001.

Riesenfeld, H. *The Gospel Tradition and Its Beginnings: A Study in the Limits of Formgeschichte*, 1957.

Gerhardsson, B. *Memory and Manuscript*, ²1964.

Zimmermann, H. *Neutestamentliche Methodenlehre*, ⁴1974, 144-52.

Jesus did not recite his teaching to his disciples like a rabbi, who had his pupils learn the most important decisions and theses by heart, so that they could be handed on without alteration (contra Riesenfeld and Gerhardsson). The united testimony of the Gospels is that Jesus did not teach like the scribes, but with an incomparable εξουσια ("authority," Mark 1:22, 27 par.; Matt. 7:29, and elsewhere). Earliest Christianity understood his message as it was handed on in the churches as the word of the living and present Lord. Thus in the course of the traditioning process the sayings of Jesus received different forms. Many sayings of the historical Jesus continued to be repeated without modification, others received clarifying additions, and many were considerably reformulated. Sayings and rules originated as oracles of Christian prophets; parables were composed which were associated with the name of Jesus, were taught as his instruction and accepted as such. The broad range of materials preserved in the synoptic tradition as preaching of Jesus may be divided into the following categories:

a. Prophetic Sayings. The speech of a prophet is characterized by short, terse formulation, usually introduced by the expression, "Thus says the Lord." Jesus never uses this introductory formula, but speaks in his own authority of the near advent of the kingdom of God, e.g. Luke 6:20 par.; 10:23 par. But prophetic sayings can also have originated in the early church—as the example of Revelation 2–3 shows.

b. Wisdom Sayings. This form is conditioned by the tradition which had already developed in Judaism. Thus it is not surprising that parallels are found in the surrounding world for many wisdom sayings of the synoptic tradition, and many sayings were taken over from it, as for example the so-called Golden Rule (Matt. 7:12), the statement that a prophet has no honor in his own country (Mark 6:4), or the saying that each day has enough troubles of its own (Matt. 6:34). But sayings are also found in the wisdom materials which were not formed after preexisting patterns, but were first shaped in the preaching of Jesus, as for example the complex of sayings in Matthew 6:19-34 par.

c. Legal Sayings. This description applies not only to church rules, but also to those "sentences of holy law" which concisely set forth, in absolute terms, what is authoritative and must be observed, e.g. Mark 8:38 par., Matthew 7:6, and the antitheses of the Sermon on the Mount (Matt. 5:21-48). By the combination of individual legal sayings into a series of rules the church is instructed concerning what it should do, or a disciplinary rule for its life together is provided, as in Matthew 18:15-22.

d. Parables. In Jesus' parables, events and experiences from daily life are narrated. Then the salient point of comparison of the picture is related to the subject matter being dealt with, e.g. Mark 4:26-29: the miracle of the harvest portrays the coming of the kingdom of God. From the broad range of materials in the parable tradition, those items which can be traced back to the historical Jesus can be ascertained with some confidence (see J. Jeremias, *The Parables of Jesus*, [6]1963). Editorial work is found mostly in the introduction and conclusions, in order to apply the parable to the situation of the church. Allegorical features found their way into the parables or into appended interpretations intended to make the meaning of the parable more concrete, e.g. in Mark 4:13-20. New parables came into being in the church tradition in order to interpret the new situation of the church, e.g. Mark 12:1-12 par.

e. Christ-sayings. The sayings which speak of the goal of Jesus' having been sent, in the form "I have come . . ." (Mark 2:17 par.) or "The Son of man has come . . ." (Mark 10:45 par.) originated altogether as church creations, for they look back on the concluded work of Jesus and express the meaning of his coming in terse formulations.

f. Conflict and Didactic Sayings. On the boundary between the sayings-tradition and the tradition of Jesus' deeds we find pericopes which first picture the situation and then give a debate between Jesus and his opponents or describe a dialogue with the disciples. The dialogue is mostly introduced by a question directed to Jesus, carried further by a counter-question from Jesus and the answer of his partner, and then reaches its high point with the concluding word of Jesus, e.g. Mark 12:13-17 par.

In the oral tradition individual sayings and stories were often brought together into larger complexes. Not just one parable of the Kingdom was told, but several in a series (Mark 4:1-34 par.), and several controversy-dialogues could be brought together (Mark 11:27–12:40 par.). The framework of the Sermon on the Plain, within which a series of sayings had been brought together (Luke 6:20-49), has been expanded by Matthew to the extensive composition of the Sermon on the Mount (Matt. 5–7). The mnemonic device was often used in which a series of sayings was connected by key words, e.g. Mark 9:33-50, where the following key-word connections are found: v. 36/37 παιδιον ("child"); v. 37/38 εν τω ονοματι ("in the/my/your name"); vv. 42, 43, 45, 47 σκανδαλιζω ("stumble, sin"); v. 48/49 πυρ ("fire"); v. 49/50 αλισθησεται/αλας ("salt" [v.]/"salt" [n.]).

Such connections were built into the oral repetition of the sayings-tradition in order to impress the material better into the hearer's memory. The evangelists then arranged the sayings and stories which came to them in the tradition and provided them with editorial framework by means of which their own emphases were expressed and the particular understanding of Jesus' message which was important to them was emphasized.

#25 The Tradition of Jesus' Deeds

Cf. bibliographies to #23 and #24.

Lohse, E. *The History of the Suffering and Death of Jesus Christ,* 1967.

Zimmermann, H. *Neutestamentliche Methodenlehre,* [4]1974, 152-60.

a. The Passion story. The oldest Christian confession bore witness to the death and resurrection of Jesus Christ as God's act for us: Christ died for us, for our sins (see pp. 32-33). The tradition of Jesus' path of suffering describes how the event of Jesus' death on the cross came about. Critical analysis of the Synoptic Passion story enables us to reconstruct the oldest form of this report of Jesus' Passion.

In three sayings it is solemnly affirmed that the Son of man must suffer many things, die, and be raised (Mark 8:31 par.; 9:31 par.; 10:33-34). The third of these has the most elaborated form, and declares that the Son of man will be delivered to the chief priests and scribes, who will condemn him to death and deliver him to the Gentiles, who will mock him and spit on him, scourge and kill him, and that after three days he will rise from the dead (Mark 10:33-34 par.). Behind this statement a short account is visible, which began with the arrest of Jesus and narrated a brief summary of the most important stations of the Passion: Jesus' arrest, condemnation, and handing over by the Jewish court, transfer to the Roman authorities, mocking, scourging, crucifixion.

A comparison of the Synoptic and Johannine Passion accounts confirms that the oldest form of the Passion story began with the arrest of Jesus, for the Johannine account also begins directly with the narration of Jesus' arrest (John 18:1). To be sure, the course of the story varies in details from that of the Synoptic Gospels, but again the following stations of Jesus' path of suffering are named: handing over by the Jewish court, transfer to the Roman authorities, mocking and scourging of Jesus, crucifixion. The synoptic Passion story begins earlier with the decision reached by the Jewish authorities to put Jesus to death (Mark 14:1-2 par.). From this we can recognize that the short account of the oldest tradition has been extended backward by adding to the Passion story individual stories that were originally handed on independently, for instance the story of the anointing of Jesus (Mark 14:3-9 par.; cf. Luke 7:36-50), and the pericope of the establishment of the Eucharist (Mark 14:22-24, 25 par.; cf. I Cor. 11:23-25), which has been inserted into the Passion story by means of an extensive editorial framework (Mark 14:12-26). The Passion story is then once again extended backward by adding more material so that the whole context begins with the story of Jesus' entry into Jerusalem (Mark 11:1-11 par.). Then follows the collision with Jesus' opponents, who resolve to destroy him (Mark 11:18 par.), a long cycle of conflict-dialogues (Mark 11:27–12:44 par.), as well as Jesus' speech about the events of the end-time (Mark 13 par.).

b. Miracle stories. An extensive complex of miracle stories is contained in the synoptic tradition. Among these are included, on the one hand, terse narratives which do not really focus on the miracle, but on the saying of Jesus which forms the high point of the pericope: one must do good on the sabbath (Mark 3:4 par.). On the other hand we find stories which picture the event with much edifying detail, as for example Mark 5:1-43 par. In these stories the specific characteristics found in the miracle stories of the surrounding world recur again and again. In the Jewish and Hellenistic stories are found comparable parallels not only for the exorcisms and healings, but also for the nature miracles of Jesus (e.g. the stilling of the storm in Mark 4:35-41 par.). By telling stories of Jesus in which he triumphs over evil spirits, sickness, and the powers of nature, the early church intended to declare that in him salvation had dawned.

c. Christ-stories. We may use this term to describe those pericopes in which the meaning of Jesus' appearance is portrayed in a self-contained narrative, as in the stories of Jesus' baptism and transfiguration, but also in the birth stories of Matthew and Luke, and above all in the Easter stories. These stories are permeated through and through with the believing confession of the church, which sought with the help of legendary features to describe the incomparable, unique glory of Jesus.

d. The pericope of the death of John the Baptist (Mark 6:17-29 par.), in which no specific Christian trait is contained, is difficult to classify. The story, for which the Jewish historian Josephus offers a counterpart (Ant. 18:116-19), has been inserted by Mark because it had been mentioned that Herod Antipas had considered Jesus to be the resurrected Baptist (Mark 6:14-16 par.). It can best be described as a "tale" handed on independently in the tradition, which narrated the death of the Baptist with legendary features.

#26 Redaction Criticism of the Gospels

Schmidt, K. L. *Der Rahmen der Geschichte Jesu*, 1919, [2]1964.
Conzelmann, H. *The Theology of St. Luke*, 1961.
Rohde, J. *Rediscovering the Teaching of the Evangelists*, 1968.
Marxsen, W. *Mark the Evangelist*, 1969.
Perrin, N. *What Is Redaction Criticism?* 1969.

a. The framework which serves to connect the individual stories is only loosely connected to them and offers no data at all for arranging the pericopes into chronological or biographical order. Thus for example according to the present Markan arrangement the whole complex of stories in chapters 4–5 took place on one day. Jesus preaches to the people and tells them parables (4:1-34). Then in late afternoon he goes in the boat across the lake of Gennesaret (4:35-41). That would be a distance of five or six miles, so that they could not have arrived on the other side until late evening. But then three miracle stories are added on, without considering the temporal framework which made it already evening: the healing of the demoniac (5:1-20), the return trip across the lake (5:21), and then in conclusion the healing of the woman with the hemorrhage and the raising of the daughter of Jairus (5:21-43). It is impossible that all these events happened on the same day. Mark 4:1 is also connected to preceding material: according to 3:9 Jesus ordered a boat to be made ready, then follow healings and miracles (3:10-11) and the calling of twelve disciples (3:12-19) as well as a controversy with the Pharisees (3:20-35). Then according to 4:1, Jesus began teaching from the boat on the shore of the lake. It can thus be clearly seen that the framework by which the individual stories are held together serves only as linkage, not for the presentation of historical data. In the Gospel of Matthew the individual units of tradition have throughout been woven together into larger structures, so that to the Savior who ministers in word, as pictured in the Sermon on the Mount (chapters 5–7) there is juxtaposed the Savior who ministers in deeds, pictured in a series of miracle stories (chapters 8–9). And in Luke the mass of material not taken from Mark is collected into the "small insertion" (6:20–8:3) and the "great insertion" (9:51–18:14). Therefore none of the synoptic evangelists presents a geographically and chronologically trustworthy report of Jesus' activities, for the outline and means of representation used by the evangelists are in each case theologically determined.

b. Redaction-critical investigation of the Gospels is concerned with the work of the evangelists themselves, and directs its attention principally to the editorial connections which they have used to connect and arrange the individual units of tradition. Although form-critical study of the Gospels at first led to the conclusion that the evangelists were "only to the smallest degree, authors, but were mainly collectors, transmitters, editors" (Dibelius), this view has since been considerably modified. Through the arrangement and editing of the transmitted material the evangelists accented what they considered important, emphasized their leitmotifs, and gave guidance in how Jesus' words and deeds should be understood. Their activity was therefore by no means limited to the collection and transmission of traditions, but by the way in which they arranged the material into contextural structures and formulated editorial connections, they proved themselves to be theologians who intended to present a particular message by the way in which they portrayed the activity of Jesus. The distinctive theological emphases of Matthew and Luke may be seen by studying the details of how each of them reworked their source materials from Mark and the Q tradition. In contrast, the theology of Mark cannot be determined by comparison with a source, but exclusively from the analysis of the introductory and concluding formulas which the evangelist composed for the pericope, and from the summaries and editorial statements composed by him.

#27 The Gospel and the Gospels

Schniewind, J. *Evangelion I*, 1927; *II*, 1931.
Friedrich, G. "ευαγγελιον," in *TDNT*, 2:707-37.
Bornkamm, G. "Evangelien, formgeschichtlich," in *RGG*[3], 2:749-53.
Stuhlmacher, P. *Das paulinische Evangelium, I. Vorgeschichte*, 1968.
Voegtle, A. *Das Evangelium und die Evangelien*, 1971.
Talbert, C. *What Is a Gospel?* 1977.

a. The word ευαγγελιον ("gospel") originally meant the reward given to one who brought good news, and then the good news itself. In the OT, only the verb ευαγγελιζομαι ("evangelize, preach the gospel") is used in a theological sense, in order to describe the glad tidings which announced that Yahweh had begun his kingly rule (Isa. 52:7). The messenger of glad tidings brings good news to those who suffer, and announces the year of God's grace (Isa. 61:1-2). The NT says that this messenger of good news promised in the Scripture is Jesus. He reads forth the words of Isaiah 61:1-2 in the synagogue and concludes with the brief statement: "Today this scripture is fulfilled in your hearing" (Luke 4:16-21). This means that the words of the Scripture have become reality, that the joyous time of fulfillment has dawned.

The concept ευαγγελιον ("gospel") was not foreign to the NT world, being used above all in the ancient ruler-cult. In the Hellenistic world the ruler had been honored as an epiphany of the god since the time of Alexander the Great. In the oriental provinces of the Roman Empire such worship was then offered to the Roman emperors. Thus an inscription from Priene in Asia

Minor of 9 B.C. declares that the birthday of the god was the beginning of good news (ευαγγελια) for the world published in his behalf. After the birthday announcement came other ευαγγελια, such as the announcement of the emperor's having come of age, his accession to the throne, and his accomplishments, which were praised throughout the empire.

In distinction from the understanding of ευαγγελιον and ευαγγελιζομαι widely current in the Hellenistic world, the Christian community proclaimed that there was only one gospel (Gal. 1:6-9), the gospel of the crucified and risen Christ (I Cor. 15:3-5), who is proclaimed as Son of God and Kyrios (Rom. 1:3-4). The concept ευαγγελιον describes both the content of the proclamation and the preaching event, as can be clearly seen from the juxtaposition of both meanings in I Corinthians 9: εκ του εθαγγελιου ζην (v. 14) means: to earn one's living from the practice of preaching the gospel; the εξουσια (μου) εν τω ευαγγελιω is the authority which the messenger of the gospel has (v. 18*b*). But when Paul says ινα ευαγγελιζομενος αδαπανον θησω το ευαγγελιον ("that in my preaching I may make the gospel free of charge," v. 18*a*), he thinks rather on the content of the good news which may not be confused or burdened down with anything else, just as he does in the expression καταγγελειν το ευαγγελιον ("proclaim the gospel," v. 14). Thus the gospel is not only a report of a past event, but declares the presence of salvation and is thus itself a part of the saving event.

b. The joining of the kerygma with the tradition of Jesus' words and deeds, as presented for the first time in the Gospel of Mark, took place on the basis of the theological reflection that the gospel, which announces the saving event, is indissolubly bound to the story of Jesus. Since the traditions which told of Jesus' words, deeds, and suffering were brought together under the leitmotif "gospel," the whole tradition was given a kerygmatic stamp. Consistent with this, Mark introduces his work with the words αρχη του ευαγγελιου Ιησου Χριστου ("the beginning of the gospel of Jesus Christ," 1:1) and thereby indicates that the good news of Jesus Christ has a certain starting point, given by the beginning of Jesus' public ministry. This starting point corresponds to the outline presupposed by the speech placed in Peter's mouth by the author of Acts: "The word which was proclaimed throughout all Judea, beginning from Galilee after the baptism which John preached: how God anointed Jesus of Nazareth with the Holy Spirit and with power; how he went about doing good and healing all that were oppressed by the devil, for God was with him. And we are witnesses to all that he did both in the country of the Jews and in Jerusalem. They put him to death by hanging him on a tree; but God raised him on the third day and made him manifest" (Acts 10:37-40). If the beginning and end points are given with the baptism of Jesus by John, and the cross-resurrection events, then this framework provided by the events themselves is filled in by the traditions of Jesus' words and deeds arranged according to their subject matter, not in a chronological or biographical order (see p. 115).

The Gospel of Mark can be described as a Passion story with an extensive introduction (M. Kähler). But Matthew and Luke, both of whom used Mark as a source, reach back further and begin with the stories of Jesus' birth and childhood, telling a continuous story of Jesus' life. The Gospel of John begins even earlier, by extolling the preexistent Logos in the introductory hymn. But all four Gospels agree in placing their main emphasis on the Passion and Easter. They tell of Jesus' ministry, suffering, death, and resurrection in order to offer a challenge to, and an invitation to, faith (John 20:30-31). The literary form "gospel" is thus a genuinely Christian creation for which there were no direct models in ancient literature. If in the second century A.D. the Gospels were described by Justin as απομνημονευματα των αποστολων ("memoirs of the apostles," Apol. I. 66), then he obviously thinks that they contain the recollections of the apostles. But in fact they cannot be compared with the memoir literature widely circulated in antiquity, for they do not even hint that they are offering the kind of data that might be used to write a *vita Jesu*.

c. The content of the testimony which the Gospels present is the one gospel. Thus when the canon was formed and the individual books were provided with titles, they were accordingly called: Gospel according to Matthew, according to Mark, according to Luke, according to John. The one gospel message was delivered in a fourfold witness, with each of the four evangelists rendering the message in his own way. The effort of the Syrian Tatian to make one gospel-harmony from the four books (see p. 239) originated in the consciousness that there is only a single gospel message. The interest of the so-called apocryphal gospels, which began to appear around the middle of the second century, gravitated in a different direction, in that legendary anecdotes, apocryphal sayings of Jesus, stories told in the style of memoirs, and much else besides was combined with material familiar to us from the canonical Gospels so that the kerygmatic character receded and a freely created complex of Jesus-materials emerged. The ancient church, which did not acknowledge these works but accepted only the four Gospels into the canon, thus made a well-grounded decision.

As a result of this, a change in the linguistic usage was brought about in the second century, in that Justin, Irenaeus, and others spoke not only of the one gospel, but also referred to the writings which reported the deeds, preaching, Passion, and resurrection as Gospels, so that from then on four Gospels were spoken of. In this way the concept ευαγγελιον ("gospel") became a term for the four books which were taken into the canon as witnesses of the story of Jesus.

VI.

The Synoptic Gospels and the Acts

#28 The Synoptic Problem

Throckmorton, B. H. *Gospel Parallels,* [3]1967.
Huck, A., and Lietzmann, H. *Synopse der drei ersten Evangelien,* [11]1970.
Aland, K. *A Synopsis of the Four Gospels,* 1972.
———. *Synopsis Quattuor Evangeliorum,* [9]1976.

a. The synoptic problem is posed by the fact that the first three Gospels obviously have extensive similarities, but also considerable differences. The interrelationship of the first three Gospels can be clearly seen when their texts are placed in parallel columns so they can be viewed together (thus "synopsis"), and an exact comparison is made.

(1) The similarities are seen first in the outline: Jesus' ministry begins after his baptism by John, followed by miracles and preaching in Galilee, then the journey to Jerusalem, and at the end the report of Jesus' crucifixion and resurrection. From the outline of the Synoptic Gospels one receives the impression that Jesus' public activity lasted about a year. In contrast, the Gospel of John alternates several times between Galilee and Jerusalem

as the setting for the events which seem to extend over a period of about three years.

There is also considerable agreement in the order of individual pericopes. For example, in all three Gospels the stories of the healing of the paralytic, the calling of the publican, the dinner party at the publican's house, and the question about fasting are told in exactly the same order (Mark 2:1-22 = Matt. 9:1-17 = Luke 5:17-39). The two sabbath-conflicts which immediately follow in Mark are similarly directly joined to the preceding speech by Luke (Mark 2:23–3:6 = Luke 6:1-11), but are not found in Matthew until 12:1-14.

Moreover, there exists a noticeable relationship within the individual pericopes in which phrases and sentences are found in verbatim agreement. Thus for example the saying of Jesus to the paralytic is formulated the same way in all three Synoptics: ινα δε ειδητε οτι εξουσιαν εχει ο υιος του ανθρωπου αφιεναι αμαρτιας επι της γης ("but that you may know that the Son of man has authority on earth to forgive sins"), but rather than completing the sentence thus begun, a fresh start is made: λεγει [Lk: ειπεν] τω παραλυτικω: σοι λεγω εγειρε αρον τον κραβατον σου και υπαγε εις τον οικον σου ("he says" [Luke: said] "to the paralytic—'I say to you, rise, take up your pallet and go home,'" Mark 2:10-11 par.). The request of Joseph of Arimathea for the body of Jesus is reported three times in the same words: ητησατο το σωμα του Ιησου ("he asked for the body of Jesus," Mark 15:43 = Matt. 27:58 = Luke 23:52). And the saying "whoever would save his life will lose it; and whoever loses his life for my sake [and the gospel's] will save it" occurs three times in the same form (Mark 8:35 = Matt. 16:25 = Luke 9:24). Noticeable agreements occur also in pericopes which are found in only two Gospels, where a parallel is lacking in the Third Gospel, as for example in the report of the speech of John the Baptist (Matt. 3:7*b*-10, 12 = Luke 3:7*b*-9, 17).

Finally, it is striking that OT quotations in all three Gospels often appear in similar wording—even when the quotation has another formulation than that of the OT or the Septuagint (LXX). So for example we find in Mark 1:3 = Matthew 3:3 = Luke 3:4 ευθειας ποιειτε τας τριβους αυτου ("make his paths straight") (sc. of the Lord = Jesus), while the LXX of Isaiah 40:3

has ευθειας ποιειτε τας τριβους του Θεου ημων ("make straight the paths of our God").

These agreements, for which a multitude of other examples could be presented, sufficiently prove that the relationship between the three Synoptic Gospels cannot have resulted from mere chance—"since all three evangelists report the same events of course they sometimes used the same expressions"—but that a relationship of literary dependence must be present. In order to determine this relationship more precisely, we must however notice that despite the numerous similarities there are also considerable differences of various sorts among the three Gospels.

(2) The differences are seen first in the outline: Matthew and Luke both add birth stories to Mark, but they do not agree with each other. Matthew begins with the genealogy of Jesus arranged in a pattern of 3 × 14 members, which begins with Abraham and comes up to Jesus (Mat. 1:1-17), but Luke in contrast does not introduce until later a genealogy which begins with Joseph and goes back through a chain of seventy-seven members to Adam (Luke 3:23-38). There is nothing in Mark comparable to the Sermon on the Mount of Matthew 5–7, and in Luke only a considerably shorter parallel (Luke 6:20-49). A series of central parables of Jesus (e.g. the good Samaritan, the prodigal son, the unjust steward, the rich man and Lazarus) are found only in Luke, without any parallel in Matthew or Mark. While all three Gospels report the discovery of the empty tomb (Mark 16:1-8 = Matt. 28:1-10 = Luke 24:1-11), the story continues in Matthew with the appearance of the resurrected Lord to the disciples in Galilee (Matt. 28:16-20), but in Luke only in and around Jerusalem (Luke 24:13-53).

Considerable variation is also found in the order of the pericopes. Thus Mark 6:1-6 (= Matt. 13:53-58) tells of the debut of Jesus in his hometown of Nazareth, and his rejection; Luke in contrast reports Jesus' first sermon in Nazareth at the very beginning of his public ministry (Luke 4:16-30). In Mark (1:16-20 = Matt. 4:18-22) the call of the first disciples is briefly related, but in Luke the call of Peter follows the miraculous catch of fish (5:1-11). While Mark first tells of the great crowds and Jesus' healings, then of the call of the twelve apostles (Mark 3:7-12, 13-19), the order is reversed in Luke (6:12-16, call of the twelve apostles; 6:17-19, crowds and healings), and corresponding sections are lacking altogether in Matthew (but cf. Matt. 12:15-21; 10:1-4). A large number of sayings found in the Sermon on the Mount in Matthew (5–7) have no parallels in Mark and are scattered by Luke over chapters 6–16 (cf. e.g. the Lord's Prayer in Matthew 6:9-13/Luke 11:2-4).

Also within the same pericope numerous important differences are to be found. In the parable of the great supper given in Matthew 22:1-14 and Luke 14:15-24, the same material is obviously presupposed in both places. But Luke describes a great banquet, and Matthew a wedding celebration given by a king for his son. In the story of the rich young man who addressed Jesus as διδασαλε αγαθε ("good teacher"), Jesus' response according to Mark 10:18 (= Luke 18:19) is: τι με λεγεις αγαθον ("why do you call me good?"), but according to Matthew 19:17: τι με ερωτας περι του αγαθου ("why do you ask me about what is good?"). Although the course of the Passion story in all three Gospels is essentially the same for extensive passages, the last words of Jesus are different. According to Mark 15:34 (= Matt. 27:46) he quotes the verse from the Psalms, "My God, my God, why have you forsaken me?" This saying is lacking in Luke, who puts in its place three other sayings of Jesus on the cross (Luke 23:34, 43, 46). The relation of the three Synoptic Gospels to one another is thus characterized by a broad range of materials used in common, as well as an impressive number of larger and smaller differences.

b. In the earlier attempted solutions the effort was made to explain how the Gospels of Matthew, Mark, and Luke were related to one another. The problem was first clearly seen in the time of the Enlightenment. Prior to that time, the opinion of Augustine prevailed, that Mark was an abbreviated form of Matthew, whose Gospel was regarded as the oldest and most important writings among the Gospels. In other respects during the Middle Ages and the Reformation period the statements of the three Gospels were generally harmonized as much as possible. Post-Reformation Protestant Orthodoxy expended much ingenuity in smoothing out the contradictions between the evangelists. But the Enlightenment could no longer be satisfied with such explanations of individual passages. Here for the first time the synoptic problem was recognized and ways to its solution were proposed.

(1) According to the primitive-Gospel hypothesis, advocated above all by Lessing, our Gospels are different translations and excerpts from an old apostolic writing in Aramaic, the gospel of the Nazarenes. There were supposedly different revisions of this gospel in circulation, which supposedly explains the different forms of our three Synoptic Gospels. But this hypothesis was only the expression of unprovable conjectures.

(2) The fragment hypothesis or *diēgēsis* hypothesis does not presuppose a comprehensive primitive gospel, but that various accounts of individual events in the ministry of Jesus were in circulation, from various apostles and disciples. Schleiermacher adopted the view that later the Gospels were assembled from such brief accounts *(diēgēsen)*. He was, to be sure, correct in observing that in the Synoptic Gospels collected materials from quite different origins had been used, but this theory only explained the similarities within individual stories, and not the similarities between the order and structure of the Gospels as a whole.

(3) The tradition hypothesis builds on Herder's insight of the significant role played by the oral tradition. At the beginning there was supposedly a gospel handed on orally, from which our three Gospels were later derived. There can be no doubt that the oral tradition played a decisive role in the early history of the material of which our Gospels are composed. But the complicated problem of the agreement and differences between the Synoptic Gospels cannot be solved without positing literary connections among them.

(4) The utilization hypothesis reckons with direct literary dependence among the Synoptic Gospels. Near the end of the eighteenth century Griesbach supposed that Mark knew both Matthew and Luke, from which he composed an abbreviated version: for example Mark 1:32 οψιας δε γενομενης οτε εδυσεν ο ηλιος (lit. "but evening having come, when the sun had set") is explained as a combination of Matthew 8:16 οψιας δε γενομενης (lit. "but evening having come") and Luke 4:40 δυνοντος δε του ηλιου (lit. "but the sun having set"). This hypothesis has partisans even today, most recently W. R. Farmer (*The Synoptic Problem,* 1964). In this view Matthew is supposed to be the oldest Gospel, then Luke, and finally Mark was written by using the two Gospels already present. But against this stands all the evidence that Mark is the earliest

Gospel (see below), which was first presented by Lachmann (*de ordine narrationum in evangeliis synopticis, ThStKr* 8 [1835] 570ff). Moreover, the relation of the Synoptics to one another cannot be explained by positing only that they used one another, for all sorts of connections also exist between Matthew and Luke in those sections for which there is no Markan parallel. The complicated relationship of the similarities and differences between the Synoptics did not in fact find a satisfactory solution until the advent of the so-called two-source hypothesis, which is today almost universally accepted.

c. The two-source theory affirms: (1) The Gospel of Mark is the oldest of the three Synoptic Gospels and was used as a source by Matthew and Luke. (2) In addition to Mark, both Matthew and Luke, independently of each other, used a second source, the so-called sayings-source Q, which consisted almost exclusively of sayings of Jesus. The basic evidence for this theory was presented above all by H. J. Holtzmann (*Die synoptischen Evangelien*, 1863) and P. Wernle (*Die synoptische Frage*, 1899).

(1) That the Gospel of Mark must be the oldest of the three Synoptic Gospels is compellingly proven by the following evidence: first, the outline of the Gospels shows that Mark must have lain before the two other evangelists as their model and point of departure. Matthew and Luke go their separate ways in the birth stories with which they each begin, and first begin to agree with each other in the report about John the Baptist, that is, exactly at the point where Mark begins. The same phenomenon is present at the conclusion: Matthew and Luke have agreements with each other where each is parallel to Mark, but when Mark ends at 16:8 they go their separate ways in relating the Easter stories. From that is to be inferred that Mark lay before them as a source.

This conclusion is confirmed by an investigation of the order of the individual pericopes. The order of Mark 2:1-22 agrees with that in Matthew 9:1-17 and Luke 5:17-39 (see p. 122). Then Matthew goes his own way (9:18–11:30). Luke 6:1-11 corresponds to Mark 2:23–3:6, but Matthew does not become parallel to Mark again until 12:1-14. Luke follows the order of Mark to 6:19, then branches off at 6:20ff. The material in the so-called Sermon on the Plain (Luke 6:20-49) has already been used by Matthew earlier in the Sermon on the Mount (Matt. 5–7). That means:

Matthew once departs from Mark's order, but Luke agrees with it. Then Luke branches off from Mark, but this time Matthew continues to agree with Mark. But Matthew and Luke never have a common order which differs from the Markan order. Therefore Mark must be the oldest of the three Gospels and have served as a source for the other two.

Almost all the material in Mark is repeated by Matthew. Of the 666 verses contained in Mark, we find more than 600 in Matthew. Since Matthew consistently condenses and tightens the expansive style of Mark, this means that with minor exceptions Matthew takes over the whole of Mark's material. On the other hand, Luke took over only around 350 verses from Mark. For several Markan pericopes Luke has parallels which have been differently formulated (e.g. the preaching of Jesus in Nazareth, Mark 6:1-6; Luke 4:16-30). The whole complex Mark 6:45–8:26 is lacking in Luke. (See p. 128.) On the one hand, Luke has eliminated double traditions; on the other hand, he has drawn heavily on non-Markan tradition. Only the following have no parallel in Matthew and Luke: Mark 4:26-29; 7:31-37; and 8:22-26, as well as the verses 1:1; 3:20-21; 7:3-4; 12:33-34; 14:51-52; 15:44-45. This small amount does not affect the conclusion: the contents of the Gospel of Mark lay before Matthew and Luke and were adopted and adapted by them.

A comparison of the contents also leads to the conclusion that Mark was the model for Matthew and Luke. Thus in Mark 8:29 the confession of Peter reads "You are the Christ," while in Matthew 16:16 it is "the Christ, the Son of the living God," and in Luke 9:20 "the Christ of God." Thus the terse formulation in Mark has been expanded or commented upon by both Matthew and Luke. According to Mark 15:39 the Gentile centurion beneath the cross says, "Truly, this man was the Son of God." Matthew 27:54 reads, "Truly, this was the Son of God." This reformulation avoids calling Jesus a "man." In contrast, in Luke 23:47 the centurion says, "Truly, this was a righteous man," because a pagan can hardly be expected to have made a complete Christian confession. While Matthew makes modifications on the basis of theological considerations, Luke seeks to describe the situation more accurately from a historical point of view.

Finally, language and style also prove the priority of Mark. Mark writes in a simple style, mostly connecting one sentence after another with και—και ("and—and") and constructs no artful periodic sentences. The historical present as used in everyday speech predominates. Matthew often changes a Markan λεγει to ειπεν ("says" to "said"), and the historical present is hardly found in Luke at all. While Mark 2:11 uses the slang word κραβαττος ("bunk") for the pallet of the lame man, Matthew says κλινη ("bed," 9:6) and Luke κλινιδιον ("bed," 5:24).

The question as to the form of the Gospel of Mark used by Matthew and Luke has been answered by many scholars by positing a shorter *Urmarkus* (primitive Mark). In support of this they have not only pointed to that body of material unique to Mark which has no parallel in Matthew or Luke, which therefore could be a secondary addition, but have especially pointed out those places where Matthew and Luke agree against Mark. Thus in Mark 6:14 Herod Antipas is named βασιλευς ("king"), while Matthew and Luke describe him as τετρααρχης ("tetrarch"). Mark 10:30 reads εκατονταπλασιονα ("hundredfold"), but both Matthew and Luke have πολλαπλασιονα ("manifold"). But Herold Antipas did not have the title of "king," so that Matthew and Luke make the appropriate correction. And the textual agreements which Matthew and Luke have in common against Mark can in many instances be traced back to the fact that the text of Matthew, by far the most prevalent in church use, has influenced the textual form of Luke. As for the sections peculiar to Mark, the most likely explanation is that these few passages were independently omitted by Matthew and Luke. Mark 4:26-29 is after all a matter of one more seed-parable, and Mark 7:31-37 and 8:22-26 are miracle stories much like those already included in other sections of their Gospels. Luke may intentionally have left out the complex of materials in Mark 6:45–8:26 in order to avoid repetitions and passages which presuppose specifically Jewish associations. There is therefore no compelling evidence that the Gospel of Mark used by Matthew and Luke was essentially different from the Mark which has come down to us. So no change needs to be made in the first tenet of the two-source theory, that the gospel of Mark is the oldest of the three Synoptic Gospels and was used as a source by Matthew and Luke.

(2) In addition to the agreements which derive from the use of

Mark as a common source, Matthew and Luke have in common a not inconsiderable amount of material—around 200 verses—which almost without exception are composed of sayings of the Lord and are to be traced back to the sayings-source Q. These materials are found in Matthew principally in the great speech-compositions of chapters 5–7, 10, 13, 18, 23-25, in Luke primarily in the passages 3:7–4:13; 6:20–7:35; 9:51–13:35. These points of contact cannot be explained by supposing that Matthew is dependent on Luke or Luke on Matthew, for how, for example, would one explain that Luke has scattered the material in the Sermon on the Mount over many chapters? Or can one suppose that Matthew omitted the three parables of the lost sheep, the lost coin, and the lost son of Luke 15, only to include a different version of the parable of the lost sheep in another place (18:12-14)? The agreements between Matthew and Luke in non-Markan passages must be traced back to a source which each of the two evangelists used independently of the other.

The material common to Matthew and Luke which is not derived from their use of Mark comprises essentially the following passages: the preaching of John the Baptist, the temptation of Jesus, a great speech of Jesus (Sermon on the Plain/Mount), the story of the centurion of Capernaum, sayings about the Baptist, a missionary discourse, the Lord's Prayer, sayings about discipleship, the parables of the mustard seed and leaven, parable of the great supper, an eschatological discourse, and the parable of the talents/pounds. Thus at the beginning there stood the tradition of John the Baptist, and at the end instruction about the last things. This collection of sayings of Jesus presupposed by Matthew and Luke contained no Passion story, for in the Passion stories of Matthew and Luke, no features are found in common in those passages which deviate from Mark.

Since in Matthew the sayings have been gathered together and composed into extensive speeches, we may say with regard to the faithfulness with which the sayings-source was reproduced that the original order of the sayings in Q is more likely to be preserved by Luke. On the other hand the wording of Q is better preserved by Matthew, who consistently remains closer to the original Semitic linguistic form of Q than does Luke who has often revised the sayings into a more Hellenistic form. Since Papias of Hierapolis in the second century A.D. reported that

"Matthew collected the logia in the Hebrew language, and each one translated them as best he could" (Eusebius, H. E. III 39, 16), it has been supposed that he could have referred to the so-called sayings-source ("logia"). But such suppositions have no basis. The collection of sayings used by Matthew and Luke as a source must have already been in a Greek form, for only under this presupposition can the extensive agreements in wording be explained. Papius was certainly not thinking of Q, but of the Gospel of Matthew itself (see p. 142).

The sayings-source may be compared with those collections of sayings found in the wisdom tradition and in the tradition of the sayings of famous rabbis. An instructive parallel is presented by the Christian-Gnostic Gospel of Thomas which contains exclusively sayings of Jesus, although of course it was not composed until later. (See J. M. Robinson, "Logoi Sophon—On the Gattung of Q" [1964], in H. Koester—J. M. Robinson, *Trajectories Through Early Christianity*, 71-113.) Behind the collection, which had been composed from sayings of Jesus, there stood a distinctive theological understanding of his mission, a theological understanding which did not speak of Jesus' Passion, but saw in him the teacher and the coming Son of man who would appear at the Last Day for judgment. (See H. E. Tödt, *The Son of Man in the Synoptic Tradition* [1965] pp. 235-70; D. Lührmann, *Die Redaktion der Logienquelle*, 1969; P. Hoffmann, *Studien zur Theologie der Logienquelle*, 1972; S. Schulz, *Q—Die Spruchquelle der Evangelisten*, 1972.)

Was Q in fact a written source? J. Jeremias ("Zur Hypotheses einer schriftlichen Logienquelle Q" [1930], in *Abba*, 1966, 90-92) has especially called attention to the following observations: (1) the deviation in vocabulary—e.g. in the Beatitudes or the Lord's Prayer—is so considerable that one can hardly suppose that the evangelists would have made such substantial changes in a written source. (2) In many places Matthew and Luke present the sayings in a completely different order. Thus for example Luke 13:22-30 corresponds to the following Matthean parallels: 7:13-14; 25:10-12; 7:22-23; 8:11-12; 19:30 (20:16). Matthew 5–7 is parallel not only to the Sermon on the Plain but to other sections of Luke dispersed over many chapters. How could a common source have been used for such places? (3) The sayings are sometimes connected by various series of key words; such connections are an indication of oral tradition. Thus after Matthew 5:15 ("gives light") comes v. 16 with the key word "light/shine"; but in Luke 11:33 the parallel saying is in a completely different context. In Matthew 23:37-39 the prophecy of the destruction of Jerusalem stands at the end of the judgment speech against the Pharisees; but in Luke the parallel saying is connected to the statement that a prophet must die in Jerusalem (Luke 13:33-35).

These observations urge that the effort to reconstruct Q be done with care and with the possibility on the one hand that sometimes the one and sometimes the other evangelist could have omitted something from Q, and on the other hand that the sayings-source of Matthew and that of Luke may not have been completely identical. For all that, it is not adequate to regard Q as only a firmly solidified layer of oral tradition. Rather, the following reasons indicate that Q must have been a written document: (1) despite many deviations in detail, there is still a recognizable outline followed by both Matthew and Luke which begins with the preaching of the Baptist and ends with Jesus' eschatological instruction; (2) only by positing a written Q can we obtain a satisfactory explanation for the so-called doublets. Both Matthew and Luke have taken over several sayings from Mark and then a second time from Q, as for example the saying about gaining or losing one's life, first from Mark 8:35 = Matthew 16:25 = Luke 9:24, but then also Matthew 10:39 = Luke 17:33. Or another example: the statement that to the one who has, more will be given, and from the one who has not, even what he has will be taken away, first Mark 4:25 = Matthew 13:12 = Luke 8:18, and then Matthew 25:29 = Luke 19:26. These doublets, to which an obvious list of other examples could be added, result from the fact that Matthew and Luke had before them not only one, but two written sources—Mark and Q—and found many of the same sayings in both sources, and in several cases took over both forms. Even if Q cannot be as clearly determined as a source for Matthew and Luke with the same precision as is the case with Mark, this does not mean that the necessity of having to reconstruct Q calls in question the second thesis of the two-source theory, which may be regarded as proven: in addition to the Gospel of Mark, Matthew and Luke independently of each other used another source which consisted almost exclusively of sayings of Jesus.

In addition each of these two evangelists used their so-called special materials, i.e. materials which came from neither Mark nor Q (see below pp. 143 and 148). But this does not mean that in addition to Mark and Q there were other written sources. To be sure, there have been attempts to show that there was probably a larger number of written sources for the Gospel. Thus E. Hirsch (*Frühgeschichte des Evangeliums,* 1941) postulated no fewer than eleven sources which the Synoptics are supposed to have reworked. (For a critique, see M. Lehmann, *Synoptische Quellenanalyse und die Frage nach dem historischen Jesus,* 1970). But rather than additional written sources, Matthew and Luke had the oral tradition of the community, the nature and characteristics of which have been illuminated by the form-critical investigation of the synoptic tradition. Thus form criticism and the two-source theory supplement each other in that they make understandable the course of the Jesus-tradition from its beginnings up to the literary fixation by the evangelists. (See K. Grobel, *Formgeschichte und synoptische Quellenanalyse,* 1937.)

#29 The Gospel of Mark

Werner, M. *Der Einfluss paulinischer Theologie im Markusevangelium,* 1923.
Conzelmann, H. "Geschichte und Eschaton nach Mc 13" (1950), in *Theologie als Schriftauslegung,* 1974, 62-73.
Luz, U. "Das Geheimnismotiv und die markinische Theologie," *ZNW* 56 (1965) 9-30.
Niederwimmer, K. "Johannes Markus und die Frage nach dem Verfasser des zweiten Evangeliums," *ZNW* 58 (1967) 172-88.
Roloff, J. "Das Markusevangelium als Geschichtsdarstellung, *EvTh* 27 (1969) 73-93.
Marxsen, W. *Mark the Evangelist,* 1969.
Schweizer, E. *The Good News According to Mark,* 1970.
Kuhn, H.-W. *Ältere Sammlungen im Markusevangelium,* 1971.
Wrede, W. *The Messianic Secret,* [4]1971.
Pesch, R. *Das Markusevangelium I,* 1976; *II,* 1977.
Gnilka, J. *Das Evangelium nach Markus I,* 1978; *II,* 1979.

a. Contents: The Gospel of Mark relates Jesus' ministry in Galilee (1-10) and his path of suffering in Jerusalem (11-16).

First the beginning of Jesus' ministry is portrayed (1:1-13), then his first public appearances in and near Capernaum (1:14-45). Then comes a series of conflict stories in which Jesus encounters Pharisees and scribes (chapters 2–3). Jesus' parables are told (4:1-34), then a cycle of miracle stories (4:35–5:43). Then come some individual stories (6:1-33): Jesus is rejected in Nazareth (6:1-6), sends out his disciples (6:6-13), who return shortly thereafter (6:30-33). In between, the story of the death of John the Baptist is related in connection with the report of Herod's view of Jesus' identity (6:14-29). Then two sections with very similar outlines are presented: (6:34–7:37; 8:1-26) a feeding story (6:34-44; 8:1-9); crossing the lake (6:45-56; 8:10); conflict story (7:1-15; 8:11-13); instruction of the disciples (7:17-23; 8:14-21); Jesus and the Canaanite woman (7:24-30, without parallel in chapter 8); a healing story (7:31-37; 8:22-26).

The three predictions of Jesus' suffering (8:31; 9:31; 10:32-34) determine the whole context of the section in which the announcement of Jesus' Passion occupies the central place (8:27–10:52). To the story of Peter's confession at Caesarea Philippi is joined the first Passion prediction (8:27-33) as well as instruction about the suffering involved in discipleship (8:34–9:1), then Jesus' transfiguration and a discussion with the disciples as they descend from the mountain (9:2-13) and the healing of the epileptic boy (9:14-29). To the second Passion prediction (9:30-32) are joined discussions with the disciples (9:33-50) and a somewhat catechetical complex of materials (10:1-31—concerning marriage, children, and property). The third Passion prediction (10:32-34) is followed by the dialogue with the sons of Zebedee (10:35-45) and the healing of a blind man (10:46-52).

Chapters 11–13 describe Jesus' last days in Jerusalem: first his entry (11:1-10), cleansing the temple (11:11, 15-19) and cursing the fig tree (11:12-14, 20-26), then follows a cycle of conflict stories (11:27–12:44) and finally the apocalyptic speech of Jesus (13). The story of Jesus' Passion and resurrection is told in 14:1–16:8, which suddenly ends with the statement that the women fled in terror from the empty tomb and said nothing to anyone because they were afraid.

b. This raises the question of the original conclusion of the Gospel of Mark. Of course the appearance of the risen Lord in Galilee is announced in Mark (14:28; 16:7), but is not reported. Was there such a report in an original conclusion to the book which is now lost? Such hypotheses have often been proposed, but never with convincing reasons. It is clear that Matthew and Luke knew a Gospel of Mark which ended at 16:8, from which point each of the evangelists goes his own way. It is extremely unlikely that Mark's Gospel had already lost its original conclusion in the very earliest time, even before Matthew and Luke became acquainted with it. The Gospel can end with 16:8, because the Easter message has already been proclaimed and needs no further illustration. God's deed in raising the Crucified One from the dead calls forth from the human side the response of fear and trembling.

Very early it was felt to be a lack that Mark told no stories of Jesus' appearance, so what were considered to be appropriate additions were made. The secondary conclusion found in Mark 16:9-20 had already been added in the second century, and presupposes an acquaintance with the Easter stories of the three other Gospels (see p. 19; vv. 9-10: John 20:11-18; vv. 12-13: Luke 24:13-35; v. 14: Luke 24:36-49 and John 20:19-29; v. 15: Matt. 28:18-20; v. 19: Luke 24:50-53). This later addition is lacking in the old codices ℵ and B as well as in Clement of Alexandria and Origen. The manuscripts L, Ψ, and 099 have a shorter conclusion following verse 8, in which it is said that the women informed Peter and the disciples of the resurrection, and that the Risen One then sent out the message of eternal salvation into all the world. Finally, Codex W has a brief appendix between vv. 14 and 15, the so-called Freer Logion, which tells of the post-Easter encounter of Jesus with the disciples. These different supplements show that the ending of Mark was already felt to be a problem very early. But in fact Mark ended his Gospel at 16:8.

c. Possibly Mark already had some written collections of material, e.g. 2:1–3:6 (Kuhn), but his main source was the oral tradition. He so arranged the individual units of tradition that they set forth the message of the gospel: whatever is narrated about the earthly ministry of Jesus is told in reference to the kerygma of the cross and resurrection. For this purpose the evangelist makes especial use of the motif of the hidden messiahship. It is repeatedly reported that Jesus heals the sick, drives out demons, and performs extraordinary deeds. But then it is constantly added that Jesus commanded people to keep quiet about it (1:25, 34; 3:12; 5:43; 7:36; 8:26, 30; 9:9). Wrede, who was the first to recognize the significance of this motif, thought that the messianic secret was intended to explain a seeming contradiction. The earliest church which after Easter confessed its faith in Jesus as the Messiah still had a clear memory that the earthly Jesus had not stepped forth publicly as the Messiah. Relief from this embarrassment was sought by explaining that Jesus was already the Messiah during his pre-Easter ministry, but had kept his true rank a secret. But this explanation is off-target, because there never existed anywhere in early Christianity any tradition which did not understand Jesus' ministry in a messianic sense. Rather, at the beginning of the Christian tradition there stood the thesis: Jesus is the Messiah. The evangelist himself indicates why he writes a book of "secret epiphanies" (Dibelius) in that in the last passage in which the command to silence appears, he explains its meaning: the disciples may not speak of Jesus' glory until the Son of man is risen from the dead (9:9). Thus the divine revelation can only be spoken of in such wise that Jesus' whole ministry is seen in the light of the cross and resurrection. In this way the series of secret epiphanies points to the one revelation of God in the cross and resurrection of Jesus. The messianic secret therefore excludes an interpretation of the historical Jesus which is not oriented to the confession of the crucified and risen Christ (Luz). Therefore, within the Passion story there is no longer any need to refer to the secret, for it is no longer possible to doubt that the one who confesses himself to be Messiah and Son of God (14:61-62) is the crucified and Risen One.

Thus the whole presentation of the ministry of Jesus stands under the sign of the cross (3:6). Jesus' preaching can only be grasped by those to whom the mystery of the kingdom of God is given (4:10-12), that is, those who recognize that the one who proclaims the dawning of the kingdom of God (1:14-15) is himself the content of the good news (1:1). The evangelist wants to communicate this message not only to the Jews, but also to all peoples (13:10).

d. The Gospel of Mark does not give the name of its author. The messenger recedes completely behind the message which he must deliver. Even indirect references are lacking which could give us some clue to his identity. Of course people have toyed with the idea that behind the reference to the young man who was present at the arrest of Jesus, but who himself escaped capture by leaving his garment behind (14:51-52), we may have a hidden reference to the author. But such conjectures lack any foundation.

The tradition of the early church traces the Gospel of Mark back to Mark, the co-worker of Peter. Papias of Hierapolis (middle of the second century) reported, according to Eusebius (H. E. III 39:15): "Mark, who was the interpreter of Peter, wrote down exactly everything as he remembered it—not however in the correct order (ου μεντοι ταξει)—of those things said and done by the Lord. For he had neither heard the Lord nor been his disciple, but rather later, as I have already said, (he became a follower of) Peter, who gave his teaching as the circumstances called for it—not as one who gives a compilation of the sayings of the Lord. Therefore Mark made no mistake in that he wrote everything out just as he remembered it, for he was concerned for only one thing: to omit nothing of that which he had heard, and not to falsify anything." These statements are obviously intended to defend Mark against two objections: (1) against the objection that everything in Mark is not written correctly, lacks proper order, has left out much, and so forth. To this Papias responds that Mark relied on the teaching of Peter, an oral source, and had no written sources at his disposal. In this connection the reference to the oral tradition at the basis of Mark is certainly appropriate, so that from this point of view ου μεντοι ταξει is sufficiently justified. (2) The objection that the author of the Gospel of Mark was no apostle is repelled by the argument that he was a disciple of an apostle who could avail himself of the tradition of Peter. In this it is unclear what is to be understood by "interpreter of Peter." Was there need for an interpreter, where the Greek language was in common use? Or is it meant that Mark was the transmitter of the tradition from Peter? However, there is hardly anything to be seen in the Gospel of Mark of specifically Petrine tradition. To be sure, Peter is especially prominent in a few pericopes (e.g. 1:29-39; 8:27-33; 14:53-72), but it by no means follows that the Gospel of Mark rests directly on Peter's teaching. Rather, the Papias fragment intends to increase the respect for the author of Mark by connecting him to the primary apostle. Since the situation evidently did not permit giving the Gospel the name of an apostle, but required that Mark's name continue firmly attached to it, the tradition that the Gospel was in fact written by a man named Mark could have a historical kernel.

The NT mentions a John Mark in different connections, who came from the earliest Jerusalem church (Acts 12:12), at first accompanied Barnabas and Saul on the so-called first missionary journey (Acts 12:25; 13:5), but then separated from them (Acts 13:13; 15:37-38). Later he again appears to be found in the company of Paul (Philem. 24; Col. 4:10; II Tim. 4:11), and in I Peter 5:13 he is named in association with Peter in Babylon (= Rome). It is however hardly conceivable that a man from Jerusalem could really have been the author of the Gospel of Mark. In 11:1 it is said that Jesus and his disciples had come into the vicinity of Jerusalem, to Bethphage and Bethany on the Mount of Olives. In fact, however, Bethphage lay directly on the east edge of the city, in contrast to Bethany, which lay a short distance from Jerusalem on the southeast slope of the Mount of Olives. In that time the road passed Bethany by, which lay to the south, and went directly to Bethphage and into the city. The way of describing the location is thus not appropriate, and must have been written by someone who did not know the geographical relationships around Jerusalem. We find other instances where geographical data about Palestine and descriptions of the customs of Jewish life are inexact (Niederwimmer; Schweizer). Therefore the Mark of Jerusalem was not the author of the Gospel of Mark, but an otherwise-unknown Christian of the second generation, who perhaps bore the name of Mark.

Just as the effort to find a distinctive Petrine theology in Mark is fruitless, so also no particular Pauline traits can be found. Of course both Mark and Paul make use of the concept ευαγγελιον ("gospel," Mark 1:1; I Cor. 15:1-5, and so forth), both sound the note αββα ο πατηρ ("abba, father," Mark 14:36; Gal. 4:6; Rom. 8:15), and both speak of the substitutionary death of Christ (Mark 10:45; I Cor. 15:3-5). But these points of contact are to be explained by the use of a common Christian tradition taken up by both Mark and Paul, so that there can be no talk of the influence of Pauline theology on the Gospel of Mark (Werner).

The author of Mark writes in a simple, unsophisticated style. He joins short sentences together with και—και ("and—and"), or continues the next sentence with ευθυς ("immediately, next"). Artful periodic constructions are absent; the narrative is mostly told in the present tense and in direct address. Now and then slang expressions are used (2:11: κραβαττος ["bunk"]); one and the same word can be used three times in one verse (4:1: θαλασσα ["sea"]). In several places the original Aramaic expressions of the oldest tradition of Jesus words is still preserved, as for example 5:41 *Talitha cumi;* 7:34 *ephphatha;* 14:36 *abba;* 15:34 *Eloi, Eloi, lama sabachthani*.

e. Concerning the time and place of writing, the ancient church tradition preserved in Irenaeus (adv. Haer. III 1, 1) and in the so-called anti-Marcionite Gospel prologues reports that Mark was written soon after the death of Peter. This tradition is probably correct concerning the date. There is no indication in Mark—including the apocalyptic speech in chapter 13—that the destruction of Jerusalem is presupposed. Many exegetes however consider it possible that Mark was not written until after A.D. 70. But the date shortly before A.D. 70 is more probably correct. Marxsen understands Mark to have been written in Palestine during the Jewish war (A.D. 66–70) and to have been permeated with the eschatological hope of the Christians that the approaching parousia would occur in Galilee (14:28; 16:7). But the book is neither oriented toward an expectation of the imminent eschaton—chapter 13 reckons with a series of apocalyptic events which still must happen before the end—nor characterized by Palestinian features. The language and theology are throughout conditioned by the Hellenistic surroundings. It could thus be possible that, in accordance with the tradition of the ancient church, Rome was in fact the place of origin. Of course that cannot be proved, certainly not by appealing to a few Latinisms which are present in Mark's text, as for example μοδιος ("bushel," 4:21); *legion* (5:9); *speculator* ("messenger," 6:27); *census* (tax, 12:14); *quadrans* (Roman coin, RSV "penny," 12:42); *praetorium* (15:16); *centurio* (15:39, 44-45); the four night watches correspond to the times of the changing of the sentries in the Roman army (6:48; 13:35). In 10:11-12 it is presupposed that a woman can divorce her husband—which corresponds to Roman law, not Jewish. But all these items without exception are Latinisms which were carried by Roman soldiers into all parts of the Roman Empire. Thus they provide no reliable evidence of the place where Mark was written. All we can say is that the Gospel of Mark was written shortly before A.D. 70 somewhere in the domain of Hellenistic Christianity.

#30 The Gospel of Matthew

Kilpatrick, G. D. *The Origins of the Gospel According to St. Matthew*, 1946, [2]1950.

Stendahl, K. *The School of St. Matthew*, 1954, [2]1968.

Trilling, W. *Das wahre Israel*, 1959, [3]1964.

Kürzinger, J. "Das Papiaszeungnis und die Erstgestalt des Matthäusevangeliums," *BZ NF* 4 (1960) 19-38.

Munck, J. "Die Tradition über das Matthäusevangelium bei Papias," in *Neotestamentica et Patristica: Festschrift für O. Cullman*, 1962, 249-60.

Strecker, G. *Der Weg der Gerechtigkeit*, 1962 [3]1971.

Hummel, R. *Die Auseinandersetzung zwischen Kirche und Judentum im Matthäusevangelium*, 1963, [2]1966.

Bornkamm, G., Barth, G., and Held, H. J. *Tradition and Interpretation in Matthew*, 1963.

Walker, R. *Die Heilsgeschichte im ersten Evangelium*, 1967.

Schweizer, E. *The Good News According to Matthew*, 1975.

a. Contents: The Gospel of Matthew may be described as an expansion of Mark, which extends beyond Mark especially by assembling the collections of sayings into long discourses and by the addition of Matthew's special material, as for example in the birth story. Chapters 1–2 contain the birth story of Jesus, preceded by the genealogy (1:1-17), then the narration of his birth in Bethlehem (1:18-25), the adoration of the Magi (2:1-12) and the flight to Egypt, the slaughter of the children in Bethlehem and the return to Nazareth (2:13-23).

In 3:1–4:11 the beginning of Jesus' ministry in Galilee is described: John the Baptist, baptism, temptation, the preparation for the beginning of his public ministry (mostly following Mark).

The section 4:12–13:58 deals with Jesus' ministry in Galilee. His first public activity is reported (4:12-17), then the calling of the first disciples (4:18-22). A short summary which speaks of Jesus' ministry in word and deed (4:23-25 = 9:35) provides the framework for the great complex of material which first relates Jesus' words (Sermon on the Mount, chapters 5–7) and then his deeds (miracle stories, chapters 8–9). Then follows the missionary address to the disciples (9:36–11:1). Next Jesus and the Baptist are compared and contrasted (11:2-19), to which are joined woes pronounced against the Galilean cities (11:20-24) and Jesus' thanksgiving to the Father and call to salvation

(11:25-30). Chapter 12 then takes up the Markan outline again (Mark 2:23–3:35). Chapter 13 contains an extensive composition of seven parables, after which comes the rejection of Jesus in Nazareth (13:53-58 = Mark 6:1-6).

The section 14:1–20:34 is held together by a framework which portrays Jesus on a journey: first in Galilee and neighboring areas (14:1–16:12 = Mark 6:14–8:21), then on the way to Jerusalem. As in Mark, Peter's confession and the announcement of the Passion forms a clear turning point. Jesus enters upon the way to Jerusalem (16:13-14). Matthew 16:13–18:9 corresponds mostly to the Markan source (Mark 8:27–9:50). Chapter 18 brings together many sayings into a discourse about life in the church. Chapters 19 and 20 take up Mark 10:1-52, adding only the parable of the workers in the vineyard in 20:1-16.

Chapters 21–25 picture Jesus' last days in Jerusalem, 21–22 essentially following Mark 11–12. The last of the extensive discourses composed by Matthew is appended to the cycle of conflict stories taken over from Mark: the speech against the Pharisees and scribes (chapter 23) and about the last things (chapters 24–25). To chapter 24 cf. Mark 13; chapter 25 contains three parables.

The Gospel is brought to an end with the story of the Passion and resurrection of Jesus (26–28).

b. The message of the Gospel of Matthew is clearly set forth particularly in the long speech compositions, which are concluded each time with the expression, "And when Jesus had finished these sayings" (7:28; 11:1; 13:53; 19:1; 26:1). The didactic character of the book is clear on the one hand from the manner in which the miracle stories are sometimes abbreviated in order to let the saying of Jesus emerge as the point (Held). Thus Mark 2:1-12 is reduced to eight verses, (Matt. 9:1-8) and Mark 5:1-20 is even more tightly compressed (Matt. 8:28-34). On the other hand, the dialogues containing the conflict sayings are elaborated by adding additional sayings or OT quotations, so that for example Mark 2:23–3:6 is expanded to become the more comprehensive complex Matthew 12:1-14. For the evangelist it is therefore the teaching of Jesus which stands in the foreground of his presentation, which is emphasized once again at the conclusion. All peoples are to be instructed to observe what Jesus has taught (28:19-20).

A noticeable feature of this teaching, as Matthew develops it, is the constant reference to the OT. Over against the synagogue, Matthew wants to show that it is in Jesus, the Messiah of Israel, that the Scriptures are fulfilled, and that therefore it is the Christian community which is the heir of the promises. This proof is set forth in the long series of "reflection-quotations" *[Reflexionszitate]:* "This took place to fulfill what was spoken through the prophet" (1:22; 2:15, 17, 23; 4:14; 8:17; 12:17; 13:35; 21:4; 26:56; 27:9). Thereby the author calls for careful attention to the relationship of prophecy and fulfillment in order to demonstrate the realization of what the prophets had proclaimed (cf. e.g. 21:5 = Zech. 9:9). Because Jesus is the Messiah of Israel promised in the Scriptures, his genealogy is placed at the beginning of Matthew's Gospel, which traces Jesus' descent in a pattern of 3 × 14 members from Abraham via David and the generation of the Exile to Joseph and Jesus (1:1-17). He is the Son of David, the king of the Jews (2:2), who is born in Bethlehem (Mic. 5:2 = 1:18-25). He fulfills the Law and the Prophets (5:17-20) and as the New Moses interprets the Torah with full authority (5:21-48). His mighty works are signs that the words of the prophets are now being fulfilled (11:2-6). As the Messiah he is at the same time the Suffering Servant described in Isaiah 53 (8:17; 12:18-21).

But that which was inconceivable in fact happened. Jesus is the Messiah of Israel, but his people rejected him. The Gentile Pontius Pilate washed his hands to emphasize that he was not guilty of the death of Jesus. But the Jews cried out, "His blood be upon us and upon our children" (27:24-25). Despite his rejection by the Jews, he remained the Messiah sent to them, and it was as king of Israel that he died on the cross.

The Gospel of Matthew is deeply rooted in the Jewish heritage, does not permit one iota or dot to pass away from the Law (5:18-19), and makes everything depend on the doing of righteousness (5:20). Jewish Christians continued to keep the law, to observe the sabbath (24:20), to fast and pray (6:1-18), and to participate in the temple and sacrificial rites (17:24-27; 5:23-24). What the scribes say concerns the Christian too (23:2), although the scholars do not do what they teach. The mission of Jesus was directed to Israel, although he knew that it was to the lost sheep of the house of Israel that he was sent (15:24), and thus he sent his disciples not to the Gentiles and Samaritans, but to the house of Israel (10:5-6). The resurrected Lord however sent his disciples into all the world, in order to convert all nations through baptism and teaching (28:19-20).

Alongside all the sharp polemic directed against the synagogue, Matthew's church is nevertheless concerned to continue in dialogue with the Jews (Hummel). But the church—the term εκκλησια is found in the Gospels only in Matthew (16:18; 18:17)—is in need of instruction from the Scripture and from Jesus' words in order to carry on this dialogue. The way of Israel is held before its eyes as a warning (21:43), in order that they not fail the test. It may be, of course, that the coming of the kingdom of God will be delayed, but the church should be ready at all times (25:1-13). The parenesis constantly points to the last judgment, which will reveal who has built his house on the sand and who on the rock (7:24-27). Then the chaff will be separated from the wheat (3:12), the weeds from the good grain (13:24-30, 36-43), the good from the bad fish (13:47-50), the sheep from the goats (25:31-46). Ecclesiology and eschatology are therefore closely related to each other in Matthew (Bornkamm).

c. The tradition of the ancient church names as the author of the Gospel of Matthew that disciple and apostle whose call is related in 9:9 and whose name is given in 10:3 as "Matthew the publican." But not a syllable of the Gospel of Matthew hints that he was the author. Just as in Mark, the name of the messenger recedes completely behind the message which he delivers.

The ancient church tradition derives from the testimony of Papias from the middle of the second century (Eus. H. E. III. 39:16): "Matthew assembled the logia in the Hebrew language, and each one translated them as well as he could." No doubt Papias is thinking here of the Gospel of Matthew, not of some collection of Jesus' sayings, and certainly not of the sayings-source Q (see pp. 129-30). Papias' statement was later elaborated. Thus Irenaeus says (adv. Haer. III. 1:1) that Matthew wrote his Gospel among the Hebrews in their language, and Origen (Eus. H. E. VI. 25:4) appeals to the tradition that Matthew wrote his Gospel in Hebrew for Jewish Christians. Eusebius himself was of the opinion that (H. E. III. 24:6) "Matthew, who at first preached among the Hebrews, later decided to turn to other nations. At this time he wrote out in his native language the gospel which he had been preaching, for he sought to provide a replacement in writing for what the Hebrews lost by his departure." These allegations are all in general agreement, and may all be traced back without exception to the testimony of Papias. They had an enduring effect—all the way to the decision of the Pontifical Biblical Commission of June 19, 1911, that the apostle Matthew was the first to write a Gospel, which he composed in Hebrew or Aramaic, and that this Gospel was *quoad substantiam* ("in substance") identical with the canonical Matthew. But since the two-source theory has attained general acceptance, this traditional view has been abandoned in large circles of Roman Catholic scholarship.

Papias' statement obviously intended—just as was the case with Mark—to defend Matthew against objections which had been raised against its linguistic form. Thus what Papias is talking about is not merely that the evangelist manifests a certain Hebrew way of thinking (so Kürzinger). There can be no doubt that Papias refers to an original Hebrew or Aramaic composition of the gospel. But this statement just does not fit the content of Matthew, which does not—as the two-source theory already proves—go back to an original Semitic text. It can therefore offer no reliable information about the origin of the Gospel of Matthew, but supposedly explains certain differences between Matthew and the other Gospels. Thus the testimony of Papias throws no light on the issue of authorship. It does however provide some insight into the process of coordinating the Gospels and the beginnings of the canon (Munck).

The Gospel of Matthew itself clearly contradicts the claim that its author had been an eyewitness of the ministry of Jesus. This is seen in that the author does not write on the basis of what he has personally seen, but makes use of sources which he interprets—Mark and Q—and draws from the tradition which has come down to him—the so-called special Matthean material—which he assembles into a document created according to his own plan. He even follows his Markan source when Mark has a quotation from the OT which deviates from the original text, as e.g. Mark 1:3 = Matthew 3:3 (see p. 122). Matthew follows Mark carefully also in other places in which Mark has introduced OT material into his text, e.g. Matthew 19:4 = Mark 10:6 (Gen. 1:27); 19:5 = Mark

10:7-8 (Gen. 2:24). But where the evangelist himself cites the OT directly, without any dependence on Mark or Q, he mostly does not follow the LXX text, but his own version of the original text. Thus his use of the OT also reveals that the evangelist is dependent on sources which he interprets.

The language of the Gospel of Matthew is consistently a higher level of Greek than that of Mark, in many places containing rather elevated expressions such as: πελαγος της Θαλασσης ("the depth of the sea," 18:6); παλιγγενεσια ("rebirth" RSV "the new world," 19:28); βατταλογεω ("babbling"; RSV "heap up empty phrases," 6:7); and word-plays such as αφανιζουσιν . . . οπως φανωσιν ("they disfigure their faces that their fasting may be seen of men," 6:16); κακους κακως απολεσει ("he will put those wretches to a miserable death," 21:41); κοψονται και οψονται ("they will mourn and they will see," 24:30) [the Greek word-plays are not apparent in English translation].

The use and reinterpretation of sources which lay before the evangelist, as well as the linguistic form of his work, thus lead to the compelling conclusion that the author could not have come from among the circle of the twelve. The name of Matthew was quite early related to the one named as an erstwhile publican in 9:9 and 10:3 in order to be able to trace its origin back to an apostle. But in fact the name of the author remains unknown. From the Gospel itself we can only ascertain that its author came from Jewish Christianity. The way he uses the Scripture and his rootedness in Jewish tradition point clearly to these antecedents. Jewish mannerisms and customs are not explained, but presupposed as already understood by the readers. Thus in 15:2, in contrast to Mark 7:1-4, it is not explained why the Jews have ritual hand washing before meals. And in 23:5 "phylacteries" and "fringes" (on the robes of the scribes) are mentioned without explaining what they are. Both author and readers are thus acquainted with Jewish customs. They are at home with the Scripture and its methods of interpretation, as is shown in the elaboration of the didactic and conflict sayings and the long series of "reflection-quotations." If one can hardly infer from this that behind the Gospel of Matthew there stands a Christian school which, like the rabbis, had developed its own particular tradition of interpretation (Stendahl), still the author of Matthew is without doubt a Jewish Christian who had received a scribal education and knew how to use it as "a scribe who has been trained for the kingdom of heaven" (13:52) for the elaboration of the Christian message and its defense over against Jewish objections.

Recently the contrary thesis has been advocated in different forms, that the Jewish-Christian elements of the Gospel of Matthew are to be assigned exclusively to the evangelist's tradition, but that Matthew himself was a Gentile Christian rather than a Jewish Christian (Trilling, Strecker), for whom in the situation after the destruction of Jerusalem the time of Israel had ended and Israel had been finally rejected (Walker). It is true that the evangelist no longer limits the commission to preach the gospel to Israel but knows that the disciples are sent into all the world (28:19-20). But that does not mean a rejection of the commission to preach the gospel to Israel, which was valid during Jesus' earthly ministry, but rather emphasizes the fundamental change that was brought about by the resurrection and exaltation of Christ. Thus the evangelist does not advocate a narrow Jewish Christianity restricted to Israel; he belonged to the Jewish-Christian circles which sought to preserve the heritage of Israel on one hand, while on the other hand they acknowledged the existence of the Gentile church and therefore knew that the Christian message must be shared with the whole world.

d. The time and place of composition may be determined on the basis of the following considerations. The Gospel of Matthew presupposes the existence of the Gospel of Mark, so it must have been written later. In 22:7 it is said in the parable of the great supper that the king became angry about the rejection of his invitation and abuse of his messengers, "sent his army and burned the city." This is an unmistakable reference to the destruction of Jerusalem in A.D. 70. According to the Gospel of Matthew the Christian congregation stands over against the synagogue, but they are not yet absolutely separated from each other. Thus Matthew can be dated around A.D. 90. For the place of origin one can think most easily of Syria, since Christians and Jews lived there in close proximity to each other, and Matthew indicates the presence in his church of both an imposing Jewish Christianity and a rapidly growing Gentile Christianity.

#31 The Gospel of Luke

Streeter, B. H. *The Four Gospels*, 1924.

Schweizer, E. "Eine hebraisierende Sonderquelle des Lukas?" *ThZ* 6 (1950):161-85.

Schürmann, H. *Quellenkritische Untersuchung des lukanischen Abendmahlsberichtes I-III*, 1953-57.

———. *Das Lukasevangelium* I, 1969.

Lohse, E. "Lukas als Theologe der Heilsgeschichte" (1954), in *Die Einheit des NT*, 1973, 145-64.

Strobel, A. "Lukas der Antiochener," *ZNW* 49 (1958):131-34.

Rehkopf, F. *Die lukanische Sonderquelle*, 1959.

Conzelmann, H. *The Theology of St. Luke*, 1961.

Klein, G. "Lukas 1, 1-4 als theologisches Programm" (1964), in *Rekonstruktion und Interpretation*, 1969, 237-61.

Flender, H. *St. Luke: Theologian of Redemptive History*, 1967.

Osten-Sacken, P. v. d. "Zur Christologie des lukanischen Reiseberichts," *EvTh* 33 (1973):476-96.

Schneider, G. *Das Evangelium nach Lukas*, 1977.

a. Contents: The outline of Luke is characterized by a threefold division: the ministry of Jesus in Galilee—the travel narrative—Jesus in Jerusalem.

Chapters 1–2 contain the stories of Jesus' birth and childhood, in which the greatness of the Christ is emphasized by relating them to the stories of John the Baptist's birth and childhood. In 3:1–4:13 the beginning of Jesus' ministry is described, including the preaching of the Baptist, the baptism of Jesus, his genealogy, and his temptation. Jesus' ministry in Galilee is portrayed in 4:14–9:50, in which Luke mainly follows Mark with the exception of the "smaller insertion" of 6:20–8:3. This collection of materials contains first the Sermon on the Plain (6:20-49), then the story of the centurion of Capernaum (7:1-10), the raising of the widow's son at Nain (7:11-17), sayings of Jesus about the Baptist (7:18-35), the story of Jesus and the sinful woman (7:36-50), and the reference to the women who followed Jesus (8:1-3).

The "travel narrative" is contained in 9:51–19:27, which portrays Jesus on the way to Jerusalem. To this belongs the "greater insertion" of 9:51–18:14 which presents exclusively non-Markan material. This section includes such important passages as the hostile Samaritans (9:51-56), different would-be followers of Jesus (9:57-62), the sending out and return of the seventy (10:1-20), the parable of the good Samaritan (10:25-37), sayings against the Pharisees and scribes (11:37-54), the three parables of the lost sheep, lost coin, and lost son (chapter 15), the parables of the unjust steward and the rich man and poor Lazarus (chapter 16), the story of the grateful Samaritan (17:11-19), sayings about the kingdom of God and the coming of the Son of man (17:20-37), the parables of the unjust judge and of the Pharisee and the publican (18:1-14). The thread of the Markan source is again taken up in 18:15: the blessing of the children, the rich young man, the third prediction of the Passion, and the healing of the blind man at Jericho (18:15-43). Then comes the story of the publican Zacchaeus (19:1-10) and the parable of the pounds (19:11-27).

In 19:28–21:38 Jesus' ministry in Jerusalem is portrayed with extensive dependence on Mark: first the triumphal entry into Jerusalem (19:28-38), the lamentation over the city (19:39-44), the purification of the temple (19:45-48); the chain of controversy dialogues (chapter 20), all of which correspond to Mark 11:27–12:40, then the eschatological discourse (chapter 21), which corresponds to Mark 13. In the report of the suffering, dying, and resurrection of Jesus (chapters 22–24) Luke is partly dependent on Mark, and partly on other traditions, especially in the Easter story (24:13-53: appearance to the disciples on the road to Emmaus, the appearance in Jerusalem, and the ascension).

b. The question of Luke's sources has been thoroughly discussed by scholars but without arriving at a consensus. It is clear in the first place that Luke has taken over the material he uses from Mark in great blocks:

4:31–6:19 (except 5:1-11)	=	Mark 1:21–3:19
8:4–9:50	=	Mark 4:1–9:41
18:15-43	=	Mark 10:13-52
19:45–22:13	=	Mark 11:15–14:16

Within the Markan materials, passages have been omitted which deal with specifically Jewish issues (Mark 7:1-37); above all, Luke has smoothed out the material and improved it stylistically. He often replaces a Markan και ("and") with δε ("but, then," and so forth). In many places the verb has been shifted from the beginning to the end. Transitions between the pericopes are smoothed out by replacing the artless conjunctions ευθυς ("immediately, next") or παλιν ("again") with a participial construction or a subordinate clause. But Luke has basically preserved the order of the pericopes in Mark—with two small exceptions: in 6:12-19 the call of the twelve disciples is placed before the summary account of Jesus' healing the throngs, in order to set the stage appropriately for the Sermon on the Plain. And in 8:16-21 the saying about the true relatives has been placed at the conclusion of the teaching in parables and before the story of the storm on the lake, so that the true relatives appear as the proper hearers of the teaching in parables. Thus though Luke has reworked the Markan material editorially, he has almost always left the order of the pericopes undisturbed in the great blocks of material which he took over from Mark.

This method of handling the material which may be observed in Luke's use of Mark is also to be supposed for Luke's adoption and editing of the Q tradition. That is to say, Luke took over the sayings-tradition essentially in the order in which he found it, but editorially reworked the way it was formulated. Speech material is found principally in the sections 3:7–4:13, 6:20–7:35, 9:51–13:35. We cannot say for sure whether the Q document used by Luke was the same as Matthew's or not (see p. 131). It would be easy to suppose that Q circulated in different forms. It is also possible that some Lukan passages for which there is no Matthean parallel derive from Q or the Q form used by Luke.

In addition to Mark and Q, Luke used a considerable amount of material from sources peculiar to him. The passages which have no parallel in either Mark or Matthew comprise almost half of Luke: the birth stories, elements of John's preaching, Jesus' genealogy, the opening sermon in Nazareth, long sections of the lesser (6:20–8:3) and greater insertions (9:51–18:14), sections of the Passion story—the Lord's Supper tradition, for example, deviates in part from Mark—and of the Easter story. If one combines the passages peculiar to Luke with the Q material, one sees that these sections are not only much more extensive than the sections taken from Mark but also comprise lengthy coherent units: chapters 1–2; 3:1–4:30 (essentially): 6:20–8:3; 9:51–18:14; 19:1-44 (except for vv. 28-38): 22:14–24:53 (essentially, with exceptions such as 24:1-12). From this observation Streeter concluded that the sections which do not derive from Mark represent an independent gospel (except for 1–2), and that Luke inserted the Markan passages only secondarily into this framework. Luke's special materials (L) plus Q formed the so-called Proto-Luke, which was the primary source for our Gospel of Luke, while Mark was only the later secondary source. In order to support this theory he points to such phenomena as the absence in Luke of a series of Markan pericopes which are replaced by parallels from some other tradition placed in another context, as for example the opening sermon in Nazareth (4:16-30) instead of Mark 6:1-6; the anointing of Jesus (7:36-50) instead of Mark 14:3-9; the question of the greatest commandment (10:25-37) instead of Mark 12:28-31. Streeter would like to explain this state of affairs by supposing that Luke gave his first priority to Proto-Luke, and in those cases in which he had two versions of a pericope—one in Proto-Luke and one in Mark—he preferred that of Proto-Luke and omitted the Markan version.

Against this Proto-Luke theory, however, is to be objected that the materials peculiar to Luke are of the most various sorts and that in the text of the Gospel of Luke there is absolutely no indication that they had been united with the Q materials to form a coherent document before being incorporated into the Gospel of Luke. Moreover the Gospel of Luke has been reworked linguistically by the hand of the evangelist to conform to his own style, so that stylistic criteria give no basis for separating out the sources. This objection applies also to E. Schweizer's attempt to distinguish a Hebraizing source among Luke's special materials. Hebraisms are mostly to be traced back to the "biblicistic" style of the author, whose language has been conditioned by the Greek translation of the OT, rather than being taken as a criterion of source analysis. That Luke's composition in fact proceeded from Mark—and not a hypothetical Proto-Luke—as the basis can be seen from a number of observations, e.g. that the three Passion-predictions in Mark are part of a somewhat symmetrical structure, separated by approximately the same amount of text, but in Luke this pattern has been broken up by the insertion of long sections from Q and Luke's special material, so that the Passion predictions are widely separated from each other: Luke 9:22, 43ff; 18:31ff. By taking over many traditions from Q and his special material, Luke has considerably reshaped the Markan source, especially the twofold structure Galilee-Jerusalem into a more elaborate threefold structure: Galilee—the journey—Jerusalem. Luke has carefully worked with his sources, but has combined them into a composition which bears the stamp of his own theology.

The question of Luke's sources is therefore to be answered in terms of the two-source theory, for Mark and Q are the only written sources used by the author which we can determine with confidence. His extensive special material probably came to him through oral tradition. Some exegetes, however, advocate the view that Luke had a separate written source for the Passion story (Schürmann, Rehkopf), since not inconsiderable deviations from Mark are found, e.g. in the story of the institution of the Lord's Supper. This supposition could be correct, but the evidence for it however is not compelling, since the deviations from Mark could also go back to the evangelist himself, who made editorial changes in his sources in order to emphasize the particular message which he wanted to express in his composition.

c. The message of the Gospel of Luke is briefly summarized in the preface (1:1-4) with which Luke has introduced his book (Klein, Lohse). By beginning with a statement about his sources, the method by which he uses them, and the goal of his book, Luke follows a pattern customary among Hellenistic authors. He first mentions predecessors who have already written accounts of the events handed on in the tradition by eyewitnesses and ministers of the Word. Thus when he speaks of "many," this corresponds to the typical expression in such prefaces, and does not permit any inferences to be made as to the number of sources which Luke actually had before him. Then Luke specially emphasizes two basic methodological principles: (1) to report everything accurately from the beginning (ανωθεν) (v. 3). When he mentions at the first those who were eyewitnesses from the beginning (v. 2), he obviously means by αρχη the beginning of the public ministry of Jesus, which corresponds to earlier tradition (Mark 1:1, see p. 118). By ανωθεν Luke probably refers to the fact that he begins even further back, with the stories of Jesus' birth and childhood (chapters 1–2). (2) To report everything in order (καθεξης) (v. 3). Luke did not write as a modern historian concerned to document the exact chronological order of the events he reports. But he did seek to fit the units of tradition together into an understandable order by smoothing out the transitions between the individual pericopes and to point out the hand of God at work in the one great path of history that leads from the people of Israel through the ministry of Jesus into the church's present.

By beginning and ending his Gospel with scenes in the temple, Luke emphasizes the uninterrupted continuity of salvation history. In 1:1 he announces that the theme of his presentation is the intention to report περι των πεπληροφορημενων εν ημιν πραγματων ("of the things which have been accomplished among us"). That means that those events are to be spoken of which have happened as the realization of salvation history—not only in the story of Jesus, but also εν ημιν ("among us"), that is in the church. This thematic intention comes to expression in various ways in the course of the presentation. Thus the so-called "great insertion" is introduced with the words εγενετο δε εν τω σθμπληρουσδαι τας ημερας της αναλημψεως αυτου ("when the days drew near for him to be received up," 9:51). By Jesus' being "received up" is meant both his way to Jerusalem and his exaltation at the ascension. The whole "travel narrative" thus stands under the heading of the fulfillment of salvation history which is already in process of realization. That this continues in the church is especially emphasized in Acts 2:1: και εν τω συμπληρουσθαι την ημεραν της πεντηκοστης ("when the day of Pentecost had come"), that is, "as the day of Pentecost which was a part of salvation history arrived." Thus the foreword to the Gospel of Luke already refers to the Acts which with the Gospel forms a single two-volume work. The life of Jesus is "the midst of time" (Conzelmann), toward which the time of promise ran its course, and from which the time of the church continues its way.

d. The name of the author is nowhere named in the Lukan two volumes. No statement of Papias, similar to those about Mark and Matthew, has been preserved. The ancient church tradition begins with the statement of Irenaeus that Luke, the companion of Paul, recorded in his book the gospel which Paul preached (adv. Haer. III. 1.1). Probably this tradition, which relates Luke to Paul and thereby brings the third Gospel at least indirectly in relation to an apostle, is somewhat older than Irenaeus. If Marcion placed only the Gospel of Luke beside the ten letters of Paul which he made into his canon (see p. 20), then it is to be supposed that he already knew the tradition that Luke, the traveling companion of Paul, was the author of the Gospel of

Luke. The so-called anti-Marcionite prologue elaborates more extensively, in that it says: "Luke was an Antiochene of Syria, a physician by profession, a disciple of apostles. Later he accompanied Paul until his martyrdom. After he had served the Lord unflinchingly, without wife or children, he fell asleep at the age of eighty-four in Bithynia, full of the Holy Spirit. Since there were already Gospels—Matthew's written in Judea, Mark's written in Italy, he wrote, led by the Holy Spirit, this whole Gospel in the region of Achaia, announcing in his preface that other (Gospels) had already been written, and it was necessary to present an exact account of the saving events to the believers among the Greeks so that they would no longer be pulled this way and that by the Jewish mythologies, or be deceived by the heretical and vain illusions which pervert the truth." In order to evaluate these statements from the ancient church tradition critically we need to investigate whether the Lukan two volumes contain any supporting evidence for the claim that Luke, the physician, who for a time was one of Paul's fellow workers (Philem. 24; Col. 4:14; II Tim. 4:11), is the author of the Gospel of Luke. Two questions are of particular significance in this connection:

(1) Are there indications that the author of the Gospel of Luke was a physician? Sometimes the information about sick people is reported more precisely, thus for example Luke 4:38, where Peter's mother-in-law was suffering from a high fever, or Luke 5:12, where the leper was "covered" with leprosy. Other examples are Luke 8:44; 13:11; Acts 28:8-10. While Mark 5:26 says that the woman with the hemorrhage had spent all her money on physicians, but still grew worse and worse, Luke 8:43 lacks this comment. Shall we suppose the author of the Gospel of Luke to have been a physician who did not want to include anything detrimental to his professional class? But in fact the descriptions of sicknesses nowhere are more precise or technical than those usually found in the Hellenistic literature of that time. Moreover, in antiquity there was not yet a highly developed medical technical terminology. There is thus no proof that the author of the Lucan two volumes was a physician.

(2) More important is the question of the relationship of the Gospel of Luke to Pauline theology. The problem of whether influences of the apostle's theology are to be found in Acts is still

to be discussed (see p. 161). So far as the Gospel of Luke is concerned, there are no traces of peculiarly Pauline ideas. Neither in the parable of the prodigal son (15:11-32) nor that of the Pharisee and the publican (18:9-14) is there any recognizable direct connection with the Pauline doctrine of justification.

The statement of the ancient church tradition that the author of the Gospel of Luke came from Antioch can hardly represent an independent tradition (see Strobel), but could easily have originated later, by inferring from Acts 11:28 D, where the so-called "we-sections" begin, that the author of the two volumes was an Antiochene. The data from the ancient church tradition thus receives no support from an investigation of the Gospel of Luke and Acts. The Lucan work itself only makes it clear that the author was a Gentile Christian with a Hellenistic education who wanted to send forth the Christian message in the Hellenistic world by publishing his presentation of the story of Jesus and the beginnings of the church.

e. Concerning the place and time of composition, we can say with confidence that the Gospel of Luke originated after Mark. The apocalyptic saying in Mark 13:14 is repeated in Luke 21:20 with a clear reference to the destruction of Jerusalem which has already occurred: "But when you see Jerusalem surrounded by armies, then know that its desolation is near." And a few verses later it is said, "And Jerusalem will be trodden down by the Gentiles, until the times of the Gentiles are fulfilled (v. 24)." Also 19:43-44 refers unmistakably to the fall of the city: "For the days shall come upon you, when your enemies will cast up a bank about you and surround you, and hem you in on every side, and dash you to the ground, you and your children within you, and they will not leave one stone upon another in you; because you did not know the time of your visitation." The Gospel of Luke must therefore have been written after A.D. 70. Since the evangelist wrote about the same time as Matthew—but independently from him—the origin of the Gospel of Luke is to be dated about A.D.90.

The place of composition can no longer be determined. The so-called anti-Marcionite prologue names Achaia. But the Gospel of Luke itself indicates only that it must have originated somewhere in the realm of Hellenistic Christianity.

#32 Acts

Jeremias, J. "Untersuchungen zum Quellenproblem der Apostelgeschichte" (1937), in *Abba,* 1966, 238-55.
Dibelius, M. *Studies in the Acts of the Apostles,* 1956.
Bultmann, R. "Zur Frage nach den Quellen der Apostelgeschichte" (1959), in *Exegetica,* 1967, 412-23.
Klein, G. *Die zwölf Apostel,* 1961.
Wilckens, U. *Die Missionsreden der Apostelgeschichte,* [2]1963, [3]1974.
Conzelmann, H. *Die Apostelgeschichte,* 1963, [2]1972.
Vielhauer, Ph. "On the 'Paulinism' of Acts," in *Studies in Luke-Acts.* Edited by Keck and Martyn, 1966.
———. Review of *Apostelgeschichte,* by H. Conzelmann. *GGA* 221 (1969):1-19.
Burchard, Ch. *Der dreizehnte Zeuge,* 1970.
Haenchen, E. *The Acts of the Apostles,* 1971.
Plümacher, E. *Lukas als hellenistischer Schriftsteller: Studien zur Apg.,* 1972.
———. "Wirklichkeitserfahrung und Geschichtsschreibung bei Lukas," *ZNW* 68 (1977) 2-22.

a. Contents: Chapters 1–12 deal with the spread of the Word in Jerusalem and Palestine. First the life of the earliest church in Jerusalem is described (chapters 1–5): introduction to the book, Jesus' ascension (1:1-14), choice of the apostle Matthias (1:15-26), the Pentecost story (2:1-41), a summary account of the life of the earliest church (2:42-47), the healing of a lame man by Peter and the sermon in the temple (3:1-26), Peter and John before the Sanhedrin (4:1-31), summary account of the life of the earliest church (4:32-37), Ananias and Sapphira (5:1-11), healing miracles by the apostles (5:12-16), the apostles before the Sanhedrin, the counsel of Gamaliel (5:17-42).

The following section (6:1–8:3) speaks of the appointing of the seven (6:1-7), the accusation of Stephen, his speech defending himself, and his death (6:8–8:1*a*), and then the persecution of the church (8:1*b*-3). Following this, the mission in Palestine and Syria is portrayed (8:4–12:25): the beginnings of the mission in Samaria (8:4-25), Philip and the official from Ethiopia (8:26-40), the conversion of Saul (9:1-30), Peter in Lydda and Joppa (9:31-43), Peter and the centurion Cornelius in Caesarea (10:1–11:18), the first Christians in Antioch (11:19-30), the persecution of the church by King Herod Agrippa (12:1-25).

Chapters 13–28 narrate the spread of the Word in the Hellenistic world until it reaches Rome. The "first missionary journey" brings Paul first to Cyprus, Antioch in Pisidia, Iconium, and Lystra (13–14). The apostolic conference takes place in Jerusalem (15:1-35). The "second missionary journey" goes through Asia Minor to Troas, the crossing to Europe, then to Philippi, Thessalonica, Berea, Athens, Corinth, then the return trip via Ephesus and back to Antioch (15:36–18:22). The following stations are named in the "third missionary journey" (18:23–21:14): Apollos in Ephesus (18:24-28), Paul in Ephesus (chapter 19), the trip to Macedonia and Greece, then the continuation of the journey via Troas to Miletus (20:1-16), Paul's parting address to the elders in Miletus (20:17-38), the continuation of the journey and the stay in Caesarea (21:1-14).

Then comes an extensive report of the trip of Paul to Jerusalem, his arrest, and his imprisonment in Caesarea: first his arrival in Jerusalem and his visit to the church (21:15-26), then Paul's arrest (21:27-40), his long speech defending himself (22:1-29), Paul before the Sanhedrin (22:30–23:11), the attempted assassination of Paul by the Jews (23:12-22), the delivery of Paul to Caesarea (23:23-35), and his imprisonment there (chapters 24–26). Paul is brought by ship to Rome and at the conclusion of the book enters the city—even though as a prisoner—to proclaim the Christian message there "openly and unhindered" (28:17-31).

b. The question of the sources of Acts must be discussed separately for the two major parts of the book. In the second half of Acts some sections are reported in the we-form, so that one could easily suppose the author is using the so-called "we-source." Thus 16:10 suddenly shifts to the we-form: ". . . immediately we sought to go on into Macedonia." The first person plural is then used until 16:17. After a long interruption the we-form returns in 20:5-15 (Philippi to Miletus), then in 21:1-18 (Miletus to Jerusalem), and finally 27:1–28:16 (Caesarea to Rome). Should we suppose that these sections are based on notes taken by a traveling companion of the apostle? To properly evaluate the we-sections it is important to note that they are no different from the rest of Acts in language and style. It follows that the we-sections must have had the same author as the rest of the book. Does this mean that a co-worker of Paul's stands behind the book? This conclusion may not be derived from the we-sections, for in the novels and stories in the Hellenistic literature this stylistic device of shifting from the narrative report to the first person was variously used in order to give the presentation more vividness. Thus the second half of Acts also uses this form, but always abandons it when Paul is portrayed as acting alone: in Philippi, Miletus, Jerusalem, and Rome. The "we" permits us to draw no conclusions concerning a source for Acts, but was used "in order to present the author of Acts to his readers as a widely traveled man" (Plümacher, *ZNW* 1977 14). The author thus presumably had available for the second half of Acts only a list of the stations visited by Paul (Dibelius). An exact reconstruction of this itinerary is not possible; however, it is probably the case that the author of Acts not only had individual items of tradition, but also used a brief travel narrative (Vielhauer), since individual places are sometimes mentioned without any details of what happened during Paul's visit there (14:24-26; 17:1; 20:13-15). Thus the enumeration of the stations of Paul's journeys was already present in the materials available to the author, and he could have made this itinerary the basis of his presentation.

Many scholars have advocated the view that a connected source was used for the first part of Acts. It could appear that a new beginning is made in 6:1, which for the first time speaks of μαθηται ("disciples") and refers to Hellenists in the earliest church. According to Jeremias, who builds on views taken over from Harnack, the section 6:1–8:4 is continued in 9:1-30, in that the story of what happened to Paul, the persecutor of the church, is continued. In 11:19-30 the spread of the Word from Antioch is described, then 12:25–14:28 and 15:35ff tell of the missionary work which radiated from Antioch. According to Jeremias this so-called Antiochene source comprised 6:1–8:4; 9:1-30; 11:19-30; 12:25–14:28; 15:35ff. Bultmann is also inclined to accept an Antiochene source, to which he assigns the following passages: 6:1-12*a*; 7:54–8:4; 11:19-26; 12:25; 13:2. But these theses cannot be proven, for Acts is linguistically so unified that criteria for separating sources on the basis of style are entirely lacking. Haenchen is more probably correct when, following the line of Dibelius, he finds no extensive written source for the first part of Acts, but regards the author of Acts as having had at his disposal only individual units of tradition such as lists of names (1:13, the twelve apostles; 6:5, the seven; 13:1, prophets and teachers in Antioch) and brief narratives from the earliest church (1:18-19, the death of Judas; 5:1-5, Ananias and Sapphira, and so forth).

The speeches presented in chapters 2, 3, 4, 5, 10, 13, and 17, though they contain some traditional expressions (see p. 31), are still basically the compositions of the author, formed to fit the context in which they stand (Wilckens). The speech of Stephen in chapter 7 is a different matter, for there a connected source might have been used, since some statements—e.g. 7:58*b*-59*a*; 8:1, 3—can only be satisfactorily explained as interpolations into a traditional text (Vielhauer and others). But the three descriptions of the conversion of Paul (chapters 9, 22, 26) are not to be traced back to written sources. Rather, with a view to edification the author of Acts has himself three times narrated the tradition of Paul's conversion in different ways and thereby underscored its great significance for the history of the young church (Burchard). Thus, rather than having an abundance of tradition at his disposal, the author of Acts has only a modest amount of traditional material available. He shows his skill in the way that he took the data and reports with which he was acquainted, and combined them artfully into a connected narrative which he constructed from the individual stories.

c. Acts was written to convey a certain message. The later tradition attempted to characterize this by giving the book the title πραξεις αποστολων ("the Acts of the Apostles"). There existed in antiquity a rich πραξεις ("acts")—literature, which told of the deeds of outstanding men such as Hercules, Alexander the Great, and others, often with novelistic decorations. But in fact Acts contains no description of the "deeds of the apostles" at all, but rather tells of the ministries first of Peter, then of Paul, who is never called an apostle (except in 14:4, 14). Alongside "Acts of the Apostles" the ancient church also was acquainted with other descriptions for our book of Acts, as in Irenaeus: *Lucae de apostolis testificatio* ("Luke's witness to the apostles," adv. Haer. III. 31:3) and in Tertullian: *commentarius Lucae* ("Luke's Commentary," *de jejunio* 10). Obviously in the earliest times the work circulated without a title.

The introduction to Acts makes reference to the preface of Luke: the πρωτος λογος ("first book") deals with [περι] παντων ων ηρξατο ο Ιησους ποιειν τε και διδασκειν ([concerning] "all that Jesus began to do and teach," 1:1) until his ascension. Then comes a transition to the description of the spread of the Word in the world, in that the theme is announced in 1:8: "But you shall receive power when the Holy Spirit has come upon you; and you shall be my witnesses in Jerusalem and in all Judea and Samaria and to the end of the earth." The course of the narrative is determined by this theme: first the earliest church in Jerusalem, then the extension of the church into Palestine and Samaria, and finally into all the ancient world. The picture which the author wishes to present is rounded off at the end in that he is able to portray Paul in Rome κηρυσσων την βασιλειαν του Θεου και διδασκων τα περι του κυριου Ιησου Χριστου μετα πασης παρρησιας ακωλυτως ("preaching the kingdom of God and teaching about the Lord Jesus Christ quite openly and unhindered," 28:31). It would not fit the assignment the author has given himself in his thematic statement if he told of the martyrdom of Paul. The course of Christian preaching has reached the capital of the ancient world. With that, the work of Luke which was to deal with the περι των πεπληροφορημενων εν ημιν πραγματων ("the things which have been accomplished among us," Luke 1:1), is brought to its conclusion.

In accord with the theme developed by Luke, all the preachers in Acts deliver one and the same message. Acts knows no difference between the doctrine of Peter and that of Paul; not a word is mentioned concerning the sharp conflict which occurred between the two in Antioch (Gal. 2:11-21). The life of the early church is described as a peaceful fellowship of all who belong to it. And where a problem emerges, as in the welfare of the Hellenistic part of the church (6:1), it is settled quickly in a manner satisfactory to all concerned. Like Peter and James, so also Paul is a faithful observer of the law inherited from the fathers. He circumcises Timothy (16:3), travels to the Jewish festivals in Jerusalem, readily subjects himself to the leadership of the Jerusalem mother church, and personally pays the expenses for the rituals of some Nazirites (21:25ff). The report of the apostolic conference makes no mention of Paul's refusal to circumcise Titus (Gal. 2:3). The portrayal of the ministry of Paul gives no indication of how he had to struggle for the freedom of the gospel from the law. Paul and the original apostles rather work harmoniously together at their common task of spreading the Word.

The content of the Christian message is expressed in terms of an unsophisticated Christology: God legitimized Jesus by his miracles (2:22). Nevertheless the Jews rejected him and crucified him (2:23), while Pilate wanted to let him go free (3:13). Jesus' death fulfilled the OT prophecies of the death and resurrection of the Messiah. By the resurrection, God exalted him and set him at his right hand (2:36; 5:31; 13:23). He is thereby made to be κυριος and σωτηρ, so that in his name salvation comes to all the world (4:12). The requirements for receiving this salvation are repentance and conversion (2:36; 3:19) and baptism (2:38 and frequently). Whoever belongs to Jesus will be saved in the coming judgment (10:42; 15:11; 17:31); for as the αρχηγος της ζωης ("Author of life") he leads to eternal life (3:15; 5:31).

This worldwide proclamation of the Christian message also shapes the attitude of Acts toward Jews and Gentiles. The missionaries always go first to the synagogues and preach to the Jews, where they are regularly rejected and then turn to the Gentiles (13:46; 18:6; 28:28 and often elsewhere). The Christians knew how to talk about the fulfillment of OT prophecies, and proclaimed nothing different from what Moses and the prophets had said (26:22). They agree with the Pharisees in their faith in the resurrection of the dead (23:8); and also the Gentile Christians fulfill the minimal requirements of the law (15:20, 29; 21:25). Thus the Christians can rightly claim to be regarded as true Israelites and to enjoy the protection of the Roman government.

The Christian message also fulfills the hopes of the Gentiles, for the unknown God they are looking for has now revealed himself (17:22-31). Paul appears before Roman officials and governors as a witness for Christ, who give him a sympathetic hearing. King Agrippa is so impressed by his speech that he says he is almost persuaded to become a Christian himself (26:28). Paul could even have been released from prison, if he had not already appealed to Caesar (26:32). Thus the message is delivered to all the world, going from Jews to Gentiles and also gaining the attention of people in high places.

d. The problem of how Acts is to be evaluated as a historical document may be clearly resolved on the basis of those places where comparative material is available. Thus the descriptions of Paul's activities can be checked at some points on the basis of authentic documentation. While Paul only refers to his conversion incidentally in a subordinate clause (Gal. 1:15-16), Acts reports this three times in considerable detail (chapters 9, 22, 26). Concerning the further course of events, Paul assures the Galatians of the reliability of his statements by appealing to God as his witness (1:20). His first visit to Jerusalem did not follow until three years later and lasted only two weeks, during which time he saw only Peter and James the Lord's brother (1:18-19). After that, he did not return to Jerusalem until fourteen years later at the apostolic conference (2:1). The picture is different in Acts: after his conversion Paul returns from Damascus to Jerusalem and is introduced to the mother church by Barnabas (9:26ff). Then Barnabas and Paul make a second visit to Jerusalem as delegates of the church of Antioch (11:30), in order to help relieve the distress of the suffering mother church. Finally, they travel once more from Antioch to Jerusalem in order to attend the apostolic conference (15:1ff). Here we have a clear contradiction. While Paul explicitly declares that he visited the Jerusalem church only once between his conversion and the apostolic conference, according to Acts he was there twice. Acts immediately brings Paul into contact with Jerusalem because worldwide Christianity had its beginning and reference point there, so Paul as the chosen instrument of God must be brought into relationship with the mother church. Acts is not thereby reporting the historical circumstances but is developing the theological conception of the continuity of salvation history. The factual course of events is thus to be derived not from Acts, but from Galatians 1–2 alone.

Acts 15 may also be compared with Galatians 2:1-10. Paul emphasizes that an agreement was made concerning the division of missionary assignments and the collection for the Jerusalem church from the Gentile Christians. Acts gives a lengthy description of the meeting in Jerusalem with long speeches of Peter and the Lord's brother. James' speech quotes Amos 9:11 according to the LXX—not according to the Hebrew text, as one would have expected by a Jerusalem Jewish Christian—and declares that he is in favor of requiring the Gentiles to observe only the minimal requirements of the law in order to enable Jewish Christians and Gentile Christians to live together (15:20, 29). In contrast, Paul emphasizes that the Jerusalem authorities imposed no further requirements on him (Gal. 2:6). It follows that the so-called Apostolic Decree, as reported in Acts 15:20, 29, could not have been promulgated at the apostolic conference. Rather, the author of Acts used a document which originally pertained to the churches of Antioch, Syria, and Cilicia (Acts 15:23) which he inserted as the concluding accomplishment of the conference in Jerusalem. The description of the apostolic conference is thus developed in Acts from an edifying and solicitous point of view, while the historically correct report is found in Galatians 2.

In the remaining chapters which deal with the message and ministry of Paul, there is no discernible awareness either of Pauline theology or of the letters of the apostle. The author obviously did not know Paul's writings and had only rather general ideas of his teaching. The struggle concerning Christ as the end of the law has been forgotten, justification by faith alone is no longer spoken of, Paul is rather a missionary and preacher of the *una sancta ecclesia* (Vielhauer). Only those representatives who are in proper connection with the Holy City bring the true message. Thus the beginnings of the Samaritan mission must also—after the fact—be inspected and legitimized by Jerusalem (chapter 8). Finally, in regard to the picture given by the author of the earliest days of the church, it is probable that he had received from the tradition only a few reports, some lists and formalized expressions of early Christian preaching. Quotations from the OT are consistently given according to the LXX, thus do not rest on old tradition which reaches back to the beginnings of Palestinian Christianity. These data compel us to the conclusion that Acts does not present an exact historical report, but sketches a portrayal of the spread of the Christian message which corresponds to the picture of the earliest period of the church which was current in the time of the composition of Acts.

e. The composition of Acts must be seen in connection with the origin of the Gospel of Luke. The tradition ascribes both to "Luke the beloved physician." Since this claim certainly does not fit the Gospel of Luke, one must also decide in the case of Acts that an author who possessed such a minimal awareness of

Pauline theology could not have been the traveling companion of the apostle. Acts was certainly written after the Gospel, but may not be dated much later, since the preface Luke 1:1-4 already refers to Acts (see p. 150). It is sometimes supposed that the author knew the work of the Jewish historian Josephus, who published his *Antiquities of the Jews* in Rome A.D. 93/94, but this cannot be proven. The possibility of dating Acts as a part of the opposition to Marcion in the period 120–130 has also been considered (Klein), but one can hardly regard the book as having been written so late, since it does not yet know any developed early catholic church structures, and also does not advocate the idea of a *successio apostolica* (Conzelmann). Thus one should consider the end of the first century as the most likely time for the book's composition. As in the case with the Gospel of Luke, the place of origin cannot be definitely determined; the most we can say is that it belongs to the realm of Hellenistic Gentile Christianity.

f. The text of Acts presents a few special problems, since the Egyptian-Alexandrian and the Western text—represented by D and E as well as by $P^{38, 41, 48}$ and the old Latin translations—differ from one another in many places. Thus the "we-sections" begin in D already in 11:28, in that the situation of the Antioch church after the arrival of the prophets from Jerusalem is described with the words, "And great joy prevailed. And when we came together, one of them, named Agabus, spoke. . . ." The text of the so-called Apostolic Decree in 15:20 and 29 has been shortened from a four-member to a three-member form which no longer speaks of "what is strangled"—that is, meat not slaughtered in the prescribed manner—but only of commandments understood in a moral sense: idolatry, blood (= murder), and fornication are prohibited. The problem of the relationship of the Egyptian-Alexandrian and the Western texts has been thoroughly clarified (Dibelius, Haenchen). Of course the question of the original text must be examined from case to case, but in the vast majority of cases the form of the Western text proves to be the result of secondary modifications, elaborations, or embellishments. In the second century the text of Acts had not yet been frozen as an unchangeable holy text, but was basically still open to modification. The Western text, the beginnings of which certainly reach back to this early time, undertook in many places to make clarifications or accommodation to the situation which had changed since Acts had been written. Thus the insertion of the "we" in 11:28 served to make the account more vivid. And the transformation of the Apostolic Decree into a list of ethical commandments was to show that it was not a matter of cultic questions, but of moral instruction of the apostles for the whole church. Elsewhere changes or additions are found which embellish or clarify the narrative, as for example 6:8: Stephen did great signs and wonders before the people, where D adds a liturgical formula, δια του ονοματος κυριου Ιησου Χριστου ("through the name of the Lord Jesus Christ"); 12:10: Peter is freed by the angel and led out of the prison, D adds: "and they descended the seven steps."

VII.

The Gospel and Letters of John

#33 The Gospel of John

Wellhausen, J. *Erweiterungen und Änderungen im 4. Evangelium,* 1907.
Schwartz, E. "Aporien im 4. Evangelium," *NGGW,* 1907/08.
Windisch, H. *Johannes und die Synoptiker,* 1926.
Hirsch, E. *Studien zum vierten Evangelium,* 1936.
———. "Stilkritik und Literaranalyse im vierten Evangelium," *ZNW* 43 (1950/51):128-43.
Schweizer, E. *Ego Eimi,* 1939, ²1965.
Jeremias, J. "Johanneische Literarkritik," *ThBl* 20 (1941):33-46.
Bultmann, R. "Johannesevangelium," in *RGG*³, 3:840-50.
———. *The Gospel of John,* 1971.
Ruckstuhl, E. *Die Literarische Einheit des Joh.-Ev.,* 1951.
Dodd, C. H. *The Interpretation of the Fourth Gospel,* 1953.
———. "Some Johannine 'Herrenworte,'" *NTS* 2 (1955/56):75-86.
———. *Historical Tradition in the Fourth Gospel,* 1963.
Noack, B. *Zur johanneischen Tradition,* 1954.
Wilkens, W. *Die Entstehungsgeschichte des vierten Evangeliums,* 1958.
Haenchen, E. "Johanneische Probleme" (1959), in *Gott und Mensch,* 1965, 78-113.
Schulz, S. *Komposition und Herkunft der johanneischen Reden,* 1960.

Lohse, E. "Wort und Sakrament im Johannesevangelium" (1960/61), in *Die Einheit des NT*, 1973, 193-208.
Braun, H. *Qumran und das NT II*, 1966, 118-44.
Becker, J. "Die Abschiedsreden im Johannesevangelium," *ZNW* 61 (1970):215-46.
Schneider, F., and Stenger, W. *Johannes und die Synoptiker*, 1971.
Schnackenburg, R. *The Gospel According to St. John*, I-II, 1980.
Cullman, O. *The Johannine Circle*, 1976.

a. Contents: Chapter 1 forms the introduction: the prologue (1:1-18), then the testimony of the Baptist (1:19-34), and the first disciples (1:35-51).

The first major section describes the revelation of the glory of Jesus before the world (chapters 2–12). First the beginning of Jesus' public ministry is portrayed (chapters 2–4): marriage in Cana (2:1-12), cleansing of the temple (2:13-22), transition (2:23-25), Jesus and Nicodemus (3:1-21), further testimony of the Baptist (3:22-36), Jesus and the Samaritan woman (4:1-42), healing of a nobleman's son (4:43-54).

The following chapters picture Jesus' debate with the unbelieving cosmos: the healing of the sick man at the pool of Bethesda (chapter 5), the bread of life (chapter 6), Jesus in Jerusalem (chapters 7–8), healing of a man born blind (chapter 9), the good shepherd (10:1-18), Jesus at the Feast of Dedication in Jerusalem (10:19-39), transition (10:40-42), raising of Lazarus (11), anointing of Jesus in Bethany (12:1-11), triumphal entry of Jesus into Jerusalem (12:12-19), Jesus and the Greeks (12:20-36), summary of the public ministry of Jesus (12:37-50).

The second major section has as its theme the revelation of the glory of Jesus before his disciples: Jesus' last meal with the disciples (13:1-30), the farewell discourses (13:31–16:33), and the high priestly prayer of Jesus (chapter 17).

Chapters 18–20 deal with the Passion (18–19) and the resurrection of Jesus (chapter 20). The Johannine Easter story tells of the discovery of the empty grave (20:1-10) as well as the appearance of the resurrected Jesus to Mary Magdalene (20:11-18), the disciples (20:19-23), and the unbelieving Thomas (20:24-29). Then follows a brief conclusion to the whole book (20:30-31).

Chapter 21 represents an appendix which tells of Galilean

appearances: the revelation of the Resurrected One at the Sea of Tiberias (21:1-14) and his encounter with Peter and the Beloved Disciple (21:15-24) as well as a concluding word (v. 25).

b. The relation of John to the Synoptics is characterized on the one hand by some material that they have in common and on the other by considerable differences. Like the Synoptics, John also reports the story of John the Baptist at the beginning and at the end the story of Jesus' Passion and resurrection. Between the beginning and end John has a few pericopes in common with the Synoptics:

2:13-22	Cleansing of the temple	Mark 11:15-17 par.
4:43-54	Healing a nobleman's son	Matthew 8:5-13/ Luke 7:1-10
6:1-13	Feeding the 5,000	Mark 6:32-44 par.; 8:1-10 par.
6:16-21	Jesus' walking on the water	Mark 6:45-52 par.
12:1-8	Anointing of Jesus in Bethany	Mark 14:3-9 par.
12:12-16	Jesus' triumphal entry into Jerusalem	Mark 11:1-10 par.
13:21-30	Jesus foretells his betrayal	Mark 14:18-21 par.
13:36-38	Jesus foretells the denial of Peter	Mark 14:29-31 par.

In some places we even find phrases and whole sentences formulated in the same or similar wording. Thus the betrayal of Judas in John 13:21 = Mark 14:18 is announced with the words αμην λεγω υμιν οτι εις εξ υμων παραδιωσε με ("truly I say to you, one of you will betray me"). John 12:8 agrees verbatim with Matthew 26:11 (cf. Mark 14:7); so also John 5:8 with Mark 2:9, 11 par.

This data could easily suggest that in all these cases John is dependent on the Synoptics. If John knew the Synoptics, then why did he write his Gospel? Did he want to supplement them, or rather to suppress and replace them (Windisch)? But this question can only be posed after the issue of whether John was really dependent on the Synoptics has been clarified.

In order to solve this problem we must attend not only to the similarities between John and the Synoptics, but also to their differences. This is seen first in the fact that there are a considerable number of pericopes in the Fourth Gospel which have no parallel in the Synoptics. For instance, although John too has a story in chapter 20 about the discovery of the empty tomb, all his additional Easter material is peculiar to him—not only in chapter 20, but also in chapter 21, where of course the story of the miraculous catch of fish is to be compared to Luke 5:1-11. So also in the Passion story the Fourth Gospel often goes its own way. Within the portrayal of Jesus' ministry the following pericopes are peculiar to John: the marriage in Cana (2:1-12), Jesus and Nicodemus (3:1-21), Jesus in Samaria (4:1-42), healing of the sick man at Bethesda (chapter 5; but cf. Mark 2:1-12 par.), Jesus and his brothers (7:1-10), the healing of the man born blind (chapter 9), the resurrection of Lazarus (chapter 11), Jesus and the Greeks (12:20-36), washing the disciples' feet (13:4-11). The Synoptics present brief reports which tell how Jesus showed compassion to people who were poor and suffering. In John Jesus' deeds are demonstrations of his glory—seen most impressively in the resurrection of Lazarus, who already lay in the tomb four days (11:39).

Even more clearly than in the pericopes which report Jesus' deeds, the distinction between John and the Synoptics is manifest in the speeches of Jesus. The Synoptics offer throughout short sayings and parables of Jesus in which the coming of the kingdom of God is announced. In contrast, John presents long speeches which are sometimes monotonous-sounding meditations, and which always have the same content: Jesus is sent by the Father; whoever accepts him in faith has the bread of life, the light of the world, the resurrection and the life, the way, the truth, and the life, and so forth.

Finally, in regard to the Johannine outline, this too is considerably different from the Synoptics. While the Synoptics suggest a public ministry of Jesus of about one year, in which Jesus first preaches in Galilee and then makes one journey to Jerusalem, in John the scene of Jesus' activity alternates between Galilee and Jerusalem. The Passover is mentioned three times (2:13; 6:4; 11:55); four times Jesus journeys to Jerusalem (2:13; 5:1; 7:10; 12:12). According to the Synoptics Jesus' Last Supper with the disciples took place within the framework of a Passover meal (Mark 14:12-26 par.), but according to John Jesus died before the Passover meal, as himself the true Passover lamb, in the very hour that the Passover lambs were being slaughtered (John 18:28; 19:14).

call for a discriminating judgment on the question of whether the fourth evangelist used the Synoptics. To begin with, we can say with confidence that the Gospel of John presupposes the Synoptic tradition. That it was known to the evangelist is clear from the agreements between John and the Synoptics. But the considerable differences between the Fourth Gospel and the Synoptics suggest that these contacts are derived from oral traditions which the evangelist used. Certain easily remembered statements could be repeated in the same wording, even if no direct literary dependence existed. To clarify the mutual relationship between John and the Synoptics, the comparison of individual sayings of Jesus is of significance (Noack, Dodd), as for example:

John 13:16	ουκ εστιν δουλος μειζων του κυριου ("a servant is not greater than his master") ουδε αποστολος μειζων του πεμψαντος αυτον ("nor is one sent greater than the one who sent him")
Luke 6:40	ουκ εστιν μαθητης υπερ τον διδασκαλον ("a disciple is not above his teacher")
Matthew 10:24	ουκ εστιν μαθητης υπερ τον διδασκαλον ("a disciple is not above his teacher") ουδε δουλος υπερ τον κυριον αυτου ("nor is a servant above his master")
cf. John 15:20	ουκ εστιν δουλος μειζων του κυριου ("a servant is not greater than his master")

The juxtaposition of δουλος/κυριος ("servant/master") is found only in John 13:16; 15:20; and Matthew 10:24. In Matthew/Luke the contrast μαθητης/διδασκαλος ("disciple/teacher") is also found but John has αποστολος/πεμψας ("one sent/the one who sends"). Such similarities and differences indicate that this sloganlike sentence was taken from the oral tradition.

Or:

John 20:23	αν τινων *αφητε* τας αμαρτιας αφεωνται αυτοις; αν τινων *κρατητε* κεκρατηνται ("if you *forgive* the sins of any, they are forgiven; if you *retain* [the sins] of any, they are retained")
Matthew 16:19	ο εαν *δησης* επι της γης εσται δεδεμενον εν τοις ουρανοις, και ο εαν *λυσης*

επι της γης εσται λελυμενον εν τοις ουρανοις ("whatever *you bind* on earth shall be bound in heaven and whatever *you loose* on earth shall be loosed in heaven")

Matthew 18:18 οσα εαν *δησητε* επι της γης, εσται δεδεμενα εν ουραν, και οσα εαν *λυσητε* επι της γης, εσται λελυμενα εν ουρανω ("whatever *you bind* on earth shall be bound in heaven and whatever *you loose* on earth shall be loosed in heaven")

In Matthew binding/loosing—earth/heaven are juxtaposed; in John another terminology is used: forgive/retain, while earth and heaven are not mentioned. Thus also this logion, which has different forms in John and Matthew, has been taken over from the oral tradition and placed in completely different contexts by the two evangelists.

A review of the stock of traditions handled by the evangelists as a whole, as well as the investigation of passages in detail leads to the conclusion that the Gospel of John has no direct literary dependence on the Synoptics. It is assumed, of course, that the evangelist was acquainted with at least one of the Synoptic Gospels from having heard it read aloud in worship, for otherwise we could hardly explain how he had arrived at the literary form of "gospel" in which all the stories of Jesus' ministry lead toward the report of his Passion and resurrection, which stands at the end as the high point and completion of the whole. In some places historical information has been preserved in John which is not found in the Synoptics (Dodd), for example the information that Jesus' first disciples came from the circle of John the Baptist (1:35ff), or the precise description of the pool of Bethesda (5:2).

The peculiarity of the Gospel of John, which stands out clearly in comparison with the Synoptics, was once described by Clement of Alexandria thus: John recognized that the externals of the ministry of Jesus τα σωματικα (lit. "the bodily things") had been adequately presented in the other Gospels. He therefore wrote a πνευματικον ευαγγελιον ("spiritual Gospel," Eus. H. E. VI 14:7). But the difference between John and the Synoptics certainly cannot be reduced to the formula somatic-pneumatic, for John also reports "somatic" material, and the

Synoptics by no means give up all claim to presenting the "spiritual." The Fourth Gospel rather develops the testimony to Christ as it is disclosed to faith in the revealed glory of Jesus. Thus John says nothing about any hidden revelation, but from the very beginning Jesus stands before the world as the one sent by God, and before his own as the Son of the Father. The majesty of Jesus finds its consummation in the fact that he voluntarily lays down his life (10:18). His words, however, which make unmistakably clear the meaning of his deeds, proclaim that in him alone salvation and deliverance are given.

c. Johannine literary criticism seeks to clarify the question of whether the Gospel of John in its present form is a literary unit or not. Close examination reveals breaks in the narrative of the Gospel at several points. Thus 7:53–8:11 stands out most clearly, and noticeable differences are found between the long, repetitive speeches and the tersely described deeds of Jesus as in 2:1-12; 4:43-54; 12:1-8, whose spare form rather reminds one of the Synoptic pericopes. After the book has been brought to an end at 20:30-31, then chapter 21 follows with another concluding word (21:25). In 14:31 the command is given, "Rise, let us go hence." But in fact Jesus and the disciples do not "go hence," but the farewell discourses are continued in chapters 15 and 16. In 6:1 it is reported, "After this Jesus went to the other side of the Sea of Galilee, which is the Sea of Tiberias." This presupposes a trip from the west bank to the eastern side of the lake. But all through chapter 5 Jesus had been in Jerusalem. The conflict over healing the man on the sabbath in chapter 5 is taken up again in 7:15-24. And 10:19-21 continues the discussion over healing the blind man in chapter 9; but in between is found the section 10:1-18.

It was inevitable that this peculiar lack of smoothness would invite explanations in terms of the evangelist's reworking of sources. The attempt has repeatedly been made to distinguish between a primary document and its later reediting. Thus Wellhausen and Schwartz supposed that the Fourth Gospel contained a considerably shorter primary document which had then been expanded. In the primary document, 14:31 was directly followed by 18:1; everything now found in between was added later. According to E. Hirsch (1936!), a primary document, which was free of Jewish ideas, originated in the time around A.D. 100; then around 130/40 a theologian in Asia Minor gave it an ecclesiastical editing. And finally, W. Wilkens has again taken up the question of the secondary editing of a primary document in a different form: a primary version of the Gospel contained a series of signs; it was then expanded by sections of discourse which were to interpret the signs, and finally the whole was reformed into a Passion Gospel. But in contrast to the older theories, the primary document and the layers added later were all ascribed by Wilkens to one and the same author. He thereby took account of the undeniable fact that the Gospel of John is a linguistic and stylistic unity, and therefore affords no linguistic or stylistic criteria with the help of which primary document and later redaction could be separated. But once it is accepted that the Gospel of John originated from layers of material placed one over the other, but with all the layers attributed to the same author, then in fact the attempt has been given up to distinguish a primary document from later editing.

In the Gospel of John definite stylistic features are found throughout which are characteristic of the evangelist (Schweizer, Ruckstuhl), for example: (1) the possessive pronoun with the article, placed after its antecedent: the friend of the bridegroom rejoices with him αυτη ουν η χαρα η εμη πεπληρωται ("therefore this joy *of mine* is now full," 3:29); (2) the epexegetical ινα ("that, in order that")-clause is typically Johannine: εμον βρωμα εστιν ινα ποιω το θελημα του πεμψαντος με ("my food is to [lit. *that I may*] do the will of him who sent me," 4:34); (3) the use of εκεινος ("that") as an independent personal pronoun in the singular is especially frequent: απεκρινατο ουν ο Ιησους και ελεγεν αυτοις αμην αμην λεγω υμιν ου δθναται ο υιος ποιειν αφ εαυτου ουδεν εαν μη τι βλεπη τον πατερα ποιουντα α γαρ αν *εκεινος* ποιη ταυτα και ο υιος ομοιως ποιει ("Jesus said to them, 'Truly, truly I say to you, the Son can do nothing of his own accord, but only what he sees the Father doing; for whatever he [lit. *that* one] does, that the Son does likewise,'" 5:19); (4) the prefaced double αμην ("amen"; "truly") is characteristic of the Fourth Gospel αμην αμην λεγω υμιν ("amen, amen"; "truly, truly I say to you," 5:19). These and other Johannine characteristics are strewn over the whole Gospel—with one exception: 7:53–8:11 contains not a single Johannine stylistic peculiarity. Thus this pericope represents a foreign body in the Gospel of John, a stray page that perhaps originally belonged to the Gospel of the Hebrews (Eus. H. E. III. 39:17), and in many NT manuscripts has been placed after Luke 21:38.

The observation that the Gospel of John is a linguistic and stylistic unity is also a significant datum to be kept in mind for the evaluation of all efforts at source analysis. All older hypotheses were made obsolete by the works of Rudolf Bultmann. According to Bultmann the author had before him written sources which he reedited: (1) the so-called "signs source" is indicated by the references which enumerate the first (2:11) and second (4:54) signs of Jesus. Its beginning is 1:35-50, and the basic stratum of miracle stories belongs to it: the marriage at Cana, healing of the nobleman's son, healing of the lame man at Bethesda, the feeding of the five thousand and walking on the water, Jesus and his brothers, the healing of the man born blind, the raising of Lazarus as well as (perhaps) the anointing of Jesus and the triumphal entry into Jerusalem. This source ended with the summary in 12:37-38 and the conclusion in 20:30-31. (2) Alongside this the evangelist used a second narrative source, which had some relationship to Synoptic accounts, but was not identical with the formulations of these stories in the Synoptic Gospels: cleansing of the temple, confession of Peter, (perhaps) the anointing of Jesus and the triumphal entry into Jerusalem, the foot washing, and parts of the Passion story. (3) The source of the so-called "revelation discourses" is calculated to have contained a total of 157 verses: the original prologue, the conversation with Nicodemus, sections of chapters 4 and 5, the discourse on the bread of life, parts of the speech on the light of the world, the Good Shepherd, the sayings concerning resurrection and life, sections of chapter 12, and especially the farewell discourses and the high priestly prayer of Jesus. From the point of view of the history of religions, the "revelatory discourses" are characterized by an oriental Gnosticism, as it is supposed to have existed in Baptist circles. That is, it is a matter of a pre-Christian source. The evangelist John thinks and writes in continuity with the train of thought of this source, in that he annotates his source with comments from a Christian point of view, with a manner of speaking borrowed from the OT.

Bultmann's penetrating source analysis has been thoroughly

discussed among scholars. The part of Bultmann's theory which has found the most agreement is that a source for the miracle stories could have been available to the evangelist. The references in 2:11 and 4:54, as well as the terse style with which the miracle itself is presented throughout, could in fact indicate the use of a written source. It is thus thoroughly possible that a "signs source" was used, although it remains hypothetical (Schnackenburg). And one may readily think, though it cannot be proved, that for his version of the Passion story the evangelist used in part a written source different from that found in the Synoptic Gospels. But the hypothesis that the evangelist used a discourse source remains problematic. Bultmann is aware of the difficulties for this hypothesis presented by the linguistic unity of the Gospel. He wanted to overcome these problems by referring to the distinctiveness of the content of the speeches, and supposing that the evangelist wrote in continuity with the style of his sources. Bultmann sought to support his analysis with material from the prologue and proceed from there, since in the prologue the source can be clearly distinguished from the later editing—especially on the basis of the prose insertion in vv. 6-8 and 15. But since our present prologue is based on an original hymnic form and thus is a passage *sui generis*, the analysis of the prologue can have no demonstrative force for the rest of the Gospel. The speeches themselves are not arranged in rhythmical structures, so that one cannot extract lines that clearly do not fit, but are written in an elevated prose. Thus neither linguistic and stylistic criteria nor unambiguous formal characteristics enable us to distinguish source from later editing by the evangelist. It must therefore be considered improbable that a written discourse source was used by the evangelist. Rather, he elaborated the sayings that came to him in the tradition, reformulating them in a style stamped by his own theological reflection.

In order to remove the gaps in the present form of the Johannine narrative, Bultmann proposed numerous rearrangements, in an effort to restore the order of the passages as originally intended by the evangelist. In this process a few verses or parts of verses were shifted to other locations, without Bultmann being able to explain why they are found in their present location. Thus one must consider the matter more carefully. In the transmission of ancient literature displacements of the text sometimes occurred as a result of pages being inserted in the wrong place. Thus, for example, in all Greek manuscripts Sir. 33:13*b*–36:16*a* stands between 30:24 and 25, and John 7:53–8:11 has been inserted at different places in the NT by the manuscript tradition. If one reckons ca. 760 letters per papyrus page, one arrives at the following calculations: chapter 5: 3795 = 5 × 759 letters = 5 pages; 6:1-59: 4619 = 6 × 770 letters = 6 pages; 7:15-24: 763 letters = 1 page; 10:1-18: 1495 = 2 × 748 letters = 2 pages; 10:19-29: 775 letters = 1 page (Schweizer). If the Gospel of John was first written on individual pages, then it is conceivable that when they were brought together to form the book—by the editor?—individual pages were displaced from this original location. With this hypothesis one is enabled to set 6:1-59 before chapter 5, to place 7:15-24 as the conclusion of chapter 5, and place 10:19-29 before 10:1-18. But the problem of the farewell discourses presented by 14:31 is not resolvable in this way. Here one must either judge that two parallel versions of the farewell discourses have been placed one after the other by the editor, or that an originally shorter passage which ended at 14:31 has been later enlarged by the addition of chapters 15–16 (Becker). But except for the problem of the farewell discourses, the hypothesis of a displacement of pages opens up a way to avoid at least the most violent collisions presented by the present form of the book (Schweizer).

That the Gospel received yet another, final, editing is clear from the duplicated conclusion (20:30-31; 21:25). But this editing, as Bultmann has shown, not only added an appendix in chapter 21, but also made changes and additions within the Gospel itself and adjusted the statements of the Gospel strongly in the direction of the generally accepted Christian doctrine. Thereby references to futuristic eschatology (5:28-29) and the sacraments of baptism and the Lord's Supper were worked in (3:5; 6:51*b*-58; 19:34*b*, 35). These editorial additions may be distinguished from their contents on the basis of language and content and thereby can be identified as secondary (Lohse).

d. To determine the setting of the Gospel of John within the religious milieu of the Hellenistic world is no simple matter. The prescriptions of the Jewish law—e.g. the law concerning sabbath rest (5:9-10; 7:22-24)—are presupposed as known. The messianic expectation of Judaism is familiar to the evangelist and his readers, both in terms of its titles (1:20ff), and the ideas of the hidden Messiah (7:27) and of the origin of the Messiah from Bethlehem or from the family of David (7:42). Reference is repeatedly made to Jewish festivals and the customs related to them (2:13; 6:4; 7:2-3, 8, 37; 10:22; 18:28; 19:31, 42). Strikingly precise geographical data are given for Palestinian locations: for Jacob's well in Sychar (4:6), Bethesda (5:2), the location of Gethsemane (18:1), and others. Thus Palestinian tradition is visible in many places of the Gospel of John—quite apart from the fact of the abrupt separation from the synagogue (9:22; 12:42; 16:2) which had led to the fact that the Jews are pictured as a solid front, who step forth as the representatives of the world which persists in its unbelief.

The Palestinian background of the Gospel of John has been placed in a clearer light by the Qumran texts. The teaching of the Qumran community is characterized by a distinctive dualism. The children of light are separated from the children of darkness, truth stands against wickedness, obedience to the law in contrast to disobedience and despising of the Torah. Many statements of the Gospel of John are expressed in concepts very similar to those used in the Qumran texts. Thus I QS III 18ff state that the children of light walk in paths of light, but the children of wickedness in the paths of darkness. And in John 8:12 it is said: "I am the light of the world. He who follows me will not walk in darkness, but will have the light of life." According to the Gospel of John, the children of light are not those who keep the law, but those who believe (12:36). In both places the truth is not understood as theoretical knowledge, but is something which one does. In the Gospel of John, as in the doctrine of the community of Qumran, dualism is not understood in cosmic terms, but in ethical terms. "And this is the judgment, that the light has come into the world, and men loved darkness rather than the light, because their deeds were evil. For everyone who does evil hates the light, and does not come to the light, lest his deeds should be exposed. But he who does what is true comes to the light, that it may be clearly seen that his deeds have been wrought in God" (3:19-21). In the Qumran community the truth is thought of in the same way, as the obligation to right living which manifests itself in keeping the law. In contrast, the spirit of perversion leads to evil deeds. Whoever lives by the evil spirit will be afflicted with many plagues and be allotted eternal destruction (I QS IV, 12). If on the one hand there is an undeniably parallel dualistic structure in the Qumran texts and the Gospel of John, on the other hand there are also considerable differences, for in the Qumran doctrine this dualism is unrelated to the messianic expectation, while in John the contrast of light/darkness, truth/lie, life/death are determined from a christological point of view. The light of the world, the truth and the life, is no other than Christ alone (8:12; 9:5; 14:6). But the doctrine of the Qumran community never speaks of one sent by God from heaven who himself embodies those qualities. Thus the Qumran texts contribute to the illumination of the Palestinian background of the Gospel of John, but in view of the considerable differences, they cannot simply be described from a history of religion's point of view as the mother country of the Gospel of John (Braun).

In distinction from the Synoptics, the Christology of the Gospel of John is characterized by features of the kind of syncretism which occurred in late antiquity, which recur in many Gnostic texts of a somewhat later date. In the midpoint of the christological witness stands the Son sent by the Father. He was with the Father from eternity (1:1; 17:5). The Father sent him into the world (17:21). He came into the world (1:10), as light in the cosmos (3:19; 12:46). At the same time he remained one with the Father (8:16; 10:30). He acts on earth with the authority of the Father (5:27; 17:2). He brings life (5:21ff), and leads out of darkness into light (3:19; 8:12). He reveals himself as the one who he really is: bread of life (6:35, 48, 51), light of the world (8:12), the Good Shepherd (10:11), the way, the truth, and the life (14:6), and so forth. He is hated and persecuted by the world (7:7; 15:18, 24). He leaves this world, returns to the Father and is exalted (3:14; 8:28; 12:32, 34). He returns to that heavenly realm from which he came (6:62; 8:14; 16:28); he takes his own with him and draws them up away from the earth (12:32). He prepares a dwelling place for them in the house of the Father (14:2), and shows them the way to it (14:6). The response which one makes to him determines the decision which he will receive at the last judgment (3:17, 21; 12:47-48).

This basic structure of the Johannine Christology cannot be

explained as the further development of a Christology as it comes to expression in the Synoptic Gospels. It rather takes its point of departure from the kind of Christology found in the early Christian hymns such as Philippians 2:6-11 or I Timothy 3:16. In this process various motifs are taken over from the religious environment: Jewish speculations about heavenly Wisdom which came down to earth, found no place to dwell, and returned to the heavenly world; apocalyptic expectations of the heavenly Son of man who will appear at the end of time to hold the last judgment; mythological ideas of a heavenly emissary who comes into the world as the redeemer, in order to free humanity and take them with him to the world above—conceptions and ideas which were then developed and firmly connected with the name of Jesus Christ in the Christian-Gnostic systems of the second century. The question of whether pre-Christian Gnosticism was already acquainted with a redeemer figure is still debated. In the texts of the Mandeans—a Gnostic Baptist sect whose scriptures were first written down in the seventh-eighth centuries A.D.—there is found a well-developed myth of a heavenly redeemer. The Mandean community supposedly originated in Palestine and then about the end of the first or beginning of the second century emigrated to Mesopotamia. In the course of several centuries their traditions were expanded from many sources—including some with Christian origins. To be sure, their beginnings do reach back to the same times as those of Christianity, but the redeemer myth was probably not developed until Christian times, and could not therefore have been a direct model for the Christology of the Gospel of John. The Mandean texts do show, however, that on the edge of Judaism, Gnostic groups, whose world of ideas contained many syncretistic influences, were formed already in NT times.

The Gospel of John refers noticeably often to the Baptist movement. The first disciples of Jesus came from Baptist circles (1:35ff). But the evangelist brings clearly to expression that John was only a forerunner, in no way the coming redeemer himself (1:6-8). The Baptist had no other mission than to bear witness to the light. When he was asked by a delegation of the Jews if he were the eschatological emissary, he denied it three times and assured them that he was only the voice of one crying in the wilderness (1:19ff). John bears witness, in that he points to Jesus as the lamb of God (1:29, 36), confesses him to be the Son of God (1:34), and preaches that Christ must increase, but he must decrease (3:30). Jesus is therefore incomparably superior to the Baptist (5:36; 10:41). These sentences execute a polemical demarcation over against disciples of the Baptist who obviously wanted to see in him not only a prophet, but also the eschatological bringer of salvation (see Acts 18:14–19:7). Thus the Gospel of John on the one hand shows clearly that points of contact with the Baptist movement exist, but on the other hand it reveals a distinction, in that it is contested that John is the eschatological redeemer, and the Baptist is rather claimed as a forerunner and witness to Jesus.

The religious background of the Gospel of John is thus formed by Jewish circles which were open to syncretistic influences. If the Gospel of John makes use of such conceptions in describing the redemptive work of Christ, it nonetheless at the same time gives these ideas a sharp anti-Gnostic point. Thus the divine Logos did not enter the world in a disguise, but became flesh (1:14). It is not the case that some human beings belong to the Redeemer because they share in the same reality he does, as would correspond to Gnostic thinking, but live in lies, darkness, and death. Rather, he leads to salvation because he alone is truth, light, and life.

e. The question of authorship still today is answered differently. The testimony of the Gospel with regard to its own authorship is found in the editorial additions. The concluding word says, "This one—that is, the Beloved Disciple—is he who gives his testimony and who has written this; and we know that his testimony is true" (21:24). Who is meant? In chapter 21, the Beloved Disciple is placed over against Peter. The reliability of that which the Beloved Disciple has testified is also underscored in the redactional note 19:35*b*. According to the Johannine Passion story he is the trusted disciple of Jesus who lay on his breast at the Last Supper (13:23), to whom the Crucified One entrusted his mother (19:26), and the witness of the empty grave (20:1ff). Obviously it is a matter of the ideal figure of a disciple, who is not historically conceivable. In distinction from the evangelist, the redactor attempts to confer clear characteristics on the Beloved Disciple. The Synoptics name three disciples of Jesus who formed the inner circle: Peter, John, and James. It has thus often been argued that since Peter is distinguished from the Beloved Disciple, and since James was killed in A.D. 44 (Acts 12:2), the Beloved Disciple must therefore be identified with John. But chapter 21 does not make this identification, and nowhere does the Gospel of John indicate that Jesus had an inner circle of three disciples as portrayed by the Synoptics. Thus one can say only that the editing in chapter 21 wants to give the figure of the Beloved Disciple a sharper profile, but does not connect him any more closely to a particular historical figure.

It was the later church tradition which first made this identification. It is met for the first time around A.D. 180 in Irenaeus (adv. Haer. II. 1:1): John the Beloved Disciple published the Gospel in his old age at Ephesus. Irenaeus supports his claim by appealing to Bishop Polycarp of Smyrna, who in A.D. 155 at the age of eighty-six suffered martyrdom. When Irenaeus was young he knew Polycarp "and heard from him how he had contacts with John and with the others who had seen the Lord, and how he remembered their words, and what he had heard from them about the Lord, about his wonders and his teaching" (transmitted by Eus. H. E. V 20:6). How strong is this chain Irenaeus—Polycarp—John? Of course Irenaeus believes that the tradition concerns the apostle John. In fact however only John is mentioned, without any title being given or any connection indicated with the origin of the Gospel of John. The tradition that emerges in Irenaeus about the authorship of the Gospel of John by the disciple John thus cannot be traced back to earlier times. It is directly opposed by the counterthesis of the Alogi who attributed the Johannine writings to the Gnostic Cerinthus (see p. 229). Around A.D. 200 the Alogi used this view against the Montanists, who based their doctrine of the Spirit principally on the Paraclete sayings of the Gospel of John. But also the polemic of the Alogi for its part proves that around the end of the second century the Gospel of John was ascribed to John the son of Zebedee.

This view, that the Gospel of John was written by an apostle, first began to be questioned at the beginning of the nineteenth century. In 1820 Bretschneider, the general superintendent of Gotha, compared the speeches of the Gospel of John with the Synoptic Gospels and came to the conclusion that an eyewitness could not have written them. He met passionate opposition, especially by Schleiermacher, who argued that the spiritual content of the Gospel of John argues that what is described had really been experienced. The opposition was so strong that Bretschneider withdrew his theses. But the critical view reemerged a short time later. F. C. Baur and his school affirmed that the Gospel of John was not written until about A.D. 170 and presupposed the struggle with Gnosticism and Montanism. It formed the synthesis of the antitheses of earliest Christianity, as its crowning fulfillment (see p. 13). Since Baur, criticism of the view that the Gospel of John goes back to an apostle has never been silenced.

The critics base their views mainly on observations from the Gospel itself, from which they conclude that a disciple and eyewitness could not have expressed himself in this way. For support they also sought evidence in the ancient church tradition which opposed the view of Irenaeus mentioned above. In this connection two traditions received attention. The allegation of an early martyr's death of the apostle John is found in a note from Papias, but is first documented in the A.D. 430 writings of Philip Sidetes, and emerges once again in the ninth century in Georgios Hamartolos. Furthermore, the Syrian martyr calendar lists December 27 as the date for the apostles John and James. Could it be that John the son of Zebedee died an early martyr's death with his brother James? Acts 12:2 reports that James lost his life under King Herod Agrippa, but John is not mentioned. It has been often supposed, however, that the saying of Jesus in Mark 10:39 par. should be seen as a *vaticinium ex eventu*, which would support the thesis of a common early martyr's death (Schwartz). But the ancient church testimony is late and weak, and Mark 10:39 cannot be taken as proof for a common martyr's death of the two Zebedee brothers. Rather Galatians 2:9 documents that John the son of Zebedee participated in the apostolic conference, thus he lived longer than his brother. Thus the supposition that the Zebedee John died as a martyr cannot be proven and can contribute nothing to the clarification of the problem of the authorship of the Fourth Gospel.

On the other hand, there is an old church tradition which is more important, according to which there was an elder John. In a note preserved by Eusebius, Papias of Hierapolis reports of his successful efforts to obtain authentic reports about Jesus' life and teaching: "Whenever anyone came who had been a disciple of the elders, I inquired of him concerning sayings of the elders: (1) what Andrew or Peter *had said* or what Philip or Thomas or James or what John or Matthew or what any other disciples of the Lord *(had said)*, and (2) what disciples of the Lord such as Aristion and the *elder John were saying*" (Eus. H. E. III. 39.4). Obviously two persons are spoken of who bear the name of John. The first is mentioned together with other members of the circle of the twelve, who had said something but were no longer alive; the other John however still speaks, therefore is still alive as Papias writes. Thus it is presupposed that John the son of Zebedee has died, but the elder Presbyter John is distinguished from him as a personality who can still be inquired of. A connection to the Gospel of John is however not established, but it is merely mentioned that this elder John was likewise a disciple of the Lord and had emerged in a special way as a bearer of old tradition. Since the Apocalypse derived from an author named John (1:1, 4, 9; 22:8), who is not described as an apostle, but rather as a prophet and an acknowledged witness to Jesus, it would be conceivable to relate this John to the elder (see p. 230; further pp. 193-94). But it still remains a completely unprovable supposition if one attempts to find the author of the Gospel of John in the elder John mentioned by Papias.

Thus a critical review of all the statements made in the ancient church tradition establishes only that the Gospel of John was ascribed to John the son of Zebedee around A.D. 180. One could affirm apostolic authorship for the Gospel on this basis. But since neither the Gospel of John itself nor older indications in the tradition can contribute anything to the clarification of the authorship question, the identity of the fourth evangelist remains unknown. Nor is anything changed in this regard by the theory that the author was neither John the son of Zebedee nor a member of the circle of the twelve, but had been an eyewitness of the ministry of Jesus who is to be identified with the Beloved Disciple. He was supposedly a Judean and one of a special group of Jesus' disciples who came from a circle which stood on the edge of Judaism, a circle with which the historical Jesus also came in contact (Cullmann). Such suppositions remain hypothetical constructions.

Even if the name of the evangelist is no longer available, his work itself provides some information about his own way of thinking, his language, and his style. The evangelist is a Christian of Jewish origin, whose Greek style is clearly influenced by his thinking in a Semitic language. Of course the Gospel of John was not originally written in Aramaic and then translated, but Semitic linguistic forms are recognizable in the Greek style of the evangelist in many places. A few examples: (1) in place of the Semitic suffix the postpositive pronoun is used, e.g την μαρτυριαν αυτου (lit. "the testimony *of him*" 3:32); εν τη χειρι αυτου (lit. "in the hand *of him*," 3:35), and so forth. (2) The Semitic languages have no word for "no one," so instead a negative expression is used such as ανθρωπον ουκ εχω ινα . . . βαλη με εις την κολυμβηθραν (lit. "I do *not* have a *man* that he may put me into the pool," 5:7); ου δυναται ανθρωπος λαμβανειν (lit. "a *man* is *not* able to receive," 3:27); ου μη . . . εις τον αιωνα (lit. "*not* . . . forever = never," 4:14). (3) So-called *causus pendens*, i.e. a concept which is to be emphasized is placed at the beginning of the sentence and then taken up again in the following; e.g. ο ποιησας με θγιη, εκεινος μοι ειπεν (lit.: "*the one who* made me well, *that* one said to me," 5:11). (4) The placing of the verb first is typical of Semitic syntax: ειπεν ουν ο Ιησους (lit.: "said then Jesus," 4:48). (5) The asyndetic order of sentences and clauses corresponds to Semitic style. It is not as in Greek, where artful transitions are made with the help of conjunctions, particles, and so forth, but one sentence or clause simply follows another. Compare, for example, the numerous asyndeta in the prologue, 1:1-18. (6) The sentences and clauses are also frequently joined to one another simply with και ("and"), e.g. εν αρχη ην ο λογος, και ο λογος ην προς τον Θεον, και Θεος ην ο λογος ("in the beginning was the Word, and the Word was with God, and the Word was God," 1:1). Often this formal parataxis is combined, as in the Semitic languages, with a logical hypotaxis, that is, clauses are not simply juxtaposed, but one is subordinated to the other, e.g. πεντηκοντα ετη ουπω εχεις και Αβρααμ εωρακας (8:57) = "although you are not yet even fifty years old, have you seen Abraham?" Often the και has adversative meaning, e.g. το φως εν τη σκοτια φαινει, και [but] η σκοτια αυτο ου κατελαβεν ("the light shines in the darkness, *but* the darkness has not overcome it," (1:5). (7) In many places *parallelismus membrorum* is found as an indication of the art form of Semitic poetry, e.g. "He who believes in me / believes not in me / but in him who sent me /. And he who sees me / sees him who sent me" (12:44-45); "He who believes on the son / has eternal life, / he who does not obey the son / shall not see life, / but the wrath of God rests upon him" (3:36).

f. The place and time of composition must be decided from data within the Gospel. The author writes for Christian communities for which he develops the fullness of the church's testimony to Christ. He explains Aramaic or Palestinian expressions for his readers, e.g. ραββι—ο λεγεται μεθερμηνευομενον διδασκαλε ("rabbi" [which means teacher], 1:38, cf. 20:16); Μεσσιαν—ο εστιν μεθερμηνευομενον Χριστος ("Messiah" [which means Christ], 1:41); Σιλωαμ—ο ερμηνευεται απεσταλμενος ("Siloam" [which means Sent], 9:7); Θωμας—ο λεγομενος Διδυμος ("Thomas, called the Twin," 11:16); Jesus is brought to the Place of the Skull, ο λεγεται Εβραιστι Γολγοθα ("which is called in Hebrew Golgotha," 19:17). The separation of the Christian community from the synagogue has already happened (9:22; 12:42; 16:2). The community is to be supported in its debate with Judaism as well as in its demarcation from Gnosticism (1:14). This situation of the church can be most easily imagined in Syria, where Christians frequently came in contact with Jewish, and also with syncretistic movements. The Gospel of John certainly was written later than Matthew, which does not yet presuppose the final separation from the synagogue (see pp. 141-42); i.e. the time around A.D. 90 must be taken as a *terminus post quem*. The *terminus ante quem* is confirmed by an important papyrus discovery. The papyrus fragment P^{52}, published in 1935, which contains a few verses from John 18, comes from Egypt and was written A.D. ±125 (see page 238). Since the Gospel of John certainly was not written in Egypt, it must have originated before 125—supposedly around the turn of the century. Many earlier suppositions which reckoned with a considerably later date for the Gospel's composition were disproved by the small papyrus sheet P^{52}.

#34 The First Letter of John

Dobschütz, E. v. "Johanneische Studien I," *ZNW* 8 (1907):1-8.
Bultmann, R. "Analyse des 1. Johannesbriefes" (1927, in *Exegetica*, 1967, 105-23.

———. "Die kirchliche Redaktion des ersten Johannesbriefes" (1951). *Ibid.*, 381-93.
———. "Johannesbriefe," in *RGG*³, 3:836-39.
———. *A Commentary on the Johannine Epistles*, 1973.
Dodd, C. H. "The First Epistle of John and the Fourth Gospel," *BJRL* 21 (1937):129-56.
Käsemann, E. "Ketzer und Zeuge" (1951), in *Exegetische Versuche und Besinnungen I*, ⁶1970, 168-87.
Braun, H. "Literar-Analyse und thelogische Schichtung im ersten Johannesbrief (1951), in *Gesammelte Studien zum NT und seiner Umwelt*, ³1971, 210-42.
Conzelmann, H. "Was von Anfang war" (1954), in *Theologie als Schriftauslegung*, 1974, 207-14.
Nauck, W. *Die Tradition und der Charakter des ersten Johannesbriefes*, 1957.
Haenchen, E. "Neuere Literatur zu den Johannesbriefen" (1960), in *Die Bibel und wir*, 1968, 235-311.
O'Neill, J. C. *The Puzzle of 1 John*, 1966.
Schnackenburg, R. *Die Johannesbriefe*, ⁴1970.
Klein, G. "'Das wahre Licht scheint schon': Beobachtungen zur Zeit- und Geschichtserfahrung einer urchristlichen Schule," *ZThK* 68 (1971):261-326.
Wengst, K. *Häresie und Orthodoxie im Spiegel des ersten Johannesbriefs*, 1976.

a. Contents: In I John the two themes of exhortation to brotherly love and resistance to false teachers recur in constant alternation, with the result that a clear outline can hardly be detected. The *proömium* (1:1-4) introduces the first chain of thought, which describes fellowship with God as walking in the light (1:5–2:17): fellowship with God (1:5–2:2), the knowledge of God and keeping the commandments (2:3-11), admonitions to separation from the world (2:12-17).

Then follows the warding off of false teachers and the emphasizing of the command of brotherly love (2:18–3:24): warnings about false teachers (2:18-27), the Christian hope of salvation (2:28–3:3), parenesis which enjoins renunciation of sin and obedience to the love commandment (3:4-24).

Following this, exhortations to remain separate from the world by means of a correct faith are juxtaposed to exhortations to love the brethren (4:1–5:12): the spirit of truth and the spirit of error (4:1-6), love as the indication that one has been born of God (4:7-21), love to God and the overcoming power of faith (5:1-12). At the end stands a short summary (5:13-21).

b. First John is difficult to place in a specific category. The formal characteristics of a letter are almost completely lacking, having neither the customary opening nor closing formalities; there are however recognizable references to the situation of the readers (see below pp. 188-89). Thus it is not a religious tract or a manifesto directed to all Christendom, but rather a hortatory writing sent as an admonition to a limited circle of churches which were to be warned about false teaching and encouraged to remain faithful to the commandments (Bultmann).

c. In view of the numerous repetitions of the themes of brotherly love and correct faith which alternate in a rather circular movement, the issue of the unity of I John naturally suggests itself. Did the author use sources which he reworked? V. Dobschütz observed that in the section 2:29–3:10 there is a series of antithetical couplets whose members exactly correspond to each other:

1*a* = 2:29 πας ο ποιων την δικαιοσυνην εξ αυτου γεγεννηται ("every one who does *right* is born of him")

b = 3:4 πας ο ποιων την αμαρτιαν και την ανομιαν ποιει ("every one who commits *sin* is guilty of lawlessness")

2*a* = 3:6 πας ο εν αυτω μενων ουχ αμαρτανει ("no one who *abides in him* sins")

b = 3:6 πας ο αμαρτανων ουχ εωρακεν αυτον ουδε εγνωκαν αυτον ("no *one who sins* has either seen him or known him")

cf. also 3:7, 8/9, 10.

On the basis of these observations v. Dobschütz advocated the thesis that the author had annotated a source which contained such antithetically formulated sentences.

Bultmann took this hypothesis as the point of departure for his own analysis of I John, and developed it further in that he attempted to distinguish this source from its later editing. He saw 1:5*b*-10 as formulated in antithetical sentences which asserted that fellowship with God and walking in the light (vv. 6-7) belong inseparably together, just as do truth and the confession of sins (vv. 8-10). In 2:1-2 this series of theses is then commented on by the author in a homiletical style. While in 1:6-10 the exhortation to walk in the light is paradoxically placed beside the warning to understand oneself as a sinner, in 2:1-2 solace is offered to the sinner: Christ as ιλασμος ("expiation"). Thereby the series of theses is corrected from the point of view of the teaching generally accepted in the author's church: the Christian should not continue to sin. But if it happens anyway, he can rest secure in the intercessory work of Jesus Christ in his behalf.

This explanation of the section 1:5*b*–2:2 provides the criteria for the further analysis of the letter. The homiletical-annotating style of the author is distinguished from that of his source. Bultmann attributes to the source—apart from fragments of verses—the following: 1:5-10; 2:4, 5, 9-11, 29; 3:4, 6-10, 14-15 (24); 4:7, 8, 12, 16; 5:1, 4; 4:5 (6?); 2:23; 5:10, 12. The source has the same style and belongs to the same world of thought as the "revelation discourses" of the Fourth Gospel (see p. 172); that is, according to Bultmann it was originally a non-Christian source which was reworked by the Christian author of I John.

Although he basically affirms Bultmann's analysis, Braun has made important corrections: in the section 1:5-10, v. 9 twice uses the concept αμαρτιαι ("sins," pl.). This statement is inconceivable in a Gnostic source, since Gnosticism has no concept of sin. So the source must be a Christian source. In 2:1-2 this source is corrected from the point of view of "early catholicism," in that the paradox of 1:8-10 is softened. The same state of affairs is present in 2:9-11: the equation "walking in the light" = "brotherly love" makes it improbable that this passage derives directly from Gnostic-dualistic views. On the other hand Gnostic motifs are found in other places, for example, in the talk of being begotten by God. From that it follows that the source-fragments identified by Bultmann cannot be brought together into a united structure in terms of content. They contain Christian traditions (i.e. only indirectly Gnostic), but also directly dualistic-Gnostic traditions.

Objections have been raised against source analysis, i.e. the attempt to distinguish between source and redaction, both in view of the linguistic unity of the letter and in view of the structure of its contents and connected train of thought. Käsemann has contested Bultmann's analysis of 1:5*b*–2:2: 2:1-2 does refer to 1:8-10, but not as the misunderstanding of a source, but rather as the antithetical development of the same chain of thought. In 1:8ff the reader is warned against yielding to an imagined sinlessness. This warning is continued in 2:1*a* by the instruction to take the struggle with sin seriously, which one who imagines he or she is sinless is in no position to do. But what is the real situation in such a struggle? The encouragement is given in 2:1*b*: Christ is there as the one who forgives, precisely for whoever seems to be losing this struggle. That is, the warning against imaginary sinlessness makes possible the warning to struggle against sin. But this exegesis eliminates those material criteria which permitted the distinguishing of an earlier source from later editing.

Since it does not appear possible to base a source analysis on stylistic criteria, Nauck has attempted to attribute both the source and the annotations to the same author. An older text was composed as a defense against Gnosticism and then a later, expanded edition was produced by the same author in order to strengthen the church against the false teachers of a later time. But since source and later annotations are now attributed to the same hand, this means practically giving up the effort to identify a separate source. The net result of the discussion is thus to confirm the view that we are not able to interpret I John in terms of sources and redaction, but rather should think in terms of the author's having taken up and reinterpreted different traditions.

O'Neill has made a new attempt at explaining I John: the document is supposed to consist of twelve different sections, each of which is based on a poetic Jewish text. These texts were written or used in the Diaspora by a Jewish sect whose ideas had been influenced by Qumran traditions (cf. the Testaments of the Twelve Patriarchs). The author of I John then supposedly reworked these Jewish texts from a Christian point of view in order to demonstrate that they were fulfilled in Christ. Although this theory includes correct observations concerning the traditions used in I John (see below), the hypothesis as a whole remains an unproved supposition.

The traditions which I John takes up contain on the one hand Hellenistic Gnostic material, for instance the idea of the divine begetting (3:9), and on the other hand a Jewish heritage which manifests striking parallels to the statements of the Qumran community. As at Qumran, the dualism is not understood as physical-metaphysical, but as historical-ethical. Light and darkness, truth and lie, stand over against each other. But the decision for the right side must be manifest in deed. The series of antitheses separate orthodoxy and heresy and are formulated in apodictic sentences similar to the divine law of the OT. As the Qumran community separated itself from the "men of the lie," so I John distinguishes the church from the heretics. With special emphasis, I John cites and interprets early Christian creedal statements (2:22; 4:15; 5:1-5, and others). Thus for example 4:2 cites as the content of faith that Jesus Christ has come in the flesh, thereby taking up a clear anti-Gnostic position.

As was the case with the Gospel of John (see p. 174), Bultmann has also advocated the thesis that I John has been reworked by an ecclesiastical editor. The redactor has inserted references to futuristic eschatology (2:28; 3:2; 4:17) and to the substitutionary death of Christ (1:7, 9; 2:2; 4:10*b*) and thereby undertaken to assimilate the letter to the generally accepted church doctrine. But, differently than in the Gospel, these expressions are sometimes firmly anchored in the structure of the sentences and do not permit themselves to be excised (Nauck, Haenchen). But perhaps in fact the document's conclusion has been appended by a second hand. The impression is given in 5:13 that the author has reached the end: ταυτα εγραψα υμιν ινα ειδητε οτι ζωην εχετε αιωνιον, τοις πιστευουσιν εις το ονομα του υιου του Θεου ("I write this to you who believe in the name of the Son of God, that you may know that you have eternal life"). Then verses 14-21 give the appearance of a secondary expansion which contains a summary, but also introduces a new idea, in that the idea of a mortal sin appears in v. 16. A confident decision can hardly be made, but the possibility that 5:14-21 is a later addition must be kept in mind. For the rest, however, the document has been composed as a linguistic and conceptual unity. Where differences in style emerge, as in the antithetically formulated sentences, these are the result of taking over previously existing tradition, not the use of written sources.

d. Two serious charges are leveled against the false teachers who are combated in I John: their ethic is thoroughly objectionable and their Christology is false. Against the docetic Christology it is emphasized that Christ has come in the flesh (4:2-3), through water and blood (5:6), that is, in baptism and the cross. In Asia Minor around the beginning of the second century

Cerinthus advocated a heretical Christology in which "he affirmed of Jesus that he had not been born of a virgin, but originated like all other humans as the son of Mary and Joseph, only he had been more righteous and wise; and after his baptism the Christ, who came from the Almighty Power, descended on him in the form of a dove, and after this he proclaimed the unknown Father and worked miracles, but finally the Christ separated from Jesus, so that it was Jesus who suffered death and experienced the resurrection, but the Christ, as a spiritual being, remained without suffering" (Irenaeus, adv. Haer. I. 26:1). This description manifests rather similar features to the false teaching opposed in I John, but cannot simply be identified with it, especially since the position of the opponents in I John can only be inferred in rough outline.

For his part, the author of I John develops his christological confession with great vigor: Christ is the Son of God who has become flesh (4:2-3), he died an atoning death for sins (1:7; 2:2; 4:10), he is the σωτηρ του κοσμου ("Savior of the world," 4:14). Thereby he wards off the attack made by the false teachers against the church's Christology, an attack all the more dangerous since it is made by people who once belonged to the same church as the author (2:19). But their teaching now proves that they are εκ του κοσμου ("of the world," 4:5), so that they are followed only by those who are also εκ του κοσμου. In the debate with the Antichrists (2:18ff; 4:1ff), the decision must be made between the spirit of truth and the spirit of error (4:6), and the false prophets are revealed for what they are.

The ethic and manner of life of the false teachers is closely related to the Christology. Because the Gnostics do not take the physical body seriously, they have a docetic Christology (4:2-3) and do not observe the commandments (2:3-4; 5:2-3), especially rejecting the commandment of brotherly love (2:9-11; 3:10, 14-15; 4:8, 20; 5:2). But neglecting brotherly love is the same as fratricide (3:12). The author of the letter emphasizes the unity of faith and action, placing the emphasis on the ethical demand, in order to strengthen the churches against the influence of the false teachers.

e. The name of the author is not given. In any case he must have been a person of considerable stature. Since the similarities of I John to the Gospel of John are obvious, the ancient church tradition identified the author of I John with the fourth evangelist.

The agreements between I John and the Fourth Gospel have to do with both vocabulary and style, as well as the train of thought. Compare John 1:1 εν αρχη ην ο λογος ("in the beginning was the Word") and I John 1:1: ο ην απ αρχης . . . περι του λογου της ζωης ("that which was from the beginning . . . concerning the word of life"). The love-commandment is central to both documents (John 13:34-35; I John 4:20). That the believer already has life (John 3:36; I John 5:12), that the joy of the disciples of Jesus is already complete (John 3:29; 15:11; 16:24; I John 1:4) and the victory over the cosmos is already won (John 16:33; I John 5:4-5), to name only a few items, are presented both in the Gospel and Epistle of John. One could in fact rather easily surmise that both writings are to be attributed to the same author.

But a closer look reveals that there are also some important differences between I John and the Gospel. Verses 1 and 14 of John use the λογος ("logos, word") concept absolutely, while I John in contrast has περι του λογου της ζωης ("concerning the word of life," 1:1) or ο λογος του Θεου ("the word of God," 2:14). In John 14–16 the Paraclete means the Spirit of Truth, but in I John 2:1 it means the exalted Christ. In I John 1:3-7 the expression κοινωνιαν μετα [τινος] ("fellowship with" [someone]) is used four times, but is completely absent from the Fourth Gospel. On the other hand, such important terms for the Gospel as δοξα ("glory") and δοξαζω ("glorify"), and the christological expressions καταβαινω/αναβαινω ("descend/ascend") are missing from I John. And the Gospel lacks words such as χρισμα ("anointing," 2:20, 27), σπερμα ("seed"; RSV "nature," 3:9). First John speaks of the Antichrists (2:18, 22; 4:3; cf. II John 7), but the Gospel does not.

Also to be noticed are a number of not inconsiderable differences between the train of thought of I John and that of the Fourth Gospel (Dodd): (1) while in the Gospel a realized eschatology is strongly emphasized (3:18; 5:24-25), which is supplemented by the redactor's futuristic eschatology (5:28-29; 6:39, 40, 44, 54), in I John the expectation of the parousia is described with the expressions generally used in early Christianity: παρουσια ("parousia, coming," 2:28; cf. also 3:2), ημερα της κρισεως ("day of judgment," 4:17). Thus I John stands nearer to the typical early Christian eschatology than the

Gospel of John. (2) In I John the references to the atoning death of Christ are to be attributed not to a redactor, but to the author himself (1:7, 9; 2:2; 4:10; 5:7-8). In contrast, in the Fourth Gospel it is the redactor who underscored that blood and water came forth from the wound in Christ's side, thereby grounding the sacraments of baptism and the Lord's Supper in the death of Christ (19:34*b*-35). (3) Likewise the pneumatology of I John remains within the bounds of the typical early Christian ideas. The idea of the Paraclete as the Spirit of Truth is not present. (4) While for the Gospel of John the present is determined by the contrast between light and darkness (1:4-5; 3:19-21; 12:35, 46), Christ is named as the light of the world, and believers have come out of darkness into light (8:12), in I John light and darkness are thought of as a temporal series: "The darkness passes away, and the true light already shines" (I John 2:8). The christological affirmation (John 8:12) is transformed into an affirmation about God: **ο Θεος φως εστιν και σκοτια εν αυτω ουκ εστιν ουδεμια** ("God is light and in him is no darkness at all," I John 1:5). Thus I John presupposes the Fourth Gospel and reformulates its theology, because the eschatological qualification of the present, as it is developed in the Gospel of John, was perceived by the author of I John as a problem which had not been sufficiently resolved as time continued on toward its appointed end (Klein). The relation of I John to the Gospel of John can easily be compared to the relation of the Pastoral Letters to the authentic Letters of Paul, so that I John could be described as precisely a Johannine Pastoral Letter (Conzelmann), which emphasizes the importance of tradition for the life and work of the church much more strongly than does the Fourth Gospel (1:1-4).

f. The issues of the time and place of composition of I John are affected by these considerations concerning the question of authorship. The debate with Gnostic false teachers could point to Asia Minor (Cerinthus!). The similarities in content to the Gospel of John, on the one hand and to the letters of Ignatius of Antioch on the other hand, could also speak for Syria. It is not possible to be certain. The time of composition is probably about the beginning of the second century. First John was apparently written after the Gospel, but may not be dated too late, since it was possibly already known to Polycarp of Smyrna (7:1 as a reference to I John 4:2 and 3:8, among others), and certainly quoted by Justin Martyr (*Dial*. 123:9 = I John 3:2).

g. A special problem is presented by the so-called *Comma Johanneum*. In the Latin translation of the Bible 5:7-8 is found in an expanded form, in which the words *Spirit, water*, and *blood* are explained in the following words: *Quoniam tres sunt, qui testimonium dant in terra, spiritus [et] aqua et sanguis, et hi tres unum sunt in Christo Jesu. Et tres sunt, qui testimonium dant in coelo, pater, verbum et spiritus, et hi tres unum sunt* ("for there are three that bear witness in earth, the Spirit [and] the water and the blood, and these three are one in Christ Jesus. And there are three who bear witness in heaven, the Father, the Word, and the Spirit, and these three are one.") Within the entire Greek textual tradition, only four minuscules have this form of the text, which is missing from all other Greek manuscripts. This expansion of the text was understood in the Western church as New Testament documentation for the doctrine of the Trinity. It is in fact an old variation of the Latin text which originated as an allegorical interpretation of the true witnesses in order to understand them as representing the Trinity. Today it is generally and correctly recognized that the *Comma Johanneum* is a secondary addition to the text of I John (see W. Reich, "Beobachtungen zum Comma Johanneum," *ZNW* 50 [1959] 61-73).

#35 The Second and Third Letters of John

Cf. Bibliography to #34.
Bornkamm, G. "πρεσβυς κτλ," *TDNT*, 6:670-72.
Bergmeier, R. "Zum Verfasserproblem des II. und III. Johannesbriefes," *ZNW* 57 (1966):93-100.

a. Contents: The Second Letter of John (= II) begins with an introductory greeting (1:1-3). This is followed by the main part of the letter which contains an admonition to keep the commandments, above all the commandment of brotherly love, and a warning against false teachers who deny the reality of the incarnation (4-11). At the conclusion an imminent visit of the author is announced and greetings are communicated (12-13).

After a brief opening greeting (v. 1), the main part of the Third Letter of John (= III) praises the recipient of the letter for his life in the truth and his hospitality to traveling missionaries (3-8). To this is joined a sharp censure against Diotrephes, who has arrogated to himself a leading role and refuses to welcome the brethren (9-10). On the other hand a certain Demetrius is commended (11-12). In conclusion the author announces that he will soon pay a personal visit, and communicates greetings (13-15).

b. The occasion and purpose are obvious from the letters themselves. Both letters are kept short, each about the size of one papyrus page. It is not a matter of private correspondence, however, but of official communication of an elder to a congregation (II) or to an individual (III). The Second Letter is addressed to the elect lady and her children. This is not to be understood as an individual woman, but the church and its members. It is urged to keep the commandments and to reject false teachers. The Third Letter names Gaius as the recipient. The congregation to which he belongs is being tyrannized by a certain Diotrephes who has rejected the authority of the elder.

This incident involving Diotrephes has been interpreted by Käsemann (see p. 184) as follows: Diotrephes was the monarchial bishop and as such the representative of the official church leadership. He is supposed to have excommunicated the elder, who was the official in a local congregation, because of his advocacy of a Gnostic-tinged theology. The elder, now branded as a heretic, offers his resistance in III. Precisely this elder was not only the author of III, but also of the other Johannine Letters, and even of the Gospel of John, so that the witness of the Johannine writings is the composition of an excommunicated heretic.

This reconstruction however is not tenable, for the letter indicates neither that it was because of the elder's theology that he came into conflict with Diotrephes nor that Diotrephes had effected an excommunication. The title "elder" is not used as the description of an office in a local congregation, as though he were an elder within a board of elders. But the elder exercises an extra-congregational authority which is resisted by Diotrephes in a different congregation (Bornkamm). The conflict is thus to be understood as a dispute about church order on the local congregational level. As the leader of a local church, Diotrephes resists being told what to do by someone outside.

c. The author is described in both letters as an "elder." This is certainly no reference to his age, but rather a title. Since the elder represents the guarantor of apostolic tradition, the suggestion comes readily to mind—and has in fact often been made—that this elder is to be identified with the elder John of the Papias fragments (see pp. 180-81). But since the name John is not mentioned in II and III John, this view can be no more than pure supposition.

It is readily apparent that II and III are similar to I in language and content. The Second Letter takes up the two themes which are constantly dealt with in I: the admonition to brotherly love and the warning against false teachers. On the other hand there are also certain differences from I. The letter form used in II and III distinguishes them from I. The words φιλοπροτευω ("likes to put himself first," III 9), φλυαρε ("prate," III 10), and μελαν ("ink," II 12; III 13) are not found in the Gospel of John or I John. Other concepts are reminiscent of phrases from the Synoptics or from Paul, as for example εχαρην λιαν ("I greatly rejoiced," II 4; III 3); βλεπετε εαυτους ("look to yourselves," II 8): μισθον πληρη απολαβητε ("win a full reward," II 8), συνεργοι γενωμεθα ("we may be fellow workers," III 8), ο αγαθοποιων ("he who does good," III 11) (Jülicher). The concept αληθεια ("truth") in II and III is not used in dualistic contrast to ψευδος ("lie") or πλανη ("error"), as in I, but serves as the description of right doctrine or of true faith and Christian life (Bergmeier).

Bultmann would like not only to separate II and III from I, but also to distinguish II and III from each other: the letter form of II can only be a literary fiction, in which the author has made use of both I and III. The concluding remark in II 12-13 is in imitation of III 13-14 and the designation of the author by the simple ο πρεσβυτερος ("the elder") is also most likely only an imitation of III 1. (In *RGG*[3] on the other hand, Bultmann still regarded II and III as real letters, but from a different author than I.)

On the one hand, the brevity of II and III present no adequate basis for forming a confident judgment on stylistic observations. On the other hand, the above-mentioned arguments require caution. To be sure, II and III are undeniably close to I, but that does not necessarily mean identity of authorship. One can say no more than that II and III were written in the same theological school as I.

d. Place and time of composition are to be placed in the vicinity of I, i.e. the letters presumably were written in Syria—or Asia Minor—at the beginning of the second century.

VIII.

The Other New Testament Letters

Hebrews was considered to be Pauline in wide circles of the early church and therefore in most manuscripts was placed after the letters to Pauline churches and before the Pastorals and Philemon—in P^{46} it stands between Romans and I Corinthians. On the other hand, the Letters of James, I and II Peter, I–III John and Jude were called Catholic Letters (see pp. 183-94). In the course of history up to the closing of the canon, the idea developed that there were seven Catholic Letters (cf. the seven letters in the Apocalypse). Canonical recognition for some letters was contested for a long time, until it was settled by the Easter letter of Athanasius in A.D. 367 (see p. 24). The term *catholic,* which was first used to characterize a letter by the apologete Apollonius at the end of the second century (Eus. H. E. V.18:5) is intended to affirm that the whole church is addressed in such a letter. Dionysius of Alexandria names I John "the catholic letter" (Eus. H. E. VII. 25:7)—obviously, because in I John no addressee is named, so that one could suppose it was written for the whole church. In the strict sense, of course, this characterization does not fit I John, because, although the name of the recipients is lacking, still the circumstances of a particular group of churches is presupposed (see pp. 188-89). Still less can

II and III John be characterized as "catholic," for the addressees are clearly indicated (see p. 193). First Peter is addressed to Christians in Asia Minor—to be sure, a widely scattered readership, but still not the universal church. At the most, the word *catholic* could properly be used for James, which is addressed to the twelve tribes of the Dispersion, II Peter, whose addressees are "those who have obtained a faith of equal standing with ours in the righteousness of our God and Savior Jesus Christ," and Jude, which addresses "those who are called, beloved in God the Father and kept for Jesus Christ." These statements are kept general enough that they can be understood to include all Christianity. Eusebius is the first to speak of seven Catholic Letters (H. E. II. 23:24-25). In the West they were also called *epistulae canonicae,* because they were letters generally accepted as apostolic and therefore were numbered among the canonical books. In the Greek manuscripts the Eastern churches almost always placed the Catholic Letters immediately after Acts, because they were attributed to the original apostles; but in the West the seven Catholic Letters were usually preceded by the Pauline Letters.

#36 The Letter to the Hebrews

Harnack, A. v. "Probabilia über die Adresse und den Verfasser des Hebr," *ZNW* 1 (1900):16-41.
Michel, O. *Der Brief an die Hebräer,* 1936, [6]1966.
Käsemann, E. *Das wandernde Gottesvolk,* 1939, [4]1961.
Yadin, Y. "The Dead Sea Scrolls and the Epistle to the Hebrews," in *Scripta Hierosolymitana* 4 (1958):36-55.
Kosmala, H., *Hebräer—Essener—Christen,* 1959.
Grässer, E. *Der Glaube im Hebräerbrief,* 1965.
Theissen, G. *Untersuchungen zum Hebräerbrief,* 1969.
Hofius, O. *Katapausis,* 1970.
Buchanan, G. W. *Hebrews,* 1972.
Strobel, A. *Der Brief an die Hebräer,* 1975.

a. Contents: Hebrews is not divided into a doctrinal part followed by a hortatory part, but contains direct parenetical address to the readers in several different places throughout the letter. The first major section describes the superiority of the revelation of God in the Son (1:1–4:13): the Son as bearer of the final revelation (1:1-14), the magnitude of our responsibility

(2:1-4, parenesis); the temporary humiliation of the Son as the precondition for the exercise of his high-priestly office (2:5-18), the superiority of the Son to Moses (3:1-6), the warning not to miss the rest which God has promised (3:7–4:13).

The second major section presents Jesus as the true high priest (4:14–10:18): the fulfillment of all the qualifications for the office of high priest by Jesus (4:14–5:10), the turning toward the λογος τελειος ("mature understanding"), the warning against apostasy in view of the impossibility of a second repentance (5:11–6:20, parenesis). Then comes the elaboration of the doctrine of Jesus as the true high priest (7:1–10:18): Jesus the perfect high priest after the order of Melchizedek (chapter 7), Jesus the high priest in the heavenly sanctuary and mediator of the new covenant (chapter 8), the sacrifice made by the high priest (chapter 9), the inadequacy of the OT sacrifices in contrast to the sacrifice made by Christ (10:1-18).

This longest doctrinal part is followed by the longest parenetical section, the challenge to remain true to the faith (10:19–13:17): holding fast to the confession (10:19-39), a homily concerning faith (chapter 11), instructions for the congregation (12:1-29), various admonitions (13:1-21), and conclusion (13:22-25).

b. The determination of the literary character of Hebrews is made difficult by the fact that the writing begins without the customary introductory forms found in a letter, but concludes like a letter with greetings and brief personal communications. The possibility that an original introductory prescript has been lost must be excluded, for the artfully formed periodic sentence of 1:1-4 is without doubt the beginning of the document. Hebrews is characterized by its homiletical style and describes itself as a λογος της παρακλησεως ("word of exhortation," 13:22). It alternates between doctrinal instruction and parenesis, so that the chain of thought reaches its high point in direct address to the reader. Thus in Hebrews we have extracts from early Christian preaching which have been written down in order to be read to the congregation (Michel). The sermon is closely related to OT texts: Psalm 8 in chapter 2; Psalm 95 in chapters 3–4; Psalm 110 in chapter 5 (taken up again in chapter 7); Jeremiah 31 in chapter 8; Psalm 40 in chapter 10. The style is reminiscent of the Hellenistic synagogue preaching, as represented for example in Philo of Alexandria or in IV Maccabees.

The sermonlike character of the writing makes an introduction such as 1:1-4 understandable, just as it does the direct address to the community and the letterlike conclusion. The author is not writing a treatise or theological essay, but directs his writing to a particular congregation whose problems he knows, and which he wants to help by instruction and warning.

Hebrews emphasizes the incomparable greatness of the revelation which has happened in Christ. The salvation provided by Christ is described in contrast to the old covenant. Thereby sacrifice and ritual are not described from within their own point of view, but are portrayed exclusively with reference to the OT in order to show that Christ is incomparably superior to them all. He has once and for all offered the authentic sacrifice. To this proof from Scripture the parenesis is then joined. The readers obviously stand in danger of giving up or apostacizing. Thus they are told: whoever apostacizes cannot repent a second time; there is a remorse which cries in vain (6:4-6; 10:26; 12:17). The warning that a second repentance is impossible is intended only to impress the danger of apostasy upon the congregation so that no one incurs the loss of σωτηρια ("salvation"). As the αρχηγος της σωτηριας ("pioneer of [their] salvation," 2:10), the προδρομοσ ("forerunner," 6:20), the αρχηγος και τελειωτης της πιστεως ("pioneer and perfecter of our faith," 12:2), Christ has prepared the way; the wandering people of God are to follow him (Käsemann). Thus the reader and hearer are challenged to take advantage of the possibility made available by the death of Christ and appropriated by baptism, and in faithful obedience to enter into the sanctuary opened up by Christ in order to receive grace and mercy (4:16; 10:19).

c. The introduction of the document does not state who the recipients of Hebrews were, since the greeting and address of the typical letter are lacking. The title προς Εϐραιους ("to the Hebrews") was not added to the document until later. The obvious intent was to designate the addressees in a way analogous to the Pauline Letters, and it was supposed that these addressees could be inferred to be "Hebrews" from the typological-allegorical use of the OT in the letter. The superscription "To the Hebrews" is documented already around A.D. 200, first in Pantaenus (quoted in Eus. H. E. VI. 14:4), then in Clement of Alexandria, the manuscript P^{46} and in Tertullian.

In the ancient church the dominant view was that the readers were Jewish Christians. In support of this view, which is also maintained by a few exegetes today, it is said that the writing presupposes a precise knowledge of both the OT and the priestly rituals in the temple. Since the Jewish community at Qumran expected, in addition to the messianic king, also a priestly Messiah, the view has recently been advocated that the high-priestly Christology of Hebrews suggests that the readership was a group who had been members of the Qumran community who had been converted to Christianity (Yadin), or else a religious movement which had separated from the Qumran sect but had not yet come to faith in Jesus (Kosmala). But the teaching concerning the high priest in Hebrews manifests hardly any features comparable to the ideas of the Qumran community, and the form and content of Hebrews is of a thoroughly Hellenistic sort. In fact, Hebrews gives no reason at all to suppose that the readers were located in Jerusalem or Palestine. According to 6:10 they had often helped needy Christians, but the poverty-striken church in Jerusalem itself had to receive help from others. According to 2:3 they did not belong to those who had personally heard the preaching of Jesus: "It [salvation] was declared at first by the Lord, and it was attested to us by those who heard him." This statement would not fit the Jerusalem church, in which the gospel was first preached. In 10:32-34*a* persecution is spoken of, which the readers had endured soon after their conversion. But the Jerusalem congregation had to withstand more than one persecution. Thus if one wants to identify the readers as Jewish Christians, they must be located somewhere outside Palestine. But the real question is whether the readers were in fact Jewish Christians at all.

The predominant view in the more recent exegesis is that the readers were Gentile Christians. When in 6:1 it is said that the people had received instruction concerning repentance from dead works and faith in God, it is the basic elements of the missionary preaching to Gentiles which are named. In 9:14 it is said that the blood of Christ cleanses our consciences from dead works so that we can serve the living God. The pre-Christian past could not possibly be characterized by the expression "dead works" if it referred to those who once had been Jews. If detailed quotations are given from the OT, followed by long explanations, this by no means necessarily presupposes that the readers must once have been Jews (cf. Gal., Rom.!). Gentile Christians also studied the Scripture and understood its exposition. The discussions concerning temple and ritual nowhere presuppose direct acquaintance with the procedures in Jerusalem, but are derived exclusively from the Scripture. Thus Gentile Christians are addressed, who are warned of the danger of apostasy and are challenged to hold fast to their confession.

Where are these Gentile Christian readers of Hebrews to be located? The late superscription "To the Hebrews" provides no point of departure for answering this question. A few indications could point to Italy or even Rome. In I Clement, composed in Rome at the end of the first century, Hebrews is already quoted (17:1; 36:2-5). (See below.) Hebrews 13:24 sends greetings from those in Italy. Christians who, like the author, are separated from the congregation, want to strengthen their relationship with the congregation by these greetings. Thus one could suppose that Christians in Italy send their greetings to the church in Rome. The Neronian persecution lies in the past, but new trials stand before them.

d. The document provides no indication of who the author may have been. In the East the letter was regarded as Pauline from a very early time. In the West, of course Hebrews was known at an early date, but was not considered Pauline and canonical until about A.D. 350. It was only through the influence of the Eastern church that the West accepted Hebrews into the canon as a Pauline writing, in the period between A.D. 350 and 400.

As efforts to guess the name of the unknown author, the following possibilities have been proposed:

(1) For the traditional view that Paul is the author, one might first mention that the conclusion of Hebrews, like the Pauline Letters, contains personal communications, greetings, and admonitions. Timothy, mentioned in 13:23, belongs to the inner circle of Paul's co-workers. And then it could be pointed out that the theology of Hebrews is in several respects comparable to that of Paul. The new covenant which takes the place of the old is grounded in Christ's atoning death (7:18ff; 8:6ff/II Cor. 3:6ff). As the mediator of creation Christ already possessed the divine glory before his incarnation (1:1ff/I Cor. 8:6; Phil. 2:6-11). In

Hebrews Christ is proclaimed as the end of the law with reference to the cultic law, by Paul with regard to the Torah as such.

But the differences between Paul and Hebrews are much more weighty than these comparable aspects. (a) The language and style of Hebrews are considerably different from that of Paul. Hebrews contains 168 *hapax legomena* which are without parallel in the other NT writings, plus an additional 124 words which are not found in Paul. The language of Hebrews corresponds to the sophisticated Hellenistic Greek style. The opening sentence begins with an artful alliteration: πολυμερως, πολυτροπως, παλαι, πατρασιν, προφηταις ("many, various, old, fathers, prophets: in Greek all begin with 'p'"); a play on words is found in 5:8: εμαθεν αφ ων επαθεν (*emathen aph hon epathen*—"he learned through what he suffered"; the word play is lost in translation). While Paul sometimes fails to complete his sentences (anacolutha), Hebrews manifests a regular, carefully rounded sentence structure. (b) Most of Paul's letters are divided into a doctrinal and a parenetical part, while Hebrews in contrast—but corresponding to homiletical custom—is interlaced with parenetical sections which break up the doctrinal train of thought. (c) Quotations from the OT in Hebrews are never introduced by the formulas usually used by Paul, such as γεγραπαι, η γραφη λεγει ("it is written"; "the Scripture says") and others, but we find: God, his Son, the Holy Spirit, or "someone" says, and so forth. The OT is regularly cited according to the LXX, never from memory. (d) According to 2:3 the author numbers himself among those who have been instructed by those who personally heard the preaching of Jesus, i.e. by Jesus' disciples. In contrast Paul emphasizes his independence from the original Jerusalem apostles (Gal. 1–2). (e) There are also considerable differences in Christology. The title of high priest frequently attributed to Jesus in Hebrews is never used by Paul. Instead of the resurrection, Hebrews speaks mainly of the ascension of Christ by which he became High Priest. The formalized expression εν Χριστω ("in Christ") is lacking in Hebrews. (f) While Paul in Romans 10:4 speaks of Christ as the end of the law, so that the law has once and for all been excluded as a means of salvation, Hebrews is only concerned to deal with the cultic stipulations of the law. The issue of the significance of the law for salvation is no longer present for Hebrews, for the law is understood by the author as a lower level of revelation which has now been left behind (10:1). (g) There is no affirmation of the *justificatio impii* ("justification of the ungodly") in Hebrews, although Habakkuk 2:4 is cited in 10:38.

It follows from this series of contrasts that Hebrews cannot be attributed to Paul either directly or indirectly (i.e. to a disciple of Paul). Luther perceived the conflict with Paul very clearly, when in the preface to his September Bible of 1522 he described the rejection of a second repentance as contrary to all the Gospels and the Letters of Paul, but in other respects thought that Hebrews was an uncommonly fine letter which speaks masterfully of the priesthood of Christ from a solid scriptural basis.

(2) Clement of Alexandria supposed that Luke could be the translator of a letter written by Paul in Hebrew (Eus. H. E. VI. 14:2-3). But this view is meaningless, for Hebrews simply cannot be seen as the translation of an original Hebrew text.

(3) Origen was already acquainted with the hypothesis that Clement of Rome wrote Hebrews. Then I Clement, which quotes Hebrews (see above), would have to have the same author; in any case there is no evidence to support this suggestion.

(4) Since Tertullian, Barnabas has also been considered a possibility. Since he was a Levite from Cyprus, it has been thought possible to credit him with the extensive description of the Old Testament cultus. But this suggestion also is no more than supposition.

(5) Nor is the case any different with the idea which repeatedly emerges that Hebrews could have been written by Apollos. As an Alexandrian, Apollos had certainly received an education in rhetoric and biblical scholarship (Acts 18:24ff; I Cor. 1:12; 3:4ff; 16:12). But that by no means indicates it must be he who stands behind the scholarly exposition of Hebrews.

(6) The suggestion of v. Harnack, that the married couple Aquila and Priscilla wrote Hebrews, is as original as it is fantastic. The author's "we" is supposedly thereby explained. But because authorship by a woman had seemed offensive to some, the prescript was early removed and the idea that this scholarly document was to be credited to a woman was suppressed.

None of these suppositions succeeds in solving the puzzle. The name of the author will probably never be known. The matter remains where Origen left it, that God alone knows who wrote

Hebrews. Nonetheless, the theological position of the author is set forth in all clarity, an author who wants to strengthen the second Christian generation against temptation and slackness, in that in his theological model he seeks to have faith understood as simply identical with being a Christian (Grässer).

e. The approximate time of writing can be determined for Hebrews on the basis of the following considerations. The portrayal of the temple cultus does not necessarily presuppose that the temple must still be standing. Rather, the argument is always on the basis of Scripture and not on the basis of personal observation of the cultic practice, so these expositions offer no basis for deciding whether the author wrote before or after A.D. 70. On the other hand, Hebrews is already known by the end of the first century. To be sure, it is not uncontested that Hebrews is quoted in I Clement (see above), because, so it is argued, it could be a matter of both documents taking up a common oral tradition (Theissen). The echoes of the wording of Hebrews are however so strong, that it is more likely a matter of direct quotation of Hebrews. Author and readers belong to the second Christian generation (2:3), therefore the most reasonable date for the composition of Hebrews is the decade between A.D. 80 and 90.

#37 The Letter of James

Meyer, A. *Das Rätsel des Jakobusbriefes,* 1930.

Kittel, G. "Der geschichtliche Ort des Jakobusbriefes," *ZNW* 41 (1942):71-105.

———. "Der Jakobusbrief und die apostolischen Väter," *ZNW* 43 (1950/51):55-112.

Lohse, E. "Glaube und Werke: Zur Theologie des Jakobusbriefes" (1957), in *Die Einheit des NT,* 1973, 285-306.

Dibelius, M., and Greeven, H. *A Commentary on the Letter of James,* 1976.

a. Contents: James contains proverbial wisdom and pārenesis, in loosely connected series of sayings: introductory greeting (1:1), concerning temptations (1:2-18), concerning hearing and doing (1:19-27), concerning respect of persons (2:1-13), concerning faith and works (2:14-26), concerning the danger inherent in the teacher's profession, and the power of the tongue

(3:1-12), against quarrelsomeness (3:13–4:12), against worldly minded merchants and the rich (4:13–5:6), words of consolation and warning (5:7-12), rules for various situations (5:13-20).

b. The peculiar literary character of James is impressed upon the document by the parenesis which it presents (Dibelius). The document begins with a greeting in 1:1, but no letter-formulas are found at the end. James is addressed to the twelve tribes of the Dispersion (1:1). Since no particular Jewish questions are discussed in the parenesis, but generally applicable rules for living, it is obviously not Jews who are addressed, but Christians who live in the world as the Israel of God.

The introductory greeting χαιρειν (lit. "rejoice") is linked to the following verse by word association (χαραν, "joy," v. 2). The epistolary introduction has thus been prefaced to James in order to direct it to all Christians as an open letter.

The instructions for the conduct of Christians in the world make extensive use of traditional materials. Old Testament Jewish wisdom, proverbial tradition, statements from Hellenistic popular philosophy and early Christian sayings have been patched together to form a colorful wreath. The series of admonitions contains only two references to the name of Jesus: the introductory greeting in 1:1 and a second time in 2:1. The speculation occasionally expressed in earlier times, that one could have the original, purely Jewish writing simply by removing Jesus' name from these two places, is not correct. In the first place, the debate concerning the relation of faith and works in 2:14-26 cannot be made understandable from Jewish presuppositions alone; it rather necessarily presupposes the debate concerning Paul's theology (see below p. 207). And in the second place, many places in James contain echoes of and points of contact with sayings of Jesus which are transmitted in the Synoptic tradition (see below p. 206). James is therefore clearly a Christian writing, which has, however, made extensive use of Jewish and Hellenistic parenetic tradition.

A. Meyer sought to answer the question of the Jewish traditional material in James by the hypothesis that James was the reworking of a Jewish source which had been a Testament of Jacob, in which the patriarch gave his last will and testament to each of his twelve sons (cf. Gen. 49). The James of 1:1 originally meant the OT Jacob, and then there followed in order (as can still be recognized by allegorical connections) first, allusions to Isaac (= χαρα, "joy," 1:2), Rebecca (υπομονη, "steadfastness," 1:4) and Jacob's struggles and temptations (1:12ff). From 1:18 on the sons of Jacob are addressed: Reuben (απαρχη, "first fruits," 1:18), Simeon (ακουειν, "hear," 1:19), Levi (θρησκεια, "religion," 1:27), and so forth. The references to Jacob and his sons which are supposed to be present in these texts could in some cases appear to be discussible, but more often are dragged in violently, as for example when the argumentation of 2:14-26, that faith without works is dead, is interpreted allegorically as Rachel's infertility. According to Meyer this Jewish source was reworked in post-Pauline times. The extreme degree of allegorical art which this theory sees as fundamental to James raises the question of why straightforward parenesis should be clothed in a form so difficult to understand. The speculation that we are dealing with a document which was originally Jewish testamentary literature thus cannot be persuasive; still, it was correctly recognized that James takes a large proportion of his material from Jewish tradition.

The closest parallels to James in the NT are found in the parenetical sections of the Pauline Letters (I Thess. 4:1-12; Rom. 12–13; Col. 3–4) and in the Sermon on the Mount/Plain in the Gospels. The parenesis of these sections and of James is characterized by the typical features of this category of material (Dibelius): (1) Eclecticism. Sayings of various ancestry—Jewish, Hellenistic, early Christian—are patched together, often with minimal Christianizing or none at all. (2) The lack of context. The various units are for the most part linked together only loosely, frequently by no more than word-association (see p. 113), as for example χαιρειν/χαρα ("greeting/joy," 1:1, 2); λειπομενοι/λειπεται ("lacking/lack," 1:4, 5); διακρινομενος ("doubting," twice in 1:6); πειρασμον/πειραζομενος ("trial/tempted," 1:12, 13); θρησκεια ("religion," twice in 1:26-27), among others. (3) Because the material is arranged according to form and not according to content, the same motif often recurs in different places: 1:21 and 3:13ff exhort to meekness; 1:26 and 3:3ff warn against sins of the tongue; 1:2-4, 12, and 5:7ff urge endurance in suffering; 1:9ff, 2:1ff, and 5:1ff speak against the rich. (4) The lack of a specific situation. Parenetic material is intended to be universally applicable. Thus for example the polemic against the rich permits no conclusions to be drawn with regard to a particular church situation.

c. The theological setting of James may be determined more closely by a comparison of parallel statements in other writings of the NT. To begin with, noticeable contacts are found with sayings of Jesus in the Synoptic Gospels. These are, however, never introduced or cited as such, but are simply woven into the series of exhortations. Just as Jesus forbade his disciples to use oaths, this is also prohibited to Christians in James, and they are commanded that their yes should mean yes and their no should mean no (Matt. 5:34-37; James 5:12). The promise that one may pray in confidence that God hears prayer is found in a saying of Jesus (Matt. 7:7) and in James 1:5. The Sermon on the Mount ends with the compelling challenge to do the word of Jesus (Matt. 7:24-27), and in James 1:22 it is said, "Be doers of the word and not hearers only." Both Jesus and James are absolutely opposed to judging the brother (Matt. 7:1-2; James 4:11-12). A considerably longer list of such contacts could be made, and in none of them is it simply a matter of sayings which accidentally sound alike, but rather sayings of the Lord have consciously been taken up into the parenesis of James. The different forms of the sayings simply show that no literary dependence is present. Rather, orally transmitted parenetic traditions have been taken up into the Sermon on the Mount on the one hand, and have been combined into somewhat catechetical complexes in James, on the other.

All sorts of parallels exist between James and the parenetical sections of the other epistolary literature. One example: Paul puts forth a sorites in Romans 5:3-5, "we rejoice in tribulation, because we know"—and now a chain of ideas is attached—"that θλιψις ('suffering') works υπομονη ('endurance') endurance produces character (δοκιμη), and character produces hope (ελπις)." The high point is reached with hope, which represents a most beautiful result of what can be attained from θλιψεις ("sufferings"). A similar chain is found in I Peter 1:6-7: Christians rejoice, "though now for a little while you may have to suffer various trials (πειρασμοις ποικιλοις) so that the genuineness το δοκιμον of your faith, more precious than gold which though perishable is tested by fire, may redound to praise and glory and honor at the revelation of Jesus Christ." Thus here it is said: in the afflictions which Christians have to endure, faith proves its genuineness. James 1:2-4 contains a chain of thought which is closely related to both passages from Romans 5 and I Peter 1. The readers are called upon to "count it all joy, my brothers, when you meet various trials (ποικιλοις πειπασμοις), for you know that the testing (το δοκιμον) of your faith produces steadfastness (υπομονην κατεργαζεται). Let steadfastness have its full effect, that you may be perfect and complete, lacking in nothing." As in Romans 5 so also here υπομονη ("endurance, steadfastness") is spoken of as the result of trials as well as its power to stand the test. But while Paul uses the concept of θλιψεις ("sufferings"), I Peter has the same expression as James, ποικιλοι πειρασμοι ("various trials"). First Peter refers to the situation of persecution; James, on the other hand, means the difficulties of everyday life beneath which a Christian may groan. But he should accept such hardships, because thereby υπομονη is strengthened, and this then brings forth the precious fruit of perfection and blamelessness. The comparison of James 1:2-4 with Romans 5:3-5 and I Peter 1:6-7 thus shows that the concepts and chains of thought in all three places derive from oral tradition. But in James the traditional material has been placed under the heading of perfection, for which the Christian should strive.

The section 2:14-26 stands out from the network of instruction as an integrated argument which provides a theological foundation for the parenesis. The thesis, faith without works cannot save, is developed in a debate with sloganistic mottoes behind which Pauline theology certainly stood originally. But the Pauline understanding of πιστις ("faith") is hardly preserved in these slogans nor is anything said concerning the decisive issue of the law. So the argument does not proceed on the basis of an accurate knowledge of Pauline theology. Rather, the author undertakes a demarcation against misunderstood Pauline slogans in order to emphasize that cooperation of faith and works which should lead to the goal of Christian perfection.

d. As the name of the author, 1:1 gives Ιακωβος Θεου και Κυριου Ιησου Χριστου δουλος ("James, a servant of God and of the Lord Jesus Christ"). Since a personality of great prestige is thereby intended, only James the Lord's brother can be meant, for James the Son of Zebedee had died an early death (Acts 12:2). Thus the question is posed, whether James the Lord's brother could have written the Letter of James. The NT reports that the resurrected Jesus appeared to him (I Cor. 15:7), that he became a member of the earliest Jerusalem church (Acts 1:14), and later took over its leadership (Gal. 2:1-10). The tradition is found in Hegesippus that he also enjoyed great respect among the Jews and finally was condemned to death by the High Priest Ananus and died by stoning (Eus. H. E. II. 23:4ff). The thesis that it was in fact this James who was the author of our document—even with the help of a secretary (for the secretary hypothesis, see p. 48)—has been advocated especially by Kittel with the following arguments: (1) the simple self-description as a servant of God and the Lord speaks for the early days of the church, in which the earliest Jerusalem church was led by James; (2) it was by virtue of this position that he had the authority to write to the twelve tribes of the Dispersion, i.e. the Jewish Christians; (3) the multitude of contacts with the sayings of Jesus point to someone close to the historical Jesus; (4) Palestinian tradition is recognizable in the letter, as for example when 1:5, 17, and elsewhere use a passive expression in order to avoid using the name of God. Kittel would like to date the composition of James even before the apostolic conference, i.e. before A.D. 48. In that case the polemic in 2:14-16 would not be directed against the Pauline Letters, since they did not yet exist, but against rumors and reports which had come to the author's attention.

But these arguments do not persuade: (1) the self-description as δουλος says nothing to the issue of the date; (2) the twelve tribes includes all Christians, not just Jewish Christians; (3) the oral tradition of Jesus' words continued far into the second century, especially in connection with parenesis *(Didache!)*; (4) alongside traditions which without doubt do come from Palestine, the author also takes over Hellenistic tradition, from the Cynic-Stoic diatribe material. An early date—prior to the Pauline Letters—cannot be held in view of 2:14-26 (see below).

Authorship by James the Lord's brother is to be excluded especially for the following reasons: (1) language and style indicate a notably good Greek of the high Koine. Word plays are found in many places, e.g. φαινομενη—αφανιζομενη ("appears/vanishes," 4:14); διεκριθητε—κριται ("made distinctions"/[become] "judges," 2:4); αδιακριτος—ανυποκριτος ("without uncertainty"/"without insincerity," 3:17); χαιρειν—χαραν ("greeting/joy," 1:1-2); εργων—αργη ("works/barren," 2:20). Alliteration is repeatedly used: πειρασμοις περιπεσητε ποικιλοις (*peirasmois peripesete poikilois:* "you meet various trials," 1:2); μικρον μελος—μεγαλα (*mikron melos—megala:* "little member—great things," 3:5). A rhyme is found in 1:14: εξελκομενος και δελεαζομενος (*exelkomenos kai deleazomenos:* "lured and enticed"), and in 1:17*a*—perhaps accidental?—hexameter. Occasional Hebraisms are to be explained by use of the LXX, as for example ποιειν ελεος (lit.: "do mercy," 2:13); ποιητης λογου ("doer of the word") in 1:22, ποιητης νομου ("doer of the law") in 4:11; προσωπον της γενεσεως (lit.: "face of [his] birth = natural face") in 1:23 or the use of nouns in place of adjectives: ακροατης επιλησμονης (lit.: "hearer of forgetfulness") in 1:25; η ευχη της πιστεως ("the prayer of faith") in 5:15 among others. On the other hand no Aramaisms are found—a proof of the fact that the language of James is a cultivated Greek influenced by biblical expressions from the Septuagint. The thoroughly Hellenistic linguistic form of James stands against the theory that James the Lord's brother—even with a helpful secretary—could have written the letter of James. (2) The relation to Pauline theology, as determined on the basis of the statements in 2:14-26, cannot be seen as a newly initiated polemic of James the Lord's brother opposing reports which had come to him of the beginnings of Paul's activities. Rather, it is a matter of correcting some misunderstood slogans which had falsely been derived from the Pauline theology. The time of Paul is already some distance in the past; the struggle concerning the end of the law or its continuing validity has been forgotten. The author speaks unself-consciously of the law of freedom (1:25; 2:12) as the *nova lex* (new law) of the Christian community.

As James 3:1 lets us recognize, the author who is unknown to us by name must have been a teacher who gathered parenetic tradition and assembled it into a pamphlet of ethical instructions (Lohse). To this writing intended for the whole of Christianity he prefaced the name of James the Lord's brother, who was respected by Christians and Jews, and who like no other had emulated the longed-for goal, namely to attain and realize that Christian perfection which God acknowledges as righteousness.

e. The time of writing should probably be set at the end of the first century, since the time of Paul's activity already lies in the distant past. The nature of the parenesis in James, which refers to no circumstances in particular but presents rules for living which are always valid, permits no inference concerning the place of composition.

#38 The First Letter of Peter

Perdelwitz, R. *Die Mysterienreligion und das Problem des I. Petrusbriefes,* 1911.

Selwyn, E. G. *The First Epistle of St. Peter,* 1946, [3]1949.

Cross, F. C. *I Peter: A Paschal Liturgy,* 1954.

Lohse, E. "Paränese und Kerygma im 1. Petrusbrief" (1954), in *Die Einheit des NT,* 1973, 307-28.

Moule, C. F. D. "The Nature and Purpose of I Peter," *NTS* 3 (1956/57):1-11.

Boismard, M. -E. "Une Liturgie Baptismale dans la Prima Petri." *RB* 63 (1956):182-208; 64 (1957):161-83.

Goppelt, L. *Der erste Petrusbrief,* 1978.

Brox, N. *Der erste Petrusbrief,* 1979.

a. Contents: Following the salutation (1:1-2) comes a paragraph of praise and thanksgiving (1:3-12). Then the first major section gives a call to a life appropriate to the redemption which has already taken place through Christ (1:13–2:10).

Then follow exhortations concerning the conduct of Christians in particular circumstances, which are developed in the form of an extended table of household duties *(Haustafel)* (2:11–3:12). Following that, the right conduct of Christians who suffer is described, with Christ held up as an example (3:13–4:11).

Finally a new train of thought treats the sufferings of Christ once again (4:12–5:11). The letter is rounded off with a brief, concluding formula (5:12-14).

b. The recipients of the letter are described as the exiles in the Diaspora of Pontus, Galatia, Cappadocia, Asia, and Bithynia who have been chosen by God (1:1). Of course the descriptions εκλεκτοι παρεπιδημοι ("chosen exiles") and διασπορα ("Dispersion") could suggest that Jewish Christians are meant. But the life of Christians in the world as such can be described as the Diaspora, since the world is not the native land of the people of God (see James 1:1). The copious use of the OT in the letter's train of thought by no means implies that the readers must be Jewish Christians. On the contrary, several statements in the letter make it clear that Gentile Christians are addressed. Their pre-Christian past was determined by επιθυμιαι ("passions") which dominated them εν αγνοια ("in ignorance," 1:14). That could no more be said of Jews than the statement that they had been ransomed from the futile ways inherited from their fathers (1:18). The readers were once straying sheep (2:25), and the women in the church are told that they have become Sarah's children (3:6). Finally, the community is told that in the past times they have already done enough of those things which the heathen like to do, and idolatry is mentioned among other things (4:3-4)—a charge which simply could not have been made against those who were former Jews. The readers are therefore Gentile Christians in the domain of the earlier Pauline mission field.

c. The occasion and goal of the letter are clearly stated in the conclusion: "I have written briefly to you, exhorting and declaring that this is the true grace of God; stand fast in it" (5:12). It is a matter of an encouraging and monitory letter written to strengthen the readers in view of the sufferings which they must endure. The persecutions obviously do not come from the government authorities, but from the pagan civil population. Christians are falsely accused, slandered, and hauled into court (2:12, 15; 3:14ff; 4:12ff). They are blamed because they no longer participate in the pagan activities (4:3ff). The Christians should not incur suffering because of any kind of misconduct on their part; rather only that suffering which comes about for Christ's sake can be accepted in good conscience. In the parenesis, I Peter uses an abundance of catechetical material, including some which is not directly concerned with the conduct of Christians in persecution, such as the table of household duties. But from time to time the exhortations are specifically directed to the situation of Christians under persecution and supported by referring to the model of the Christ who suffered patiently (2:18-25; 3:18-22); he is the one who must be followed through suffering to glory.

d. The question has been posed in various ways as to whether I Peter reworks a source. Perdelwitz posed the thesis that the basis of 1:3–4:11 was provided by an early Christian baptismal sermon (cf. the allusions to baptism in 1:3, 23; 2:1-2). This baptismal discourse was then expanded by adding an epistolary introduction (1:1-2) and a longer supplement (4:12–5:14). While the baptismal discourse only discusses suffering hypothetically, from 4:12 on the situation of persecution is directly presupposed. This view has been widely accepted and further developed with various modifications. The document is sometimes thought of as a baptismal homily, sometimes a baptismal worship service, sometimes a Passover liturgy. The connection to the Passover is made, according to Cross, not only by the description of Christ as the lamb (1:18-19), but also by the way the word for Passover (πασχα) is echoed in the repeated πασχω ("suffer"), the repeated references to the Exodus tradition (1:13/Ex. 12:11, 2:9-10/Ex. 19:4ff), and the application of catechetical materials in the instruction. But the fact is that there are no references in I Peter which permit the inference of a Passover homily, especially since the word πασχα is not present at all.

Nor are the repeated attempts to uncover a baptismal liturgy in I Peter any more persuasive (Boismard). The references to baptism and rebirth are essentially limited to the section 1:3–2:10. The Pauline Letters also make repeated reference to baptism, in order to ground the imperative of the parenesis in the indicative of the pledge of salvation. Moreover, the theme of the letter as a whole is not baptism, but the suffering of Christians, and that not only in the section following 4:12, but also from the very beginning (see especially 2:18-25; 3:13-22; 4:12ff). Thus the theory that I Peter represents the elaboration of an early Christian baptismal sermon is not tenable either on the basis of the content of the letter or on the basis of the material it uses. Nor is the attempt persuasive to divide I Peter in two different letters: 1:1–2:10, 4:12–5:14, and 1:1–4:11 and 5:11-14, with 1:1–2:10 and 5:12-14 in both forms (Moule).

Rather, I Peter has made extensive use of orally transmitted traditional material (Selwyn, Lohse), as can be clearly recognized for example in the table of household duties (2:13–3:12). Old Testament quotations, Jewish proverbial wisdom, also expressions which derive from the Hellenistic popular philosophy are taken up into the parenesis of I Peter. The letter thus did not originate on the basis of one or more written sources—neither a homily nor a liturgy—but rather various sorts of traditions have been brought together under the theme of the suffering of Christians. In this process parenetic material was combined with kerygmatic formulations of early Christian creedal affirmations and hymns, so that the suffering of Christians is brought into the same context as the suffering of Christ (1:18-19; 2:21-25; 3:18-22). By this means the parenesis receives its proper grounding, for healing is accomplished by the wounds of Christ, so that the believers are freed to new life (2:24). The suffering of Christians is understood as a participation in the sufferings of Christ (4:13). Because of this, joy prevails in the persecuted churches (1:6-7; 4:13-14), but also the obligation to live a holy life is to be taken with redoubled seriousness.

e. The author of the letter is stated to be Πετρος αποστολος Ιησου Χριστου ("Peter, an apostle of Jesus Christ," 1:1), who in 5:1 is also described as ο συμπρεσβυτερος και μαρτυς των του Χριστου παθηματων ("a fellow elder and witness of the sufferings of Christ"). Since Babylon (5:13) serves as a code name for Rome, as in the apocalyptic tradition, the letter is to be understood as written by the chief of the apostles from Rome, the capital city of the world. But there are weighty considerations against the hypothesis that the letter was in fact written by the apostle Peter: (1) except for 5:1, there is no reference at all to the author's having personally been a disciple of Jesus, just as there is no reference to Jesus' ministry or sayings. (2) Instead, the letter is characterized by the adoption of various sorts of traditional material—parenesis, formalized expressions, creedal statements, and songs. The letter therefore does not stand at the source of early Christian tradition, but rather presupposes it as its basis.

(3) The language and style of the letter represent a fluent Koine, even using the optative in 3:14, 17, which had fallen out of use in Hellenistic Greek. (4) Many places in I Peter indicate clear connections to Pauline theology. Thus the expression εν Χριστω ("in Christ") is found outside the Pauline corpus only in I Peter (3:16; 5:10, 14), the concept χαρισμα ("gift, charisma," 4:10) is reminiscent of Pauline usage, and the verb καλεω ("call") is used in the full sense of "effective call to be a Christian" as by Paul. These contacts do not point to a literary dependence, but are rather to be explained as the influence of the continuing Pauline school tradition, the effects of which can be perceived not only in the Pastorals, but also in writings such as I Peter and I Clement. (5) The situation of the community presupposes that the time of Peter lies in the past.

Any discussion of the authorship question must take account of the note in 5:12: "By Silvanus, a faithful brother as I regard him, I have written briefly to you." This could be taken to mean that Peter dictated the letters to Silvanus (cf. Rom. 16:22). But that Peter should have dictated word for word a letter composed in good Koine Greek would be a peculiar idea indeed. Or should we rather understand that Silvanus served as Peter's secretary in the sense that he is responsible for the details of the letter, which he composed on the basis of general instructions from Peter (Selwyn)? But the fundamental objections to secretary hypotheses are also valid here (see p. 48). Even with their help it is not possible to claim even an indirect authorship by the apostle Peter, because of the considerations listed above. The reference to Silvanus will rather have been made by the anonymous author of I Peter in order to make intelligible the conscious resemblance to Pauline theology, for if a former co-worker of Paul's (I Thess. 1:1; II Thess. 1:1; II Cor. 1:19; Acts 15:22ff) now stands beside Peter, it is not remarkable that echoes of Pauline expressions are found. For the rest, the concluding notes of I Peter contain no more than was common knowledge about Peter: he was in Rome, and Mark was with him (see pp. 136-37).

f. In conclusion, we may say with regard to the time and place of composition that an unknown Christian around the end of the first century made use of a variety of types of traditional material to write a letter of encouragement to the suffering Christians of Asia Minor. He prefaced the name of Peter to the writing, which reveals clear influences of Pauline theology and thereby gave expression to the idea which had developed in the church around the end of the first century that Peter and Paul had harmoniously taught the one gospel in all the world and had confirmed it by their suffering (cf. Acts, I Clem. 5). On the basis of 5:13 we may accept Rome as the place of writing.

The letter is attested quite early; the author of II Peter expressly designates his letter δευτερα επιστολη ("second letter," 3:1) and thereby indicates that he knows I Peter.

#39 The Second Letter of Peter and the Letter of Jude

Schelkle, K. H. *Die Petrusbriefe, der Judasbrief*, 1961.

Käsemann, E. "An Apologia for Primitive Christian Eschatology," in *Essays on NT Themes*, 1964.

1. Jude

a. Contents: The Letter of Jude begins with a general address which is directed to all Christians everywhere (1-2), and closes with a doxology (24-25). The body of the letter is an urgent warning against false teachers who have appeared in the churches (3-4). Appeal is made to examples from the OT (5-7), sharp polemic is directed against the activities of the false teachers in the churches (8-19), which concludes with a warning to the reader to remain true and to reject the heretics (20-23).

b. The occasion for the writing of Jude was given by the appearance of false teachers. They have not yet separated from the churches (22-23) and participate in the love feasts (12). They want to be "spiritual" (πνευματικοι), but in reality are only "physical" (ψυχικοι) (19). This distinction shows clearly that it is a matter of Gnosticism. They deny the only Master and Lord, Jesus Christ (4), boast of dreams and revelations (8), and lead a debauched and licentious life (4, 11-12, 16, 18-19). In order to strengthen the reader against this false Gnostic teaching, the author points to warning examples from the OT (5-7), explains that they will be judged like Cain, Balaam and the company of Korah (11), and calls to memory how Enoch had prophesied the judgment of sinners (14-15). Even if an exact description of these Gnostic teachers is not possible, still the basic outline of their views is clear: christological heresy and libertine ethic.

c. "Jude, a servant of Jesus Christ and brother of James" is named as the author of the Letter of Jude (1). This is intended to refer to the brother of James, the highly respected brother of Jesus (see pp. 207-8, cf. Mark 6:3; Matt. 13:55). Hegesippus reports a tradition that near the end of the reign of the emperor Domitian two grandsons of Judas the Lord's brother were regarded suspiciously because they were descendants of David, were personally interviewed by the emperor, but were released as harmless. They became leaders among the churches and lived until the time of Trajan (Eus. H. E. III. 20:1-7). Could Judas the Lord's brother, who probably lived in Palestine, have been the author of the Letter of Jude?

In the first place, the considerations which have already been presented with regard to James speak against this supposition (see p. 208). Then the letter itself clearly indicates that it must have originated in a later time. The readers are reminded of "the predictions of the apostles of our Lord Jesus Christ" (v. 17), are exhorted "build yourselves up on your most holy faith" (v. 20) "which was once for all delivered to the saints" (v. 3). An advocate of early catholicism speaks in these sentences, for whom πιστις ("faith") means the correct doctrine which is taught by the church as the guardian of orthodoxy.

d. Thus the time of composition is to be placed at the beginning of the second century. Jude, the brother of the Lord, is appealed to in order to add weight to the polemic against the Gnostics. Since Jude quotes unself-consciously from the OT Apocrypha—Assumption of Moses (9) and the Book of Enoch (14-15)—the letter should not be dated too late. The oldest attestation for Jude is II Peter, which used Jude as a source (see below).

2. *II Peter*

a. Contents: Simon Peter writes a letter in the form of a testament "to those who have obtained a faith of equal standing with ours in the righteousness of our God and Savior Jesus Christ." After the salutation (1:1-2) introductory exhortations are expressed (1:3-21): hold fast to the precious gifts of salvation (1:3-11). Before his death the apostle once again wants to confirm to his readers the reliability of the prophetic word (1:12-21).

Next follows a detailed warning against false teachers (2:1-22): their presence is announced (2:1-3), they are threatened with judgment (2:4-11), their libertine activities are portrayed (2:12-22).

The next section deals with the parousia of Christ (3:1-13): against the view that the parousia will not happen at all (3:1-4) the author objects that God works by another standard of time than ours (3:5-13). The concluding exhortations urge the readers to authenticate themselves by their blameless manner of life (3:14-18).

b. A relationship of literary dependence exists between II Peter 2 and the Letter of Jude. The same polemic against false teachers is found in both letters: they deny the Lord Jesus Christ and lead a licentious life (2:1-2/Jude 4). They disdain and blaspheme the good angelic powers (2:10-11/Jude 8-9). They are waterless clouds driven by the wind, for whom the nether gloom of darkness has been reserved (2:17/Jude 12-13), they speak pretentiously (2:18/Jude 16), and so forth. Thus the question is, Which of the two documents was the source for the other? Jude 5-7 names three OT examples from which one can learn that God punishes the unbelieving blasphemers. They are presented in the order: Israel in the wilderness, the fallen angels, Sodom and Gomorrah. In II Peter these three are rearranged into historical order: fallen angels (2:4), the flood (2:5, instead of Israel in the wilderness), Sodom and Gomorrah (2:6). The example of the flood has obviously been taken up because it is going to be used against the deniers of the parousia in 3:6. Thus it is indicated that Jude was the source for II Peter. That this was the relationship is confirmed by the fact that the quotations from noncanonical Jewish writings (see p. 216) are missing from II Peter. While in Jude the false teachers are presented as a present danger to the community, II Peter gives the appearance of speaking of the future appearance of the false teachers in a prophetic prediction (2:1-2). But although the description of the false teachers begins in the future, the author slips back into the present tense (2:10, 12ff, 20) and even into the past (2:15, 22).

c. The occasion of the letter is not the polemic against false teachers, which is taken over from Jude and belongs to the customary content of a testament, but the problem of eschatology discussed in chapter 3 (Käsemann). The false Gnostic teachers already referred to in chapter 2 surrender the eschatological hope. After the hope of Christ's parousia had already been briefly spoken of in 1:19-20, in chapter 3 the real problem which II Peter wants to deal with comes to expression. People had mockingly asked, "Where is the promise of his coming? For ever since the fathers fell asleep, all things have continued as they were from the beginning of creation" (3:4). Against these objections the author of II Peter defends the early Christian eschatology with the following argumentation: for God, a thousand years is as a day. Thus the time that has so far elapsed is not very important. There is no doubt that the Lord will honor his promise. The Day of the Lord will come, as a thief in the night (3:9-10). Thus each one should be ready for his sudden advent, by always living a blameless life.

d. According to 1:1, the author of II Peter is Simon Peter,

δουλος και αποστολος Ιησου Χριστου ("a servant and apostle of Jesus Christ"). This claim is also maintained in the letter itself. The author speaks as an eyewitness of the transfiguration of Jesus (1:16ff) and refers to Paul as a beloved brother by whose side he stands as a colleague (3:15-16). But that Peter in fact wrote this letter must be absolutely excluded: (1) II Peter is literarily dependent on the late Letter of Jude. (2) The language and world of ideas in which II Peter is at home are extremely Hellenisticized: 1:3 uses the concept αρετη ("excellence") with reference to God, and 1:5 uses the same word in parallel to πιστις ("faith"). In 1:4 the readers are told that they will become partakers of the divine nature (φυσις), after they have escaped the corruption that is in the world because of passion. The series of examples could be extended. The language and style are considerably different from I Peter; only a small part of the vocabulary is common to both letters. (3) II Peter already presupposes a collection of Pauline Letters (3:15-16). (4) Finally, the apologia for early Christian eschatology points clearly to a setting in the second century. Second Peter is therefore a fictitious testament. The apostle Peter—thus the idea is developed in the letter—gives a kind of last will and testament to the church, in order to impress the correct doctrine upon its memory. This "early catholic" Christianity which comes to expression in II Peter belongs to the middle of the second century. Thus II Peter is to be regarded as the latest document of the NT.

IX.

The Revelation of John

As is indicated by the designation αποκαλυψις (*Apokalypsis*; "revelation"), the Apocalypse contains a revelation which describes the course of the last things from the resurrection and exaltation of Christ to his second coming and establishment of his lordship over all the world. The NT contains no other writing consisting of such contents; only individual brief passages in the Gospels and Letters contain comparable texts (Mark 13 par.; I Thess. 4:13-18; II Thess. 2:1-12; I Cor. 15:20-28, among others). To be sure, in pious circles of contemporary Judaism the expectation of the near end of the world and the beginning of God's new world was a living hope. This hope found its expression in many varieties of apocalyptic literature.

#40 Apocalyptic

Volz, P. *Die Eschatologie der jüdischen Gemeinde im neutestamentlichen Zeitalter*, 1934 = 1966.
Rowley, H. H. *The Relevance of Apocalyptic*, [3]1963.
Vielhauer, Ph. "Apocalypses and Related Subjects: Introduction," in *NT Apocrypha II*. Edited by E. Hennecke and W. Schneemelcher, [3]1965, 407-21.
Plöger, O. *Theocracy and Eschatology*, [2]1968.

Harnisch, W. *Verhängnis und Verheissung der Geschichte,* 1969.
Osten-Sacken, P. v. d. *Die Apokalyptik in ihrem Verhältnis zur Prophetie und Weisheit,* 1969.
Schreiner, J. *Alttestamentlich-jüdische Apokalyptik,* 1969.
Lohse, E. *The NT Environment,* 1971, 55-73.
Schmithals, W. *The Apocalyptic Movement,* 1973.

a. Jewish apocalyptic saw itself as standing in the succession of OT prophecy, in that it sought to express the prophetic message in a new idiom. It focused its attention not only on the course of the history of Israel and the neighboring peoples but also considered the course of world history as a whole, which it saw as rushing precipitously to its final end. This world is about to perish amid terrible catastrophes, but God's new world will descend from heaven and restore the paradisiacal glory. The sharp contrast between this world and the transcendent world was developed with the aid of conceptions taken over from Iranian religions, which were combined with the faith in one God who holds the course of history together. A final period of terrible catastrophes will erupt into this world which presently stands under the domination of satanic powers. Wars, scarcity, and epidemics will befall the human race. The earth will refuse to bring forth its fruits, women will not bear children, the structure of the cosmos will fall apart, so that the stars no longer follow their regular courses. But these "messianic woes" announce the approaching end. When the distress reaches its highest point, then the allotted time for world history has expired, and God will intervene. The final events will unfold in a certain order predetermined by God. The dead will arise from their graves, all people will appear before the judgment seat on which God and the Messiah/Son of man are enthroned. Their deeds will be read forth from books, and they will be judged in accordance with these deeds. This pronouncement of judgment is irrevocable and decides between eternal salvation or eternal damnation. After the judgment, God brings in the new world to replace the old. The blessed will dwell in this new world for all eternity, and God will be in their midst.

The knowledge of this plan for history has been made known to the apocalyptists by secret revelations. The future events are seen in dreams, visions, and ecstatic experiences. While the OT prophets received their message primarily in the form of a word from God which was then communicated in words, the divine message is communicated by the apocalyptists in the form of pictures and allegories which must be interpreted. The prophets in their time preached directly to their contemporaries, but the apocalyptists compose literary works. They enclose their message in a veil of mystery, so that it may be the more alluring, and they publish their apocalyptic writings under the name of some saint of the past. The anonymous authors of the Jewish apocalyptic literature conceal their identity behind the names of Enoch, Abraham, Jacob and his sons, Moses, Baruch, Daniel, Ezra, and others. They let these men of God of the past speak and predict the course of history. Past history is described from the days in which the OT prophets lived until the time of the composition of the apocalyptic book, as if the saint of the past had foreseen the course of history in details. Just as this prophetic vision had previously been exactly fulfilled *(vaticinia ex eventu)*, thus also the further prophecies which refer to the end events will be fulfilled. These events are imaginatively portrayed in vivid pictures. Since God has exactly determined the course of history and its periodization, numbers play a significant role in the apocalyptic presentation. Thus the number seven represents the divine fullness. Seven ages of the world succeed one another in the course of world history. The number twelve has a cosmic scope, for the world proceeds on its determined course under the twelve signs of the zodiac. But this world will finally pass away. Thus the portrayal of the end of the world and the new creation forms the conclusion of the dramatic series of scenes.

The OT saints to whom such visions were granted sealed their writings shut; they were to be opened and read only in the final period of distress. The present, in which the apocalyptists live, stands in the expectation that the end will come soon. The content of the apocalyptic writings is communicated to the believing community in order to encourage them in their time of testing: now they know about the coming end and the promised glory. Through this knowledge they are strengthened so that they can remain faithful, persevere in keeping God's commandments, and hold out until the last day.

b. Apocalyptic texts are already found within some of the later OT writings, e.g. Isaiah 24–27. The oldest apocalyptic book was written during the time of oppression by the Syrian king

Antiochus IV Epiphanes (167–164 B.C.), and transmitted under the name of Daniel. The Book of Daniel was still acceptable within the circle of OT writings. But of the large number of other apocalyptic writings which were written soon thereafter, none was able to attain canonical standing. Two books are handed down as works of Enoch, one in Ethiopic, the other in Slavic. The Ascension of Isaiah, which is preserved in Latin, records a speech which Moses gave at the end of his life. In the Testaments of the Twelve Patriarchs each of the twelve sons of Jacob gives a speech to his descendants just before his death. In the first century A.D. Jewish apocalyptists wrote books under the name of Ezra (IV Esra) and Baruch (Syriac, Greek) which deal with the apparently unresolvable problems of why God had rejected his people and had let the Holy City be razed to the ground (70 A.D.). Apocalyptic ideas also found extensive expression in the literature of the Qumran community. Since the apocalyptic texts are mostly transmitted in various translations rather than the original language, this means that after the advent of Christianity Judaism tended strongly to separate itself from apocalyptic, because the Christians provided these Jewish texts with references to the fulfillment of the eschatological hope in Christ and then read them as Christian edifying literature. But beside them stood new writings which had originated in Christian circles, which used apocalyptic tradition to affirm the Christian hope in the dawning of the new world. The Apocalypse of John, the only Christian apocalyptic document to be taken into the NT canon, draws from this broad stream of apocalyptic traditions and brings them into the service of the expression of the Christian message.

#41 The Revelation of John

Vischer, E. *Die Offenbarung Johannis, eine jüdische Apokalypse in christlicher Bearbeitung*, [2]1895.

Bousset, W. *Die Offenbarung Johannis*, [2]1906 = 1966.

Brun, L. "Die römischen Kaiser in der Apokalypse," *ZNW* 26 (1927): 128-51.

Boismard, M. E. "L'apocalypse ou les apocalypses de S. Jean," *RB* 56 (1949): 507-41.

Lohse, E. "Die alttestamentliche Sprache des Sehers Johannes" (1961), in *Die Einheit des NT*, 1973, 329-33.

———. *Die Offenbarung des Johannes*, ^{4}1976.
Strobel, A. "Abfassung und Geschichtstheologie der Apokalypse nach Kap. XVII," *NTS* 10 (1963/64): 433-45.
Caird, G. B. *The Revelation of St. John the Divine*, 1966.
Kraft, H. *Die Offenbarung des Johannes*, 1974.

a. Contents: The outline of the book corresponds to the commission with which the seer was charged (1:19): to write what he has seen (= the appearance of the exalted Christ), 1:9-20, what is (= the letters to the seven churches of chapters 2–3) and what will happen hereafter (chapters 4–22). The introductory chapter includes the foreword (1:1-3), the epistolary introduction (1:4-8), and the call vision (1:9-20). The message of the Apocalypse is then presented in seven major sections.

The seven letters are directed to seven churches in Asia Minor (chapters 2–3). Then follow the visions of seven seals (4:1–8:1). These are introduced by a preliminary vision of a heavenly scene in which the seer is permitted to view the heavenly throne room (4:1-11) and the handing over of the book with seven seals to the Lamb (5:1-14). Then the first six seal-visions are described (6:1-17), and an interlude which portrays the sealing of the 144,000 and the innumerable host before the throne of God (7:1-17). With the opening of the seventh seal a great silence pervades the universe (8:1).

The series of seven trumpet-visions (8:2–11:19) is similarly constructed to that of the visions of the seven seals. To a brief introductory section (8:2-6) are joined the first four trumpet visions (8:7-12), then the fifth and sixth visions are extensively portrayed (chapter 9). An interlude portrays an angel with an open book, the measuring of the temple, and the two witnesses (10:1–11:14). The seven trumpet-visions lead to the eschatological songs of triumph (11:15-19) and introduce the heart of the book: the dragon and the Lamb (12–14). First, the mythical background is sketched: the persecution of the woman by the dragon, her miraculous preservation in the wilderness and the downfall of the dragon from heaven (chapter 12). Then the currently relevant point is elaborated (chapter 13). Two beasts, creatures of the dragon, emerge in the scene, the first with a death blow which has been healed (12:18–13:10), the second as a propagandizing prophet of the first (13:11-18). To this is joined an anticipatory vision of the coming victory of Christ: the Lamb and his own (14:1-5), as well as the announcement and preparation for the coming judgment (14:6-20).

A further cycle of seven visions describes the increasing terrors (15–16). After a heavenly prelude (chapter 15) the seven bowls are poured out on the earth (chapter 16). The fall of Babylon is then pictured in detail (17:1–19:10). Judgment is pronounced on the harlot Babylon (17), a lament is sung for the accomplished judgment on Babylon by a choir of many voices (chapter 18), but there is rejoicing in heaven (19:1-10). The coming of Christ and the consummation are portrayed in the last major section (19:11–22:5). Christ defeats the beast and his military forces (19:11-21), he rules with his own for a thousand years, and judges Satan (20:1-10), after which the last judgment is held (20:11-15). Then come the new heaven and the new earth (21:1-8) and the New Jerusalem (21:9–22:5). In the conclusion and attestation of the book (22:6-21) the prayer for the soon coming of Christ is heard once again.

b. Contrast and comparison with Jewish apocalypses clearly reveals the character of the Revelation of John as a Christian apocalypse. In the first place, it is clear that Revelation has several points in common with Jewish apocalyptic. As in Jewish apocalyptic, where short prophetic sayings are replaced by extensively developed pictures, so also in the Apocalypse heavenly scenes and visions follow one another in a vivid series. The Jewish apocalyptists received dreams and visions which revealed how the course of history was to run until the end of this world. The seer John was made to fall into an ecstatic state (1:10; 4:1), he was carried away in the Spirit to some other-worldly place (17:3ff; 21:9ff) in order to receive mysterious revelations. These revelations deal with an event of cosmic proportions. Satan, demonic powers, angelic beings, obscure threatening armies, and mysterious forces appear in the drama, which hastens speedily to its end. The features which describe the individual scenes correspond to apocalyptic tradition. The pictures which succeed one another in rapid changes of scene must sometimes be understood in terms of the meanings commonly associated with such pictures in apocalyptic tradition. Thus in his book the seer John does not simply describe the dreams and visions which he himself has experienced; rather, he uses traditional motifs and materials which he fits together to form a series of Christian affirmations by relating them to the church's confession of the crucified, risen, exalted, and coming Lord. This recoining of the material into a new form was undertaken by a man who addressed the churches as a minister of the Word with prophetic authority. He summed up the insights granted to him in this literary work intended to serve the distressed churches as a book of encouragement and warning.

Thus the form and content of the Apocalypse are to be understood against the background of Jewish apocalyptic. But closer observation confirms not only the close relationship with the views and ideas of Jewish apocalyptic, but also reveals that the Apocalypse as a Christian book is different from Jewish apocalyptic in significant ways: (1) the Apocalypse of John is not a pseudonymous work. John the seer does not conceal his identity behind the name of some OT saint, but names his own name (1:1, 4, 9; 22:8). (2) John does not write for later generations, but for a particular readership in his own time. In the seven churches in Asia Minor, the whole church is addressed. (3) The Apocalypse of John was not sealed up for some later time (22:10), but immediately delivered to the churches as a prophetic message. Thus also there is no elaboration of retrospective "prophecy" in the form of *vaticinia ex eventu*, but the content of the Apocalypse is comprised exclusively of the eschatological events which have already begun with the cross and resurrection of Christ and concludes with his parousia and the beginning of the new world. (4) Within the book there is repeated reference to the situation of the community; the heavenly church is united with the suffering community on earth in that it too sings praises to God and the Lamb. Although the author of the Apocalypse is deeply rooted in apocalyptic traditions, he never quotes an apocalyptic writing. But there are constant allusions to the OT, whose expressions are preserved even when they are not completely capable of expressing what the seer himself wants to say (Lohse). Since the order of the last things is determined by God's decree, for the seer the language of the OT is the only appropriate means of expression for his testimony that the revelation of Jesus Christ rests on the promise of the Scripture, which it brings to completion and fulfillment

By means of investigations which pay special attention to the development of the traditions *(Traditionsgeschichte)* used in the Apocalypse, exegesis has sometimes drawn attention to the particular features of the seer's traditions and the way they are used by him. This approach reveals how eschatologically oriented the work is, since the abundance of pictures point predominately to the coming day on which the Lord will appear. The present, in which the author and his readers find themselves, is however not neglected, but understood as a part of the series of eschatological events which have already begun. This reference to the present is clearly seen in the references to contemporary history (e.g. in chapter 13).

c. The question has repeatedly been raised as to whether the Apocalypse is a literary unity. Have written sources been used? After E. Vischer had attempted to separate out a Jewish primary source, which later received a Christian reworking, various suggestions have been made as to how sources and editing might be separated from each other. But the thoroughly consistent linguistic and stylistic form of the Apocalypse has always stood in the way of such attempts. Boismard attempted to take this state of affairs into account by positing two sources that are used throughout the Apocalypse, both of which go back to the same author: an older apocalypse from the time of the persecution of Christians under Nero, which consists essentially of chapters 12–16 and parts of 17–22, and a later writing from the time of Domitian, which contained primarily materials in chapters 4–9, but also passages from elsewhere in the book, especially from chapters 17–22. Finally, the latest section was written ca. 95, the letters to the seven churches.

The impetus for attempts to identify sources has been given by a few places in the Apocalypse which do not seem to fit smoothly into their context. Thus in 11:1-2 the seer is given the task of measuring the temple, but should omit the outer court since it is given over to the Gentiles, who will trample over the Holy City for forty-two months. This clearly presupposes the situation during the siege of Jerusalem by the Romans in A.D. 70. It was hoped that the holy places would be preserved through all the terrible events. Should we then suppose that this passage was written in A.D. 70? This supposition fades away once it is recognized that the seer John obviously takes up an older tradition in chapter 11 but now uses it in a different context, for he is not interested in the temple as such, but interprets it figuratively as the church, which will be preserved by God.

Difficulties are also presented by 17:10: of seven kings (= emperors), five have fallen, the sixth is presently ruling, and the seventh is still to come. When he comes, he will remain only a short time. The beast, which was and is not, is itself the eighth (17:11). What is meant? If one begins the series of emperors with Augustus, then we have: Augustus, Tiberius, Caligula, Claudius, Nero—Vespasian. Then this would possibly be a fragment from the time of Vespasian. Or should one proceed from the hypothesis that the emperor who presently rules (sixth in the series) is Domitian, and calculate from there (Brun)? But then why should the series begin with Caligula? Does the idea perhaps stand in the background that the series begins with the first ruler who appeared after the cross and resurrection of Jesus (Strobel)? But nothing in the text supports such considerations. It is rather the case that here also the seer is dependent on old tradition which regarded the course of world history as divided among seven rulers, which he applies to illuminate the present in which the church finds itself. His view is exclusively directed to the near future in which the eighth terrible world ruler will appear, who will bring the world rulership's hostility to God to a head and thereby bring world history to its end. He is thus not interested in the question of whether the number of named kings agrees with the factual course of things in Roman history, so that also in 17:10-11 no basis is to be found for the view that a source or fragment from the time of Vespasian has been used.

The different traditions taken over by the author have been combined by him into a work which is homogeneous in language and style. He writes Greek, but thinks mostly in terms of Hebrew grammar, which he then expresses in Greek. The verb often stands at the beginning of the sentence; sentences and clauses are repeatedly connected only by "and." In 1:4 stands απο ο ων και ο ην και ο ερχομενος (lit.: "from the one who is and the he-was and the one who is to come")—not because the seer was ignorant of the fact that απο is followed by the genitive, but because he intends to express by this unchangeableness of the expression which describes God that God himself remains unchangeably the same. A pronounced Hebraism is found in 3:8, when it is said of the door ην ουδεις δυναται κλεισαι αυτην (lit.: "which no one is able to shut it"); in Greek the αυτην ("it") is redundant but is placed here because in a Hebrew relative clause the antecedent is represented by a suffix attached to the verb. Compare further 12:6: the woman fled into the wilderness, οπου εχει εκει τοπον (lit.: "where she has there a place"). He readily places a word in *casus pendens* emphatically at the beginning of a sentence, with no grammatical connection, as for example ο νικων—δωσω αυτω ("he who conquers—I will give to him") instead of τω νικωντι δωσω ("I will give to the one who conquers," 2:26; 3:12, 21). A participle is followed by a finite verb without any difference in meaning, e.g. the woman Jezebel η λεγουσα εαυτην προφητιν και διδασκει και πλανα τους εμους δουλους (lit: "the one calling herself a prophetess and she teaches and deceives my servants," 2:20). Grammatical genders are often used in what appears to be an arbitrary alternation, e.g. ζωα εν καθ εν αυτων εχων ("living creatures, each one [neut.] of them having" [masc.], 4:8), i.e. the masculine participle is used where proper Greek grammar calls for the neuter. Examples of this sort, which are met at every step as one proceeds through the Apocalypse, show both that the language and style are peculiar to the author and that they are uniform throughout. The Semitizing style gives to the words a solemn tone which reckons with the unique content of the prophetic message.

d. The author of the Apocalypse is designated by the name of John, servant of God and brother of the Christians to whom he speaks (1:1, 4, 9; 22:8). As preacher and prophet (19:10; 22:8-9) he is held in high regard by the churches of Asia Minor. He is imprisoned on Patmos—perhaps at the instigation of the Roman authorities—and cannot address the churches directly; he therefore delivers his continuing message to them in writing. Since he considers it something special to be designated a Jew, although the synagogue had forfeited this worthy name (2:9; 3:9), it is most likely the case that he himself is a former Jew, perhaps from Jewish Christian circles in Palestine. Now and then Hebrew words are introduced, which however are explained for the readers, as Abaddon (9:11) and Armageddon (16:16). Who was this John?

The ancient church tradition, as it is preserved from the middle of the second century, regards John as the apostle, the son of Zebedee, who belonged to the circle of the twelve. But this claim, which is found in Justin Martyr, Irenaeus, and others, was opposed around A.D. 200 by the counterthesis of the so-called "Alogoi"—i.e. the opponents of the logos-Gospel [John]—that the Johannine writings were a fabrication of the Gnostic Cerinthus. They directed this affirmation against the Montanists, in order to wrest the Johannine writings from them, because they were used as the favorite texts for the Montanist doctrine of the Spirit (see p. 179). The Alogoi thus contested apostolic authorship on theological grounds. But also the tradition already found in the middle of the second century, according to which the seer John is to be identified with the apostle, is not based on historical information but represents a theological claim. If an apostle had written the Apocalypse, its acceptance as belonging to the canon would have been assured. Thus the advocates of the book as well as its opponents did not know any more to say about the person of the author than they could derive from the book itself. But can the view that the apostle wrote the book be supported from the Apocalypse?

First, the relationship of the Apocalypse to the Fourth Gospel must be clarified, since according to the ancient church tradition it too was written by John the son of Zebedee (see p. 179). Closer observation reveals that the two writings are very different in both form and content. To be sure, both documents speak of life and death, testimony and attestation, victory and overcoming. But while in the Fourth Gospel the concepts light, truth, love, peace, only Son of the Father, Paraclete, the new commandment, and so forth, are frequently found, these ideas and expressions are almost completely absent from the Apocalypse. The Gospel of John proclaims Jesus as the resurrection and the life (11:25-26); whoever believes in him has already passed from death into life (5:24-25); he is already excluded from judgment (3:18). The Apocalypse on the other hand portrays a series of eschatological events which must take place before the end, the judgment, and God's new world finally arrive. While the message of the Gospel of John is entirely oriented to the present in which the eschatological crisis is already happening, the Apocalypse pictures an apocalyptic drama. The Gospel of John only rarely introduces a quotation from the OT, but the language of the Apocalypse is permeated with biblical allusions in almost every verse. These fundamental differences make the conclusion compelling that the author of the Apocalypse cannot be identical with the fourth evangelist.

Nowhere in his book does the seer indicate that he himself is an eyewitness and apostle of Jesus. Nothing is told of the earthly activity of Jesus; only cross, resurrection, and parousia are named, in accord with the common Christian confession. The twelve apostles are spoken of as a closed circle in 21:14, but no hint is given that the author reckoned himself to this number. In 18:20 the apostles are named with the saints and prophets as the choir who are to sing the victory song about the judgment that has been executed on Babylon. Their time is already some decades in the past. In the churches of Asia Minor hardly any traces of the preaching of the apostle Paul are still to be found, although it was he, after all, who had founded the first church in this province (chapters 2–3). Thus when the author introduces himself as John, that is not to be understood as a claim to be the disciple and apostle of the Lord. Rather, the identification with John the son of Zebedee was first made by later church tradition which wanted to assure John's book general acceptance in the church.

On the basis of the information provided by the Apocalypse itself, only so much may be said: the author was an early Christian prophet who exercised great authority in the churches of Asia Minor. It is conceivable that this John was identical with the elder John spoken of by Papias (Bousset; see pp. 180-81 above). But nothing may be affirmed about this with confidence.

e. The place and time of the composition of the Apocalypse may be clearly ascertained. That the book originated in Asia Minor—on Patmos—is plainly said (1:9-11). Irenaeus reports that the Apocalypse was written toward the end of the reign of the emperor Domitian (A.D. 81–96) (adv. Haer. V. 30. 3). This date is confirmed by the Apocalypse itself. Persecution had already taken place (6:9-11). But the churches stand before new sufferings and an even more severe conflict with the civil authorities, who are insisting on the worship of the emperor as divine (chapter 13). The seer seeks to strengthen Asia Minor Christianity for this struggle. Thus the Apocalypse was written in the last decade of the first century A.D. in Asia Minor.

C.

The Text of the New Testament

C.

Nestle, E., and Dobschütz, E. v. *Einführung in das griechiche NT*, [4]1923.
Lietzmann, H. "Einführung in die Textgeschichte der Paulusbriefe," in *An die Römer*, [4]1933, 1-18.
Kenyon, F. G. *The Text of the Greek Bible*, 1937, [3]1958.
Greeven, H. "Erwägungen zur synoptischen Textkritik," *NTS* 6 (1959/60): 281-96.
———. *Der Urtext des NT*, 1960.
———. "Text und Textkritik der Bibel, II: Neues Testament," in *RGG*[3], 6:716-25.
Metzger, B. M. *The Text of the NT*, [2]1968.
Zimmerman, H. *Neutestamentliche Methodenlehre*, [4]1974, 31-82.

#42 The Task of New Testament Text Criticism

a. The original copies of all NT documents have been lost; their text is preserved only in later copies. But for no other literary document of antiquity is there such an extensive and reliable manuscript attestation as for the NT. Many ancient writings are only available to us in the form of medieval manuscripts, so that more than a millennium lies between the time of composition and the oldest extant manuscripts. In contrast, the attestation of the NT goes back into the second century, so that only about one hundred years exist between the origin of the NT writings and the oldest manuscripts available to us. The task of NT text criticism consists in the critical examination of this manuscript tradition and the evaluation of the variations that occur, in order to reproduce the lost original text. In order to fulfill this task, one must be thoroughly informed about the nature of ancient manuscripts and the hereditary factors involved in their transmission and about possible sources of error which could have led to changes in the text, as well as the age and value of the materials available for the reconstruction of the wording of the original texts.

b. The common writing material in antiquity was papyrus, which was quite perishable, made by cutting, drying, and gluing together small strips of the pith of the papyrus plant. The side of the page on which the strips lay by each other horizontally is called the recto, the opposite side on which the strips are vertical, the verso. The individual pages were then combined to form a scroll, the average length of which was about ten meters—though there were rolls as long as thirty meters. The early Christian texts were written on scrolls, but there was not enough room on even the longest scroll for all the canonical NT writings. For this reason alone it is clear why the textual history of the individual parts of the NT did not develop evenly. The individual pages were as a rule divided into two columns; the scroll was usually provided with text on only one side. The text was written in a continuous script, *scriptio continua,* without leaving space between individual words or sentences, and without punctuation marks. Ancient papyri have been preserved in large numbers in the desert sands of Egypt, but elsewhere almost always they deteriorated very quickly. The codex, the book form, is to be distinguished from the more usual scroll. In NT times the codex was used only for books of notes, accounts, and rough drafts, not however for literary purposes. The Christians, however, copied their Scriptures in the codex form, the pages of which could be turned and written on both sides.

Parchment (περγαμηνα, *pergamēna*)—named after the city of Perga in Asia Minor so famous for its library—was much more valuable than papyrus. It was made from animal skins which were processed into a lasting writing material. Beginning in the time of Emperor Constantine, parchment was also used by Christians in the production of their Bible manuscripts. Since parchment was expensive, it often happened that the text already present on a parchment was erased, in order to copy a new text onto it (the so-called palimpsest). Modern scholarship has often been successful in making the older text of such a palimpsest readable. From the thirteenth century on, paper which had come into the West from the Far East was also used. For NT text criticism the oldest texts—the papyri and the early parchment codices—are by far the most important, for the reconstruction of the lost original text must be based on the oldest available manuscripts.

c. The history of the NT text is embedded in the history of the early church. In the beginning period of Christianity the early Christian writings were not yet regarded as sacrosanct, so that changes were often made in the text. The early Christian churches were poor, could often hire only bad scribes, and often possessed only a few scrolls. In times of persecution many manuscripts were destroyed, and different areas of the church often remained out of contact with one another for extensive periods. This is the explanation for the fact that the history of the text did not always proceed evenly in all parts of ancient Christianity.

d. In the copying of a text, a number of different types of errors are possible. Text criticism has to reckon with the fact that the copyists not only made intentional changes in the text, but also were subject to oversights and accidental mistakes. A few examples: (1) unintentional alterations in the text: errors of hearing could occur in the process of dictation, e.g. the substitution of an ω ("omega," long ō) for an o ("omicron," short o), Romans 5:1: ειρηνην εχωμεν ("let us have peace") instead of εχομεν ("we have"); or an η ("eta," long a) instead of an ι ("iota," short i); Acts 11:26: χρηστιανους ("good people") instead of Χριστιανους ("Christians") (the so-called *iticismus*, since η and ι in Hellenistic Greek were both regularly pronounced as ē). The *scriptio continua* could lead to errors in writing, thus in Romans 6:5 ΑΛΛΑ ("but") becomes ΑΜΑ ("together") in some manuscripts. The eye of the copyist could jump from a word or phrase which occurs in one line to an identical or similar word or phrase in another line, omitting the material in between (the so-called *homoioteleuton),* e.g. I Corinthians 7:2, where some manscripts skip from the first to the second εχετω ("should have"). A letter could be accidentally written twice, thus producing a dittography, as for example I Thessalonians 2:7 εγενηθημεν ηπιοι ("we were gentle") became in some manuscripts εγενηθημεν νηπιοι ("we were babes") by accidental doubling of the ν. Or the reverse could happen when two identical letters or syllables occur together: one could be omitted, as in I Thessalonians 1:5, εγενηθημεν εν ("we proved to be among"), where the εν ("among") is missing from many manuscripts. Since punctuation was missing from the *scriptio continua,* the end of a clause or sentence was not always clear. Sometimes important exegetical decisions depend on how such questions are answered. Thus for example if one places a comma in the midst of Romans 9:5, the second half of the sentence refers to Christ who is named in the first half, and Christ is called "God." But Paul most likely intended a stronger separation between the two clauses, since he of course often describes Christ as the Son of God, but never elsewhere as God. Thus a colon must be placed between the two clauses (see p. 41).

(2) Intentional changes in the text: in many places in the texts copyists have undertaken to make stylistic improvements, as e.g. in Mark 2:27 εγενετο ("was made"; lit.: "became") to εκτισθη ("was created") or Matthew 6:1 δικαιοσυνην ("righteousness") to the more intelligible ελεημοσυνην ("alms"). Very frequently in manuscripts of the Gospels one finds that the text of one has been assimilated to the text of the other in the corresponding passage, as for example many manuscripts of Mark 3:14 contain the addition ους και αποστολους εκαλεσεν ("whom also he named apostles," from Luke 6:13). This parallel influence or conformation was especially at work in the manner in which the text of Matthew, which was the text most widely distributed and used, influenced the texts of the other Gospels. Clarifying additions were sometimes added at particular points in the texts, as is shown for example by the various supplements to John 7:39: to ουπω γαρ ην πνευμα (lit.: "for the Spirit was not yet") some manuscripts add αγιον (Holy"), or δεδομενον ("given"), or αγιον . . . επ αυτοις ("Holy . . . to them"), or αγιον . . . δεδομενον ("Holy . . . given").

Especially important are those textual changes which affect

the content. Thus the statement in I Thessalonians 3:2, in which Paul names Timothy και συνεργον του Θεου εν τω ευαγγελιω του Κριστου ("and God's co-worker in the gospel of Christ") raised the question of whether it was possible for a human being to be God's co-worker. The multiplicity of attempted answers is reflected in the variant readings και συνεργον ("and co-worker"); και διακονον του Θεου ("and God's servant") as well as the combination και διακονον του Θεου και συνεργον ημων ("God's servant and our co-worker"). In Matthew 24:36, ("But of that day and hour no one knows, not even the angels of heaven, nor the Son, but the Father only") christological considerations have caused the words ουδε ο Υιος ("nor the Son") to be omitted in some manuscripts, on the supposition that after all Christ is omniscient too, not just the Father. Trinitarian doctrine is reflected in the addition to I Corinthians 8:6, which has received a third line in some manuscripts: και εν πνευμα αγιον εν ω τα παντα και ημεις εν αυτω ("and one Holy Spirit, in whom are all things and we in him"). Concerning the problem of the so-called *Comma Johanneum*, see p. 192. Critical investigation of the manuscript tradition must be able to recognize such changes in the text, exclude secondary readings, and thereby open the way to the original text.

#43 The Manuscripts of the New Testament

Aland, K. *Kurzgefasste Liste der griechischen Handschriften des NT, I,* 1963.

———. "Die griechische Handschriften des Neuen Testaments: Ergänzungen zur 'Kurzgefassten Liste,'" in *Materialien zur neutestamentlichen Handschriftenkunde I.* Edited by K. Aland, 1969, 1-53.

———. ed. *Die alten Übersetzungen des Neuen Testaments, die Kirchenväterzitate and Lektionare,* 1972.

———. *Novum Testamentum Graece,* [26]1979, 684-716.

The material available for NT textual criticism is comprised of papyri, majuscules, minuscules, early translations of the NT, and NT quotations in the church fathers.

a. The Papyri. As the most important papyri are to be pointed out: the Chester Beatty Papyri from the early third century; P^{45} contains extensive sections of the Gospels and Acts, P^{46} the

Letters of Paul and Hebrews (not complete, the Pastoral Letters are missing), P^{47} ten pages of the Apocalypse. The oldest fragment of a NT text is the papyrus Rylands Greek P^{52} from the early second century, which contains a few verses from John 18. In recent times some relatively large papyrus texts have been rediscovered and published: Papyrus Bodmer II P^{66} presents an almost complete manuscript of the Gospel of John from around 200, the Papyrus Bodmer XIV/XV P^{75} likewise belongs in the time around 200 and contains most of the Gospels of Luke and John.

b. The Majuscules. Until around A.D. 1000 the Greek text was written entirely in capital letters (= majuscules), after which writing in small letters (minuscules) gradually became the generally accepted practice. To designate the majuscules, capital letters are used, or a number preceded by a zero. Sinaiticus א (01) comes from the early fourth century and was rediscovered by C. v. Tischendorf in the Mt. Sinai monastery. It contains not only the OT and NT, but the letter of Barnabas and the Shepherd of Hermas as well. The א manuscript, which manifests a close relationship to B, is a very valuable witness of the Greek text and has properly received special attention in text criticism. The manuscript Alexandrinus A (02) was copied in the early fifth century in Egypt and in addition to the NT includes the two letters of Clement. The codex was named after its place of origin and was given to King Charles I of England by the patriarch Cyril Lucaris. Its value as a witness to the original text is not of the same rank as א and B. The manuscript Vaticanus B (03) derives like א from the early fourth century and contains the OT and the NT up to Hebrews 9:14, the conclusion having been lost. It has been a part of the Vatican Library collection since ancient times. This codex, which was produced with great care, is a parallel exemplar to א in offering an especially important witness to a very old Egyptian text. The codex Ephraemi Rescriptus C (04) is a palimpsest. The biblical text which was copied in the fifth century was erased and replaced by the discourses of the Syrian church father Ephraim. Little is preserved of the OT, from the NT about 5/8. Scholars were able to make the NT text readable again, and to evaluate its readings. D designates two manuscripts from the fifth/sixth centuries which offer a Latin translation alongside the Greek text. The first such manuscript is named Bezae Cantabrigiensis (05)—Calvin's successor Theodore Beza presented it to Cambridge University—and contains the Gospels and Acts. The other manuscript bears the name Claromontanus (06), named after the monastery Clermont in France, and contains the Pauline Letters. Besides these witnesses which are especially important for NT textual criticism, from among the majuscules two other Gospel manuscripts are to be especially emphasized: Freerianus W (032) from the fourth/fifth century (now in the Freer collection in Washington), and the Koridethi Gospels manuscript Θ (038), probably copied in the ninth century, and named after the monastery Koridethi in Caucasia.

c. The Minuscules. There are so many of these later manuscripts, which are designated by Arabic numbers, that they can hardly be dealt with in survey fashion. Here we must only call attention to those which are important for text criticism because they are demonstrably copied from much older, reliable witnesses. Two minuscule groups deserve special attention: the Ferrar Group named after their discoverer W. H. Ferrar (φ = 13, 69, 124, 346, 543, among others), and the Lake Group discovered by K. Lake (λ = 1, 118, 131, 209, among others). In addition to the numerous minuscules, also to be mentioned are the lectionaries, which do not contain complete texts, but only the readings designated for use in worship (designated by 1^{lect}, and so forth).

d. The Translations. The early translations of the NT are very valuable because of the early date at which they were made, for they offer an indirect witness to the Greek text used by the translator. Of course in the translation all the fine points of the Greek text which was used can no longer be recognized, for example the different past tenses of the verb or the distinction in the use of prepositions such as απο and υπο. The following translations are of special importance for NT text criticism:

(1) Syriac Translations. At the beginning of the Syriac Bible stands the Diatessaron—Eus., H. E. IV. 29:6: το δια τεσσαρων (= [harmony of] "four tones," "quartette")—a harmony of the Gospels constructed by Tatian around A.D. 170–180. It was widely circulated in the Syriac church.

However, in the fifth century the Diatessaron was forced out of use in the worship service and copies were destroyed, so that it is no longer extant. Its form can only be reconstructed from later translations. It is not even clear whether the Diatessaron was originally composed in Greek or Syriac. In Dura-Europos, on the boundary of the Roman Empire on the Euphrates, a third-century Greek fragment of the Diatessaron was found. But since this fragment only contains fourteen lines, comprehensive inferences are not possible. The Diatessaron was widely circulated in the Syriac language and exercised a not-inconsiderable influence on the further history of the Greek text.

Alongside the Diatessaron there also existed quite early the so-called Separated Gospels, that is, Syriac translations of all four Gospels. Two translations were made, probably in the fourth century. One is called the Curetonian Syriac after its editor William Cureton (syr^{cur}), and is documented by one fifth-century manuscript. The other translation was rediscovered in the monastery at Mt. Sinai, hence the name Sinaitic Syriac (syr^{sin}), the manuscript of which is from the fifth or fourth century. In the fifth century a common Syriac Bible became generally accepted, especially due to the efforts of Bishop Rabbula of Edessa, the so-called "Peshitta" (= the simple, i.e. *Vulgata*), which contained all four Gospels. Later times produced two more versions of the Syriac NT: the revision of the Peshitta arranged by Bishop Philoxenus of Mabug (Hierapolis) in 508, the so-called Philoxenian (sy^{ph}), which was once again revised by Bishop Thomas of Harkel (Heraclea) in Egypt one hundred years later (= the so-called Harclean [Sy^{h}]).

(2) Latin Translations. The oldest Latin translations were made in the second century. The different Old Latin versions (= Itala or Vetus Latina; the manuscripts are indicated by small letters a, b, c, and so forth) had so much variation from one another that a revision became necessary. Bishop Damasus of Rome (366–384) entrusted this task to the scholar Jerome. While for the OT he partly revised existing versions and partly translated afresh from the original language, for the NT he undertook a textual revision in dependence on the best manuscripts of the Old Latin translation. Perhaps only the revision of the Gospels goes back directly to his hand, with other revisers responsible for the remainder of the NT. The revised text, which as the Vulgate was

supposed to be the commonly used text, did not by any means universally prevail, and many readings of the Old Latin translations gradually forced their way back into the text. Therefore in 1546, in the fourth session of the Council of Trent, it was decided to prepare an authentic edition of the Vulgate. In 1590, under Pope Sixtus V, an official edition of the Vulgate was published; however it was so full of mistakes that it had to be replaced quickly by a new edition, which appeared in 1592 under Pope Clement VIII. But neither was this text completely satisfying. The third edition of the Clementine Vulgate of 1598 then became the official biblical text of the Roman Catholic Church.

(3) Coptic Translations. In Egypt the NT had already been translated into different dialects of the common language, Coptic, at an early date. The Sahidic translation (sa), whose text stands near to א and B, was made in upper Egypt in the third century; the Bohairic translation (bo) was completed in lower Egypt in the third or fourth century.

The other translations of the NT which originated later are not of comparable importance to those named above: the Armenian, Ethiopic, Georgian, Arabic, Persian, Old Slavic. They were either translated from a later Greek text or from another translation such as Syriac, so that their significance for text criticism is not very great. But we should mention that Ulfilas made a translation into Gothic in the fourth century, the most famous exemplar of which is the sixth-century Codex Argenteus in Uppsala.

e. Quotations in the Church Fathers. The NT is frequently quoted in the writings of the church fathers. The works of Clement of Alexandria and of Origen presuppose an old Egyptian text. However, in evaluating the quotations in the church fathers, attention must be given to two sorts of phenomena: (1) frequently the later copyists of the works of the church fathers accommodated the biblical quotations therein to the text current in their time. Therefore only critical editions of the church fathers can be used for NT textual criticism. (2) Sometimes it is not clear whether the church father is citing from a text of the NT before him, or from memory. Thus a certain caution is necessary when the NT quotations in the church fathers are introduced as evidence for text-critical decisions.

#44 The History of the Printed New Testament Text

a. After the invention of printing by Johann Gutenberg, at first only the Vulgate text was printed. A first edition of the Greek New Testament was prepared in Spain, the Complutensian Polyglot. This great undertaking, which was carried out at the initiative of Cardinal Ximenes, included not only the NT, but also the OT as well. The text of the Greek NT was ready for publication in 1514, but the papal authorization to print it was delayed. Then the Basel publisher and book dealer Froben learned of this Spanish work, decided to bring out his own edition first, and enlisted the famous Rotterdam scholar Erasmus for his project. Erasmus set to work in 1515 and prepared an edition of the Greek NT on the basis of the few Greek manuscripts which he could lay hands on. For the Apocalypse he had only one manuscript available, and it broke off at 22:16. Erasmus extricated himself from this dilemma by retranslating the final verses from Latin into Greek. The first edition of the Greek NT appeared already in the spring of 1516, which Erasmus frankly admitted he had prepared very hastily *(praecipitatum verius quam editum)*. The second edition of this work, printed in 1519, was used by Luther as he translated the NT into German.

b. The subsequent printings became the basis of the Erasmian text, which, to be sure, received some minor improvements, but no fundamental changes. The Paris printer Stephanus brought out an edition in 1551 in which the text was for the first time divided into verses, which was soon universally accepted. (The usual division into chapters goes back to Stephen Langton [1206], who later became Archbishop of Canterbury.) Also Theodore Beza in Geneva adopted the Erasmian text, although the Codex D was at his disposal and he could have taken its readings into consideration. In 1633 the printer and publisher Elzevier in Leiden produced an edition, in the preface to which he commented: *textum ergo habes nunc ab omnibus receptum, in quo nihil immutatum aut corruptum damus* ("thus you now have the universally received text in which we present nothing that has been changed or is corrupted"). In accord with this statement, this text came to be commonly called the *textus receptus*, and its general acceptance was unchallenged. Although it had come into being in a rather questionable manner, it was regarded by the old Protestant Orthodoxy as verbally inspired.

c. In the eighteenth century of course the *textus receptus* continued to be reprinted. But a few scholars began to collect variations and to print them alongside the received text, so that the reader could form his own judgment. In his *Gnomon Novi Testamenti* (1734) Joh. Albrecht Bengel cited many variant readings and made an effort to classify the witnesses to the text into groups or families. Joh. Jakob Wettstein published in 1751/52, as the fruit of many years of study, a *Novum Testamentum graecum . . . cum lectionibus variantibus*. The system adopted by him for designating the majuscules (capital letters) and minuscules (Arabic numerals) has been generally used ever since. Joh. Jakob Griesbach built on the foundations provided by these two scholars and sought to assign the manuscripts to three recensions or groups. But in spite of these beginnings which could have led to the production of a critical edition of the text, the *textus receptus* remained unshaken also in the eighteenth century.

d. The dominance of the *textus receptus* was not broken until the nineteenth century. The classical philologian Lachmann set forth the persuasive principle that the methods of classical philology should also be applied to the textual criticism of the NT. In this process the *textus receptus* should not be used as the point of departure for the discussion. Rather, the realistic goal of reconstructing the text in general use in the church around 380 should be determinative. Although Lachmann went to work very carefully with the date named by him in view, it was soon possible to reconstruct the text of an even earlier date, due to the rediscovery of many old manuscripts. Constantin v. Tischendorf was especially productive as a discoverer and collector of manuscripts. In his great edition of the NT he gave priority to the Codex א which had been discovered and edited by him. Because of the ample critical apparatus his *Editio octava* I 1869, II 1872, III 1894 (Gregory) is still indispensable even today. Alongside this edition there soon appeared other critical editions. The Englishmen Wescott and Hort gave priority to B as the best witness to what they called the neutral text (1881). Also

B. Weiss's edition considered B to be the best manuscript (1894–1900; [2]1902–1905). Soon after the beginning of the twentieth century Hermann von Soden brought out a comprehensive critical edition of the NT, which introduced a new system of sigla into the critical apparatus, but it proved to be too cumbersome and thus did not obtain general acceptance. The manuscripts were assigned to three great recensions: that of Hesychius in Egypt, that of Lucian of Antioch for the Byzantine (or Koine) text and that of Pamphilus for the so-called Jerusalem text. One must of course take into consideration that the text of the Greek NT had in fact been carefully edited by good philologians in Alexandria. But there can be no talk of three different recensions of the NT text, and there never was any such thing as a Jerusalem text.

e. In order to bring together the results of these great scholarly editions into a handy edition of the Greek NT, E. Nestle proceeded according to the following principle. He made no independent study of the manuscripts, but used the great scholarly editions as the basis for his text. Where Tischendorf, Westcott-Hort, and Weiss agreed, this wording was adopted as his text. Where two stood against one, he adopted the majority reading. Nestle's *Novum Testamentum Graece* appeared for the first time in 1898. Later editions also made much use of the work of v. Soden, especially in those cases where the three other editions offered no united results. Thus the text printed by Nestle does not reproduce the witness of a manuscript, but a form of the text arrived at on the basis of the critical editions which had already been produced. In the later editions published by Eberhard Nestle and then his son Erwin Nestle, an increasing number of readings of important manuscripts were introduced into the apparatus. The older principle of constructing the text only on the basis of previous editions was no longer maintained, as progress was made in text criticism and its methods were refined. K. Aland, who has been responsible for *Novum Testamentum Graece* for some time, has therefore abandoned this procedure. He presents us with a critically edited text with a comprehensive critical apparatus, indicating the most important variant readings, and thereby affords the user the possibility of examining the decisions made by the editor and of arriving at his own judgment. The twenty-sixth edition of

Nestle-Aland will still further expand the material offered by the apparatus. [This appeared Fall 1979. Trans.]

#45 The Present State of New Testament Text Criticism

In addition to the literature on p. 233, cf.:

Duplacy, J. *Où en est la critique textuelle du Nouveau Testament?* 1959.

Schäfer, K. Th. "Der Ertrag der textkritischen Arbeit am NT seit der Jahrhundertwende," *BZ NF* 4 (1960:1-18.

Aland, B. "Neutestamentliche Textkritik heute," *VF* 21 (1976):3-22.

Parker, D. C. "The Development of Textual Criticism Since Streeter," *NTS* 24 (1977):149-62.

Epp, E. J. "NT Textual Criticism in America: Requiem for a Discipline," *JBL* 98 (1979):94-98.

a. The attempts made during the last two hundred years to classify the manuscripts into large groups have produced a widely held consensus in recent scholarship. When a text family is spoken of, that does not necessarily mean a rigid group. Sometimes one or another member goes its own way. According to the present state of NT text criticism, the following groups may be distinguished:

(1) The Egyptian-Alexandrian Text. It is attested by most papyri, by the majuscules ℵ and B—A and C present a mixed text—as well as by the church fathers Clement of Alexandria and Origen, and by the Sahidic and Bohairic translations. The text attested by these witnesses is consistently very good; but nevertheless, it does not present a neutral text, as described by Westcott and Hort, nor can it be considered the representative of the original text.

(2) The Caesarean Text. This group, which stands very near to the Egyptian-Alexandrian text, may be established with confidence only for the Gospel of Mark. Its representatives are P^{45}, W, Θ, λ, φ. The name "Caesarean Text" was chosen because Origen possibly brought this version of the text with him from Egypt to Caesarea in Palestine.

(3) The "Western" Text. This group is represented by manuscripts from the west of the Roman Empire, above all by the two manuscripts designated D, which have a Latin text

alongside the Greek. This "Western" text is also attested by the Old Latin versions and the Western church fathers. This text sometimes branches off from the usual text in noticeable ways, especially in Acts (see p. 162). More recent studies have shown that many "Western" readings can be documented at an early time in Egypt. Thus the description "Western" may not be taken too strictly.

(4) The Koine or Imperial Text (*Siglum* 𝔎). This text is represented by the vast majority of manuscripts. Constantinople was the center from which it was widely distributed. It represents the end product of a long development which, under the influence of the text common in Syria, had smoothed out places which were linguistically rough and generally improved the quality of the Greek. The Imperial Text is therefore of less value for text criticism than the other groups, although also in this later textual group there are places where, contrary to the witness of the other families, the original reading has been preserved. The Imperial Text has been preserved by many majuscules (A and C have a mixed text, see above) and by the vast majority of minuscules. But the value of the readings offered by a group of manuscripts is not determined by the number of manuscripts in the group, but only by the relevant weight of their evidence.

b. How does one go about the work of text criticism? First, one undertakes external criticism, i.e. the age and value of the manuscripts which represent a particular reading are evaluated, along with the textual family to which they belong. But even the best manuscripts are not always right when it is a matter of deciding between a number of variant readings, for not a single one of the many manuscripts which have come down to us represents the original text itself. Mistakes can have crept into the copying of any manuscript, and one must reckon also with the possibility that the scribe intentionally made changes here and there. Thus internal criticism must be practiced alongside external criticism. Here one must evaluate the material grounds which speak for one reading and against another. In the process some help is offered by two rules of thumb which have been developed in text criticism and which have often proven their value.

The first rule states: *Lectio difficilior probabilior*—a principle already laid down by Bengel. It affirms that the more difficult expression is to be regarded as more likely original, for it would have given occasion for scribes to have made changes in order to smooth out difficult places in the text. Thus for example in the instance named above from I Thessalonians 3:2 (see p. 237), the original text is certainly represented in the words in which Paul describes Timothy as συνεργον του Θεου εν τω ευαγγελιω του Χριστου ("God's co-worker in the gospel of Christ"). Of course they are only attested by D, 33, d, e, Ambrosiaster, Pelagius, therefore predominately by Western witnesses. But all other readings can be explained as later "improvements" of the expression which appeared problematic in the original text, that the human being Timothy was a co-worker with God. B omits του Θεου ("God's") and says merely συνεργον ("co-worker"); ℵ A P 629 vg sy[h] bo replace συνεργον with the unproblematic διακονον ("servant"), so that διακονον του Θεου ("God's servant") is now read; 𝔎 pl sy[p] permit both expressions to flow together: διακονον του Θεου και συνεργον ημων ("God's servant and our co-worker"); G places only διακονον ("servant") in front, so that the formulation reads διακονον και συνεργον του Θεου ("God's servant and co-worker").

The other rule instructs: *Lectio brevior potior*. Thus when one must decide between two different readings, the shorter form should be evaluated as generally more likely to be original, because it is usually lengthened by a secondary explanation or supplement intended to exclude a possible misunderstanding. Thus for example in the instances already referred to (see pp. 236-37), John 7:39 and I Corinthians 8:6, the shorter forms are clearly recognizable as the more original. In the sentence ουπω γαρ ην πνευμα ("for the Spirit was not yet"), which Jesus spoke before his glorification (John 7:39), it was felt that it was not clear which spirit Jesus was talking about, and αγιον ("Holy") was inserted (so P[66]* ℵ, K, Θ, Ψ, *pc*), or else a comment about the spirit as the divine gift was expected, and δεδομενον ("given") was accordingly added (lat, sy, Eus.). And if I Corinthians 8:6 speaks of the confession of the one God, the Father, from whom all comes and for whom we exist, and of one Lord Jesus Christ, through whom are all things and through whom we exist, then later copyists thought that here something must have fallen out of the text, because after all the Trinitarian confession of faith must speak of all three persons. Thus an analogous formulation was added: και εν πνευμα αγιον, εν ω τα παντα και ημεις εν αυτω ("and one Holy Spirit, in whom are all things and we in him," 0142, 460, pc, Greg^{naz}). But here also there can be no doubt that the shorter two-member formulation presents the original text.

In the vast majority of cases the application of external and internal criticism produces a sure result, so that the text of the Greek NT is firmly established. On the other hand, the attempt to restore the original text by means of conjectures is a risky venture into uncertain territory. A conjecture is supported by no manuscript evidence, but expresses a mere supposition concerning the issue of how the original text could have read. Since in the past the discovery of better manuscript evidence has often revealed such speculations to be false, one must maintain a fundamental reservation concerning all conjectural emendations to the text.

In the execution of text-critical decisions not only is the weight of the relevant manuscript evidence to be taken into account, but also the exegesis of the text which keeps in view the author's linguistic usage, his train of thought, and theology is to be considered. Once one has made a text-critical decision on the basis of careful evaluation of the evidence, then the decision should be cross-checked; the reading regarded as original must be that from which all the other variants can be understood as accidental or intentional changes of the original reading.

Index of NT Passages

(Only those passages and pages are listed where some discussion of the text is found.)

Index of Authors

Index of Subjects

(*Cf. also Table of Contents.*)